Lee Rigby:
A Mother's Story

Lee Rigby:
A Mother's Story

LYN RIGBY

and Rosie Dunn

**SIMON &
SCHUSTER**

London · New York · Sydney · Toronto · New Delhi

A CBS COMPANY

First published in Great Britain by Simon & Schuster UK Ltd, 2016
A CBS COMPANY

1 3 5 7 9 10 8 6 4 2

Simon & Schuster UK Ltd
1st Floor
222 Gray's Inn Road
London WC1X 8HB

www.simonandschuster.co.uk

Simon & Schuster Australia, Sydney
Simon & Schuster India, New Delhi

The authors and publishers have made all reasonable efforts to contact
copyright-holders for permission, and apologise for any omissions or errors
in the form of credits given. Corrections may be made to future printings.

A CIP catalogue record for this book
is available from the British Library

Hardback ISBN: 978-1-4711-4947-4
Trade paperback ISBN: 978-1-4711-5903-9
Ebook ISBN: 978-1-4711-4948-1

Typeset in the UK by M Rules
Printed in the UK by CPI Group (UK) Ltd, Croydon, CR0 4YY

A Promise To My Son

I will talk about and share my Son,
To honour my boy and his memory,
Deny me that, and you deny my son's life,
Deny my son's life and you have no place
in mine.

Contents

'When I grow up, Mummy, I want to be a soldier.'

Lee Rigby, aged five

Prologue

I'm lying on the kitchen floor, curled up in a foetal-shaped ball, and I have no idea how I got here.

The tiles against my side are hard and freezing cold and my eyes scan the room, seeking clues to my brutal plight. Everything appears to be in slow motion, my brain included, and the world sounds muffled and confused, as if I've been caught in some apocalyptic blast that has knocked me to the ground.

Like a wounded wild animal I lie motionless, as screams and wails continue all around me. My body is wracked with sobs and convulsions of pain as I try and make sense of everything. Every part of my body hurts. I can hear a terrible noise somewhere in my head but it feels somehow disconnected to me.

Then I realise this is the sound of my grief. My grief for my murdered son, Fusilier Lee Rigby. This is his story.

1

The Day Everything Changed

I knew it was my Lee straight away.

From the moment I saw the blurred outline of a dead body flashing before me on a TV screen, I recognised him as my son. I can't say it was one particular thing that gave it away; the video footage on the news was grainy and unclear, and the body on the ground had been blurred to disguise identity and injuries. But just seeing the outline of the young man was enough to tell me it was Lee. I knew the shape of his body and, in a heartbeat, I recognised the dark 'HELP *for* HEROES' sweatshirt he was wearing and his favourite Timberland boots.

From that moment on my life would never be the same again. It must have been around teatime, about 5.20 p.m., when I first saw the news on the television, but by then Lee had been dead for several hours and I didn't even know it. The terror had begun to unfold at about 2 p.m. on 22 May 2013. My life had carried on as normal for a whole afternoon and I had no inkling that my beloved boy was gone forever.

Lee was a soldier serving in the 2nd Battalion, Royal Regiment of Fusiliers, and he had been with the regiment for seven years as a machine-gunner and drummer. He had already been to Afghanistan and served on the frontline but, mercifully, he'd survived and returned home safely, unlike several of his friends and comrades.

The day started without incident. It was a lovely spring afternoon and I, like most people, was enjoying the weather and looking forward to summer. I was at home in Middleton, a large suburb of Manchester, where I was running my normal daily chores for the family before getting ready to go to work early evening.

I was over two hundred miles away when Lee was attacked and killed, and it still breaks me to think I was oblivious to his pain for so long afterwards. Lee was stationed at the Royal Artillery Barracks in Woolwich, but he used to travel to work each day to the Tower of London, where he was part of a recruitment team as well as a drummer in the Fusilier Corps band. This meant he often performed with the drummers at ceremonial and recruitment events. It was part of the job he really loved. Lee was an outgoing lad and, as the Drum Corps was very social, he fitted in straight away.

The night before his murder he had worked at a recruitment and hospitality event at the Tower and, as often, the lads were in high spirits afterwards. When everything had been packed away they decided to go for drinks to wind down and enjoy themselves. A night in the pub with Army lads is not for the faint-hearted and so, when one pint turned into many, Lee and his mates ended up having a late night on the tiles.

Lee didn't arrive back at his barracks until almost 4 a.m. after a mammoth session with the boys. But despite the crazy antics of the night before, he was up and out the door a few hours later to ensure he arrived back at work at the Tower on time for 8 a.m. Many of the lads were late in that day, and arrived a couple of hours after Lee but, as it had been a successful night for the regiment, they weren't treated too harshly.

As the day wore on, the partying of the night before began to creep up on him and he looked and felt washed out. His boss took pity on him and, because he had turned up on time, he let Lee go home early sometime after midday to catch up on his sleep and recover. It's details like this that make you think fate is a very cruel mistress. Lee would normally finish work at 4 p.m. and then travel across the city back to his Woolwich barracks, arriving there about 6 p.m. It was the one day he finished early that led to him crossing the path of his monstrous killers.

Shortly after 2 p.m., Lee jumped off the train at Woolwich Arsenal Station. He was seen clearly on CCTV footage, making his way home. Lee's attackers struck as he walked down Wellington Street, near Wilson Street, just a few hundred yards from the safety of his barracks.

He was crossing the road to get to a shop when two men, Michael Adebolajo and Michael Adebowale, drove towards him in a car, knocking him over and smashing him into a post. As my son lay on the ground, they jumped from their car and began hacking at him with kitchen knives and meat cleavers. They tried to behead him, savagely cutting his head from his shoulders. They then pushed his body into the middle of the road, where he lay unconscious and dying. It was brutal, and their barbaric act took place in broad daylight.

What happened next was extraordinary. Instead of running away to avoid capture, the two men, covered in blood and still clutching their weapons, stayed put and began mingling among the growing and horrified crowd. The attack had been witnessed by a lot of people who had been going about their daily business on a busy London street.

Several women stood out that day for their immense courage and bravery and their first-hand accounts will be included later in the book. One woman tried desperately to rescue and prevent

Lee from being run over, while another lay on the ground and cradled my boy in his final moments.

The police had been called at 2.20 p.m., followed by the ordering of a specialist firearms unit after the full horror of events became clear. Before officers arrived, Adebolajo and Adebowale began ranting to passers-by, which was filmed by people on their mobile phones and later shown on television screens around the world.

Admitting that he had killed Lee, this is what Adebolajo said: 'The only reason we have killed this man today is because Muslims are dying daily by British soldiers. And this British soldier is one ... By Allah, we swear by the almighty Allah, we will never stop fighting you until you leave us alone. So what if we want to live by the Sharia in Muslim lands? Why does that mean you must follow us and chase us and call us extremists and kill us?

'When you drop a bomb do you think it hits one person? Or rather, your bomb wipes out a whole family? We must fight them as they fight us. I apologise that women had to witness this today but in our lands women have to see the same.

'You people will never be safe. Remove your governments, they don't care about you. You think David Cameron is gonna get caught in the street when we start busting our guns? Do you think politicians are going to die? No, it's going to be the average guy, like you and your children. So get rid of them. Tell them to bring our troops back and leave our lands and you will live in peace.'

His words were heard across the world, but my son lay dead on the floor so that Adebolajo could make a political point. And all the while, I still had no idea.

The firearms police arrived at the scene at 2.35 p.m. while Lee's killers still prowled the scene, ranting their venom. The men charged at the police and armed officers responded by firing eight shots. They were both wounded, but not killed, and were taken to separate hospitals. Meanwhile Lee was pronounced dead and formally identified. It later transpired that the two men expected and indeed wanted to be shot dead so they could become martyrs in the eyes of fellow fanatics.

It's so hard for me to even think about the events of that day. Any mother will understand what I mean by that. Lee may have been a grown man, a soldier who had fought for his country, but to me he was just my little boy. I made him, grew him, nurtured him in my womb and gave birth to him. I watched him crawl, toddle and grow up into the loveliest lad imaginable. I felt like I was the luckiest mum in the world to have him, and that feeling never goes away, even when your children are grown up and fending for themselves. You still want to nurture and protect them as if they were little. To try and imagine what my beautiful boy went through, such violence and pain, is a torment that will never go away. It's a daily torture for me to live with the fact that I wasn't there to protect him when he needed me most.

Ironically Lee had been really happy at the time he was killed. He had become engaged to a beautiful girl called Aimee, with whom he was deeply in love. Aimee was a soldier herself and she was posted at Camp Bastion in Afghanistan for a three-month tour of duty when Lee was murdered. It was the highlight of his day when she rang him from Camp Bastion.

Lee worried desperately about Aimee being in a war zone. Having been there himself, he knew what a horrific and dangerous place it was. All he could do was count the days until she returned safely back to him. He would ring me in distress at times when he couldn't sleep, or when he couldn't stop fretting for his girl.

'What if something happens to her, Mum? I love her so much,' Lee would say.

'Don't worry, Son, she will be home soon, safe and sound,' I tried to reassure him.

'But what if she isn't? She means everything to me.'

It was hard to hear Lee so worried and anxious about Aimee, but it was the cruellest irony ever that, while he pined and fretted for her, it would be Lee who would face the gravest peril on the streets of his own country.

Back in Manchester, two hundred and fifty miles away, I was at peace knowing that my only lad was safe once again in the UK. As a mum, I felt a warm glow of contentment knowing that Lee was healthy and happy. That's all you can ever want for your children. But my world was about to be shattered forever.

At the time, I worked as a cleaning supervisor in a local call centre, LBM, which employed about five hundred people. I had been there about three years and got on with plenty of my colleagues. I enjoyed going into work and it helped to bump up our family income on top of my husband Ian's job.

That afternoon I received a phone call from my eldest daughter, Sara, Lee's sister. I think it was just after 5 p.m., as I was on my way to work, when she told me about a soldier being killed in Woolwich. This was the first I had heard about what had gone on. Ian was driving me to work and a shiver ran down my spine when I realised it was a soldier where Lee was based. I told Ian what had happened.

'Why hasn't Lee called to let us know he's OK?' I asked him. 'He always rings if he thinks we might be worried about him.'

Ian was also concerned but did his best to reassure me.

'Don't panic, Lyn, he may not even know about it himself yet, which is why he hasn't rung you. He'll be straight on the phone to you once he hears the news himself to let you know he's fine.'

My heart was pounding at the very thought that a soldier had been struck down. I rang Lee's mobile but it just kept ringing and ringing and no one answered.

'Come on, Lee,' I begged out loud. 'Please answer so I know you're safe.'

'Maybe he's on exercise with the cadets and can't answer his phone,' I tried to reason with Ian.

'There will be a reason why he hasn't rung yet, love. As soon as he can he will be right on that phone to you. Just wait and see,' he replied.

But despite the dozens of calls I kept making I couldn't reach my son. I continued on to work to start my shift at 5.15 p.m. despite the fact I felt sick with worry and my body felt cold and shaken. At this stage I hadn't seen any news, so I had no idea what to expect.

Once I got inside the work building I knew I had to see the news. There were TV sets placed in the reception and the canteen, and it was there that my world fell apart. The rolling news about the murdered soldier was continuing, and the very second I saw the outline of the dead man's body I knew it was my son. To this day I wish with all my heart I hadn't watched it. A roar of pain rose from deep within me and I collapsed into a chair, sobbing, screaming and shouting. There was a kind and gentle security man who worked at LBM called John Brown, and he came running over to help me when he saw the state I was in.

'What's wrong, Lyn?' he coaxed. 'What's happened? Are you OK?'

'That's my Lee,' I screamed through my tears. 'That's my son, my boy.'

John tried his hardest to soothe and care for me.

'You can't be sure, Lyn, come on, let's sort this out.'

'It's him, I know it's him. I can see from here it's my Lee. I can see the outline of his body, his shoes and his sweatshirt. It's my Lee. He's dead.'

I was sobbing loudly and became distraught. I was in total meltdown and poor John, such a kind and decent bloke, picked me up and helped me walk to a private side room to stop people from staring at me in hysterics. He made me a cup of tea, as I sat and cried my heart out, and all I can remember is that the tea was very sweet. He must have put a lot of sugar in it for me.

My conviction that the body of the young murdered soldier on the television screen was Lee was not just based on fear and a sixth sense. Yes, they all played a part, but I'm sure any mum would recognise her own son, even though the body on the road had been deliberately blurred to avoid recognition, because a formal identification had not yet been made by family. At this stage, the dead man's family had not yet been told of his murder, but in my mind it was just a question of formality now.

I was in such a state that I couldn't possibly stay at work, so Ian came back to collect me and take me home. Sara and my two youngest daughters, Courtney and Amy, were there when I arrived back and we spent hours making a relentless stream of frantic phone calls trying to get some information. We phoned Lee's barracks at Woolwich but got nowhere. It was in complete lockdown and no information was being released to anyone. Sara also rang as many of Lee's Army pals as she could, but that was the same. Eventually Lee's own mobile phone went dead after his battery ran flat.

The only way I can describe that night is that it was sheer torture. Sara, who has children of her own, went back home and Ian tried to retain some normality by going to work on a night shift. I think he felt that if he did that, it might make me feel that everything was normal, and the whole thing was a huge mistake, and that Lee was alive and well and telling us he was fine. Ian was trying to keep a routine for all our sakes and not give in to our gnawing fears that Lee was dead. I also tried to keep up the pretence of normality, but I won't admit to doing it well. I tried to put my young girls to bed but they could see that I was distraught.

Amy was just eight at the time, and eventually she was so tired I got her upstairs to bed. I lay down with her and lied when I told her that her big brother Lee was safe and that he hadn't been hurt. She may have been young but she wasn't stupid, and I was far from convincing. I was trying not to sob at the same time as trying to reassure my girls that Lee was OK. There was no doubt in my mind that Lee was gone, but it broke my heart to have to lie to Amy. When I look back now, I wish I hadn't told her Lee was safe because it turned out not to be true; but it was just a natural instinct in me to protect and shield my daughter from the horror I knew we would be facing soon.

After Amy dropped off to sleep I kissed her on the forehead and crept downstairs to look after my other daughter, Courtney, who was eleven. She, like me, was convinced that Lee was the soldier whose murder saturated the news throughout the evening. Courtney refused to go to bed and we both tried to comfort each other in that darkest night. It was truly heartbreaking to hear my daughter wracked with sobs.

'I know it's our Lee, Mum. I just know it,' she choked, as I held her tight in my arms.

I tried my utmost to take her pain away.

'I know, sweetheart, but let's keep hoping this is all just a bad dream. We all want to see Lee again, so let's just hold on tight and pray he gets in touch soon.'

I didn't even believe my own words, and so Courtney and I held each other close and clung to each other for dear life, weeping and crying as the minutes passed by so slowly. We stayed that way for hours, jumping out of our skins every time the phone rang, willing it to be Lee to make all our nightmares go away. But that call never came – just a succession of anxious relatives and friends who, like us, were growing ever more scared of the inevitable outcome.

Finally exhausted by her sobbing, Courtney collapsed into bed at around 12.30 a.m. and I remember looking at my beautiful girls in their beds as tears rolled down my cheeks. How would they ever cope without their beloved big brother? He was their hero and they adored him.

It was now ten hours since Lee had been murdered and still we had heard nothing to confirm it. I watched the news footage over and over again and it was just grotesque. But I was trying to eke out some clues; something that would break me out of this nightmare and show me it wasn't Lee who had died. Speculation on Facebook was rife about who the dead soldier was but, mercifully, Lee's name was not mentioned at that point.

At just gone 2 a.m., I finally went upstairs myself. My eyes were stinging and red raw from crying. My head was pounding with pain and I felt weak and empty. It was truly horrendous being out of control and unable to protect your own children. But for one second I allowed myself to think that maybe it was all a big mistake.

Could I have got it wrong and it wasn't Lee after all? I questioned myself. I was almost too scared to allow myself any hope, but you hold on to anything in circumstances like that. After all, it was now twelve hours, half a whole day, and no one had been in touch to say Lee was dead.

'Please God, please let my Lee be safe. Please bring him home to us all,' I whispered to myself in the dark, as I sat helpless on the edge of the bed.

I would have given anything, my own life even, if I could see my gorgeous boy walk through the door one more time. I had been upstairs for only ten minutes when I heard a loud knock on the door. And that was when I knew it was all over. Finally all hope had gone.

I had been terrified of this moment and now it had arrived – the dreaded knock on the door. In that split second I knew for sure it was my beautiful boy who was dead. I tried to stand and

I fell back onto the bed. When I got up again I froze on the spot, paralysed with fear and despair. I forced myself to look out of my window and there I saw four people crammed onto my small driveway.

'No, no, please, please, not my Lee,' I wailed in the dark.

I stumbled down the stairs, and opened the door to see four men standing before me. I have never felt so desolate or bleak in my life. My legs felt like jelly, as I searched their faces in the dark, and I thought I was going to throw up on the spot.

I didn't know it at the time but they were two police officers and two Army officers. The police were Steve Kilburn and Phil Shaw, although I don't know to this day who the Army officers were. They were all wearing black suits and ties.

One of the men stepped forward slowly and, in a low voice, asked me: 'Are you Mrs Lyn Rigby?'

'Yes,' I managed to mumble and then, for some reason, I asked them to show me some ID. Don't ask me why. I had been expecting them all night, but there's no accounting for how the mind and body responds in times of crisis.

The men identified themselves as police and Army officers and showed me proof of who they were. They then asked if they could come in to talk to me. I led the way into my living room and fell onto the sofa. Then one of the men spoke the words which broke my heart forever.

'Lyn, I'm so sorry to inform you that the soldier who was murdered in Woolwich today is your son Lee.'

I let out a piercing scream. 'No, No, No,' I shouted. 'Not my Lee. It can't be my Lee. I want to see my baby. Please let me see my son.'

I screamed so loudly that it woke the little ones upstairs and they came running down, sobbing.

'Can we contact anyone for you, Mrs Rigby?' one of the men asked.

'Yes, my husband, Ian, Lee's dad,' I managed to blurt through my grief.

I was so distraught I couldn't even see the names or numbers in my phone, so one of the officers took it and managed to find Ian's number to call him. I was crying, shaking and dry-retching, and my whole world was spinning out of control around me. As the police got hold of Ian, I managed to phone Sara and I remember screaming down the phone at her.

'Sara, it's Lee. It's our Lee. He's dead.'

The phone went dead on the other end, as Sara sprang into action to get to me. My friend Sandra, who lived nearby, was with me by now and I heard a car door slam loudly. Another friend, Natalie, had arrived and I ran down the path and threw myself into her arms, sobbing. As the two women helped me back into the house, I saw my two little girls huddled on the stairs, petrified and crying. It was one of the saddest sights I have ever seen, but I was so riddled with my own grief I was completely powerless to help them. It's something I have never been able to forgive myself for. I have since spoken to them about this and apologised.

I told them: 'I'm so sorry that I wasn't there for you that night, my darlings, but I was so overwhelmed with grief I didn't know what I was doing.'

'Don't ever say sorry, Mummy,' Amy replied. 'We were all upset but seeing you like that made us cry even more.'

'You did the right thing, Mum,' Courtney chipped in. 'You couldn't look after us because you were too upset to even look after yourself. It hurt us even more to see you sobbing.'

Sara was quite amazing that night. Seeing the state I was in and, despite her own desperate sorrow, she organised for one of the police officers, Steve Kilburn, to take the children to her house to be cared for. Sara then drove to get my other daughter, Chelsea, who was working a night shift. Steve was also incredible that night at caring for us all, and he's still our Family Liaison

Officer to this date. He was so strong but gentle and protective of us, as was his colleague Phil. Later on, Family Liaison Officer Marie Snitynski joined the team and she, like the others, was so kind and wonderful to us. The team holds a special place in our affections because they couldn't have been more caring and brilliant to us and we will forever be thankful to them.

I really can't remember anything past that point. I do know Ian came home and that I was hysterical beyond description. It felt like my world was over – as if someone had ripped out my heart, thrown it on the floor and stamped all over it. I didn't know it was humanly possible to hurt that much but it was certainly a feeling I was going to have to get used to.

I must have passed out for a while because I have no other memories of that night, but I woke to find a doctor had been called to see me. The moment I opened my eyes I began to cry once again. I was in agony but, as I looked out of the window, my heart turned over as I saw that the street outside my ordinary small home was swarming with photographers, journalists and TV crews. I was scared, and I felt like I had been plunged into a living nightmare. All I had ever wanted was to be a loving wife and mum and to care for and protect my family. Now my beloved son was gone and life would never be the same again.

2

The Aftermath

I remember nothing about the day after Lee was murdered. I was so ill that, after being checked over by the doctor, I was sedated and given pills to make sure I slept. I remained out cold for most of the day and night, waking only to sob and shake at the desperate realisation that my son was dead.

I later learned that a steady stream of people arrived at our house throughout the day. Friends, neighbours and family rallied round to offer their help and condolences. But they were not the only visitors.

From 6 a.m. the media descended on our home in their droves and remained there for days to come. There must have been fifty or sixty members of the press outside our door, all waiting for some comment or sight of Lee's family. There were newspaper reporters and photographers, television broadcasters and camera crews and giant satellite vans all crammed along the road. It looked like a scene from a disaster movie. The media presence was so huge that a police officer had to be stationed on our front door around the clock for almost a week afterwards.

After we were informed that Lee had been murdered, his name

and details had been released to the media and, as a result, his picture was on the front page of every newspaper and on every TV screen, not just in this country but around the world.

Our nation was in shock and outrage. Condemnation of his murder came from far and wide, as the full horrors of Lee's death became known. Prime Minister David Cameron called two emergency meetings of the Government Cobra committee and led the way in speaking out against the atrocity.

He said: 'The people who did this were trying to divide us. They should know something like this will only bring us together and make us stronger ... One of the best ways of defeating terrorism is to go about our normal lives.'

He was right. The terrorist attack on my son in London had achieved the polar opposite of what Lee's killers had set out to do. They had wanted to turn the people of the UK against each other, sparking hatred and fighting amongst Muslims and the ordinary people of our great country. They failed unequivocally. Instead, people of all colours, races and creeds came together to stand united against the vile actions of two evil and warped men. Crucially important, the Muslim Council of Great Britain, which reflects the views of the majority of decent Muslims, went on to denounce the killings as cold and calculated murder, which had no basis in Islam.

The Secretary General of the Council, Farooq Murad, had this to say: 'The murder of drummer Lee Rigby was truly a barbaric act. Muslim communities are united in their condemnation of this crime. It was a dishonourable act and no cause justifies cold-blooded murder. We convey our sympathy and condolences to the family of Lee Rigby and we commend the dignity they have displayed since this tragic act took place.

'The attackers of Lee Rigby should reflect on their actions and seek repentance from the Almighty. They have made yet another family mourn for their loved one; they tried to sow division in our society and have once again besmirched our great religion of Islam.

'They claimed their act was done for those suffering in wars in Muslim lands. But it is my contention that the vast majority of our affected brothers and sisters would have nothing to do with this phoney act done in their name.'

There were reports of attacks and abuse faced by mosques and individual Muslims following Lee's murder, but they were in the minority and led by right-wing extremists looking to make political capital. In the main all we saw was an outpouring of grief, love and sympathy for Lee and our family.

Lee's murder put the country on high alert for further terrorist attacks and, at the scene of his killing, flowers began to mount up as well-wishers flocked to Woolwich to pay their respects. Many were weeping, and mums and their children held each other tight as they reflected on the savage slaying of a young man just twenty-four hours earlier.

Ian put out a short statement to the media to reflect our love for Lee.

It read: 'Lee was lovely. He would do anything for anybody. He always looked after his sisters and always protected them. He took a "big brother" role with everyone. All he ever wanted to do from the time he was a little boy was to be in the Army. He wanted to live life to the full and enjoy himself.'

And that was Lee in a nutshell. He was a wonderful, vibrant, kind and loving young man with a great sense of fun and mischief. Everyone who met him loved him and found his boisterous and bountiful love of life infectious. He had the loudest and most comical laugh and the brightest smile imaginable. He lit up a room when he walked in and, once met, he was never forgotten. Now all that had been snuffed out in a few moments of unthinkable violence and suffering.

Paying tribute to Lee, Lieutenant Colonel Jim Taylor MBE said:

'Drummer Lee Rigby was a dedicated and professional soldier. An experienced and talented side drummer and machine-gunner, he was a true warrior and served with distinction in Afghanistan, Germany and Cyrpus. He was a real character within the 2nd Fusiliers. Larger than life, he was at the heart of our Corps of Drums.'

His Captain, Alan Williamson, also paid tribute to him. He said: 'Drummer Rigby, or "Riggers", as he was known within the Platoon, was a cheeky and humorous man, always there with a joke to brighten the mood.'

His Regimental Sergeant Major of the 2nd Fusiliers, Warrant Officer Ned Miller added: 'Riggers is what every Battalion needs. He was one of our great characters and always there to raise a smile and make everyone else feel better.'

The tributes continued to pour in, although most of them went over my head at the time. They were all heartfelt and it was clear that Lee had been much loved by more than just his immediate family.

The following day I got out of my bed and tried to face the world. But I just kept collapsing into a heap of tears, completely unable to take in what was going on around me. When I wasn't crying, I sat still like a block of stone, numb and confused and frightened. We had been asked if we could bear to take part in a press conference and we agreed only because we wanted to share our love for Lee and pay our respects to him publicly. But it was a nightmare from start to finish.

I sat down at home and tried my hardest to put into words how I felt about my son and I could barely force my hand to write anything. I knew I wouldn't be able to say any words in public, so Ian said he would read the statement for us all.

Police officers took us to the Fusiliers' Museum in Bury, where dozens of journalists, photographers and TV crews were assembled and waiting for us. I was like a limp shell, hardly able to stand up or function unaided. As we took our places at the table to face the media, I thought I was going to pass out. There were bright lights and a barrage of strangers before me and I wanted to run away as far as possible. It was so alien to me and I could scarcely understand what was happening. Nothing felt real. My son was dead and I was sitting in front of a sea of glaring lights and cameras and people I had never met before. I wanted to be sick and I couldn't stop crying. I could barely lift my head from my chest.

Facing the media that day were myself and Ian, Sara, and Lee's wife, Rebecca. Lee and Rebecca – with whom he'd had a beautiful son, now two years old – had been separated for almost a year, but it was a heartbreaking day for all of us. No one stopped crying and I kept my head bowed and wept as my poor husband tried hard to read out our tribute to Lee without breaking down.

Reading my words, he said: 'What can we say about Lee, our hero? We are so proud of Lee. When Lee was born everyone adored him – he was a precious gift given to us. Lee's dream growing up was always to join the Army, which he succeeded in doing. He was dedicated and loved his job.

'Lee adored and cared so much for his family, very much a family man, who in turn looked up to him. He loved to banter with them but would never ever let any harm come to them. He was over the moon at becoming a dad and an uncle to his sister's children – he adored them all. Lee was a man who loved people. He had many friends growing up in Middleton and on Army duties all over the world. He believed life was for living and he will be so sorely missed by all who knew him.

'His young sisters, Courtney and Amy, have written something they would like to share: "Rest in Peace, Lee. We loved you so much. You didn't deserve this. You fought for your country and did it well. You will always be our hero. We are so upset you left us so early. Love you, Lee. Goodnight."'

How Ian managed to keep going I will never know. He knew

he had to stand strong for us all, but I could hear his voice crack-ing as he spoke proudly about Lee and our love for him. He went on to tell the media about how our worst fears were eventually confirmed.

'As soon as it was on the telly, we were trying to get hold of Lee, but obviously we couldn't. It wasn't until the middle of the night that we got confirmation it was him. When he was in Afghanistan, we tried to come to terms with it. We knew it was a dangerous place. You don't expect something like this on your doorstep. It is so very difficult.'

Ian also read out Lee's last, beautiful, loving text to me. I had kept it on my mobile phone because it was so special. Not only was it a message to me on the Mother's Day that had just passed, it was extra special because Lee never found writing or texting easy and he had made a huge effort to send this to me. I will keep it always.

We wanted to publicly thank the police, the Army and the public, who had come out and supported us so well. Messages, cards and flowers had been pouring in from all over the country from kind well-wishers. Ian ended with a special message to Lee from us and a poem that had been sent by a stranger.

'We would like to say goodnight, Lee. Rest in peace, our fallen soldier. We love you loads and words can't describe how loved and sadly missed you will be. Our hearts have been ripped apart from us. Everyone is struggling to cope with this tragedy.'

You fought bravely and with honour died.
You leave your family, so full of pride.
Sleep well, young soldier, your job is done.
Your war is over, your battle won.
Our family chain is broken and nothing is the same.
But as God takes us one by one
Our chain will link again.

I wept and sobbed through the whole event and kept my head bowed on my chest, too scared to look up at the flashing lights and TV cameras. My brain wasn't functioning but my heart was beating so hard and fast I thought it might crash through my chest. I just wanted to go home and retreat into my grief.

Back near our home, a prayer service was held at the Burnside Community Centre. Leading the prayers, the Rev. Phillip Miller addressed the hundreds of people who had turned up.

'When we have a day of emptiness and decimation, we must remember God walks with us and he walks with Lee,' he told them.

It wasn't until 26 May – the Sunday after Lee's murder – that I felt strong enough to go and visit the scene where he'd died. It was the last place I wanted to go, but I knew I had to in honour of my son. I really wanted to lay some flowers, but it was a huge struggle to keep myself together. Our police liaison officer drove us to Woolwich and I was overwhelmed when I saw that the pavements where Lee was killed had been turned into a carpet of the most lovely flowers and cards. It looked wonderful but still felt desperately unreal to me.

I laid a wreath on the ground and Sara placed a bottle of HP Sauce next to it. Lee put HP Sauce on everything, so this was a personal touch and little joke from Sara to her brother. Even though several days had passed, crowds kept coming to the site to read the messages and place more flowers. Children were also tying balloons to the railings and letting them soar into the sky with the sweetest of messages addressed to Lee. It was so touching to see how much people cared.

No one bothered us when we arrived but, very quickly, people recognised us as Lee's family and a silence fell among everyone. You could have heard a pin drop, and even babies in their push-chairs seemed to stop crying. The kind people who made the effort to offer their solidarity and compassion with us that day were so respectful to my family, and I would like to say thank you to all those who wished us well and shared our grief, even if I will never know their names.

In truth, I couldn't wait to get away, because although I knew I had to face being at the place my son's life ended, I didn't want to stay a minute more than necessary because it was way too painful and distressing. As the police drove us back to Manchester, I sat and gazed out of the window for most of the journey until we reached home, where I took myself to bed and wept until I passed out. The world was clearly spinning and people were getting on with their ordinary lives. All I knew was that I didn't want to face my future without my son.

3

The Funeral

*Do not judge the bereaved mother. She comes in many
forms. She is breathing but she is dying. She may look young
but inside she has become ancient. She smiles, but her heart
sobs. She walks, she talks, she cooks, she cleans, she works,
she IS, but she IS NOT, all at once. She is here,
but part of her is elsewhere for eternity.**

M ost women say there's no greater pain than to bear a child.
It's not true. There is no greater pain than to bury one. It
might be a time-weathered cliché, but it's a fact when they say
no parent should ever have to go to their child's funeral. It completely breaks you and I don't think it's something you can ever
recover from. The public attention and the scale of the funeral
also made it even harder to deal with, because every ounce of my
grief had to be played out in front of the whole world, when all I
really wanted to do was run away and curl up in a ball.

* Author unknown

The weeks after Lee's murder were one long blur of misery and suffering. It was like living in a groundhog day of intense pain and disbelief and no one day stood out from the rest. I couldn't eat or sleep but I cried and cried and cried. If I did pass out from exhaustion, I would wake and wish to God I had died in my sleep so that I could be with Lee. I had become a hostage to my grief and I didn't have the strength to live any more.

Every morning I would lie in my bed and sob, barely able to lift my head from my pillow, let alone get out of the bed to face the day ahead.

'Why has this happened to me?' I would moan out loud. 'Why have they taken my baby? I just want my Lee back.'

Looking back on those early times, I am wracked with guilt that I wasn't able to care for my other children because I was possessed with grief for Lee. I am so thankful for the strength and love of my husband, who stepped in and cared for us all in those horrific weeks. We were all grieving so badly but I had become unable to function at even the most basic level. My life had imploded in a way I had never believed possible. My girls and Ian tried so hard to comfort me through their own pain but they just couldn't reach me.

When I wasn't sobbing for hours on end, I became numb. I would just sit and wait for the next tide of tears to hit me. At night, when the children were in bed, I would drink to try and wipe out the pain, but it didn't work. If anything, it just made me feel even more wretched and desperate. I didn't know where to put my pain. I just knew that I was broken into a million pieces and that nothing could put me back together again.

At night, when I went to bed, I would sit for hours in my bedroom staring out of my window, up at the stars, desperate for some kind of a sign from Lee. I would look at the stars when they were out and try and imagine if that was where Lee was looking down on me. And I would talk to him incessantly in the hope that one day he would answer back. I just didn't accept he was gone for good. It was too final and too much to bear. My body and mind were not processing the reality of the situation, and I stayed in this non-functioning state for a long time.

'My darling Lee, I love you and miss you so much,' I would speak out loud to him. 'I want you here with me. I'm so sorry I wasn't there for you and that I couldn't save you. I hope you are safe and happy wherever you are, my beautiful kind boy.'

In my head I could hear his voice gently whispering to me: 'Don't be silly, Mum. I'm fine. Please don't cry any more. You have to live your life for both of us now.'

That was the way Lee had always spoken to me when he was alive. He always told me not to worry about him and would reassure me he was safe and happy. He just wanted me to have a happy life, but at that point it was an impossibility. Not without him.

The horrific circumstances surrounding Lee's murder meant that it was some weeks before the funeral could go ahead. Police investigations and post mortems had to be completed before his body could be released for burial, and the delay added to the already intense suffering we were all going through. But I think the hardest part of the waiting was that I couldn't have the final say in my own son's funeral. Even though I was Lee's mum, I was not regarded as his next of kin in the eyes of the law and the Army. Lee's estranged wife Becky was the only one who had the legal right to authorise the proceedings. It was a very complex and difficult situation.

Lee had separated from Becky a year before he died, but he'd not yet got round to changing his will, even though he had met and was engaged to Aimee, whom he planned to marry one day. This was an issue that had huge bearings on so many matters after Lee died, but it's not something that Becky was at fault for. Time after time I would find myself almost locked out of decisions regarding Lee because the authorities refused to recognise me as having any rights over my dead son. It was equally heartbreaking and infuriating, and it's something I will address later in the book, but at the time of Lee's funeral, so soon after he had been cruelly snatched from us, I was learning some of life's brutal lessons the hard way. I was not considered relevant to have any say regarding my son.

Lee was to be buried in a full and resplendent military funeral, and the planning for that was very much the responsibility of the Ministry of Defence. His murder had touched so many people that it was going to be a huge fanfare and something very public, so that people could pay their respects and show how much they cared.

The ceremonies began on 11 July 2013, the day before the main funeral was to take place. Lee's coffin, draped in the Union Jack flag, was being carried to Bury Parish Church, where his body would be guarded during an overnight vigil by his comrades-in-arms from the Fusiliers.

The procession began late in the afternoon and twenty-two family members made up the sombre cortege of cars, as it snaked its way slowly for two miles from the Red Hall Hotel in Bury towards the church that had long been a garrison chapel for the Fusiliers. The procession was led by a corps of two dozen drummers in scarlet tunics, as they marched to a beat. Another comrade carried Lee's ceremonial bearskin hat as a mark of respect. It was a really spectacular fanfare for Lee, but I could barely take any of it in because I was too distraught.

I clearly remember seeing thousands of people lining the streets as we made our way to the church, and I was overwhelmed by the heartfelt love and groundswell of public support Lee and his family were receiving. There were young people, old people, children and military veterans of all generations holding flags. The standard-bearers held their flags proudly aloft, then solemnly dropped them in honour as Lee's coffin passed by. Many shops, pubs and cafes in our home town of Middleton had also closed for the afternoon to pay their respects as we drove past.

Flowers adorned Lee's hearse and a separate car carried even more floral displays. We had chosen red and white roses and chrysanthemums, representing Lee's regimental colours, and they spelled out the words 'SON' and 'BROTHER'. Our card on his flowers summed up our feelings.

Lee, Our Hero. Taken from us far too early. But however hard it is, we'll take comfort in our thoughts of all the wonderful memories we have and the happiness you brought to our lives. You always lived life to the full but our lives will never be the same until the day we see your smiling face again. Sweet dreams, our beautiful boy. Love and miss you so much. Gone But Not Forgotten. OAFAAF [Once A Fusilier Always A Fusilier]. *Love Mum and Dad xx.*

Becky had chosen similarly simple flowers to represent her and Lee's son Jack in the words 'DADDY' and 'HUSBAND'. Shockingly, Aimee was told she was not allowed to include a floral tribute in the formal procession.

There was a calm dignity among the mourners which couldn't have been in greater, starker contrast to the horror of what had happened to Lee in the street two months earlier. The mood was proud and compassionate, and it showed just how much people cared about what had happened to him.

It wouldn't be until much later that I would appreciate just how wonderful the public were that day because, that afternoon, in the beautiful, blazing summer sunshine, I just wanted to remain cocooned in the car and hide from the world.

It must have been late afternoon when we arrived at the church and, as Lee's coffin drew into sight of the waiting crowds, they all started cheering and clapping and throwing single stems of flowers at the hearse. And then we came to a stop outside the church and the crowds fell silent. I had sobbed and sobbed the whole journey through and now we had arrived. You could have heard a pin drop as we got from our cars to watch six heartbroken fusiliers carry Lee's coffin inside. They were so emotional and I have no idea how they managed to perform their duty with such dignity and perfection. We were all dressed in black but we wore giant red poppies on our clothes as a mark of remembrance.

A very short, private service was carried out inside the chapel to welcome Lee and his family, although I can remember no words at all because I was distraught and cried throughout. When I did raise my eyes, I couldn't avert my gaze from my son's coffin. I just wanted to run to him and hold him.

Lee remained in the church, where the overnight vigil began. In total, thirty-two Fusiliers took turns at watching over him, with four soldiers changing guard every half hour. They could not move or talk, as they solemnly took charge of their fallen brother. It was an extremely tough job for them all because they too were heartbroken at what had happened to Lee. Family members returned to the hotel where we were staying, but I was in a daze. I can't remember eating anything for days and Ian was amazing at making sure our girls were looked after, as well as trying to support me. At 8.30 p.m. our police liaison officers drove us back to the church so we could spend some time with Lee.

It had been a horrendous afternoon for Aimee because Army rules said she was not allowed to be in the church for the arrival of Lee's coffin. She was devastated and had to stand outside with the crowds to watch her beloved partner being carried from his hearse. That evening, Sara sneaked Aimee into the chapel so she could say her goodbyes. The two girls had become close friends because Sara knew how much Lee and Aimee loved each other. It was a scandal the way Aimee was treated throughout and our hearts went out to her.

When I arrived that night, military chaplain, the Rev. Clare

Callanan, was there to greet us and she spoke a few words of comfort. The four drummers on guard over the coffin had just changed over and they were crying their eyes out. I went to each of them, stroked their arms and thanked them for their love and care for Lee. Whilst on guard, they were not allowed to move or speak back to me, but no words were needed to see how they felt. The padre must have been touched by their sorrow too because she went up to them all and tucked tissues into their motionless hands as tears streamed down their faces.

I then placed my hands on Lee's coffin and began talking to him.

'I love you, Lee, with all my heart,' I whispered through my tears. 'You will never leave my heart, Lee, even though you are no longer with us in this world. You will always be my beautiful son and I will love you forever. I wish I could wrap my arms around you now but one day I will be with you again. Rest well tonight, my gorgeous boy.'

That night, we all went to stay at the Red Hall Hotel, near Bury, so that we were out of the way from public and media attention. My youngest daughter Amy was not with us and was being cared for by a close friend. At eight years old, she was just too young to cope with the enormity of the funeral, and was adamant she didn't want to say goodbye to her big brother in a coffin. I drank myself into oblivion that evening until I passed out.

I woke with a very heavy heart the next morning. I opened my eyes and wanted to die. The day had finally arrived when I was expected to bury my only son and I didn't want to go through with it. As I looked up from where I was lying, I could see my black funeral dress hanging from the wardrobe and it was like reality had slapped me in the face.

I hated that dress with a passion because it symbolised only one thing – the death of my beloved child. It had taken me weeks before I could even drag myself from home to go and buy the outfit because I was in denial. I kept thinking that if I didn't acknowledge the funeral, then it wasn't really happening. Eventually, with just days to go, I forced myself to pick out the dress in which I would have to bury my son. Now I was having to steel myself to wear it.

I eased myself out of bed and went and stood under the shower for ten minutes. I closed my eyes and felt the wet spray pelt my skin like giant teardrops washing across my entire body, almost mirroring the waterfall of sorrow inside me. How could I possibly get through this day? I sat down in the hotel room and slowly began to get dressed. I put on my bra, my underwear and my tights and then I froze.

'I can't do this,' I wept, as Ian sat beside me calmly. 'I can't put on that dress because I can't bury my own son,' I choked, as my body began to shake with emotion and the sobs engulfed my body. 'I don't want to say goodbye, Ian. I can't say goodbye. That will mean he is never coming back and I will never see him again. I will never hear his voice again.'

Ian held me close in his arms and let me cry before he uttered a word. Eventually he broke his silence.

'We have to do this, Lyn, for Lee's sake. We have to be brave for our son.'

'I'm trying but I just don't know how I'm going to get through the day. I never had the chance to see him and say goodbye.'

That had always been a huge part of my grief – that I was unable to see Lee's body after he had been murdered. I understood it completely, and I had no desire to see what had been done to him, but in my rawest sorrow I wanted to hold my son in my arms one last time before I let him go. The brutal injuries Lee suffered meant that his coffin had remained closed after he was released by the coroner and the police for burial. The funeral was arranged by Wellens & Sons in Middleton, and they asked if we would like them to place some special items inside the coffin with Lee. The funeral was taking place just eight days after what would have been Lee's twenty-sixth birthday, and so we all signed a birthday card which read:

'We wish you were here to celebrate your birthday with us. We love you and miss you so much and you are always in our hearts.'

I also included a small poem and Sara put a love heart necklace inside, along with some military medals from my brother Mark from his own time during the Army. It was a huge pressure for Wellens to deal with such an enormous public funeral, but I would like to put on record that they were truly brilliant with our family and we are so grateful for everything they did for us, as we are to Baytree Flowers in Middleton for their stunning floral tributes.

Eventually, Ian coaxed me to put on the black dress I would wear to bury my son. All I really wanted to do was burn it, but I had no choice. No matter how hard I tried to block it all from my mind, this was happening and it was beyond my control. As Ian and I went to leave the room, I fell apart again.

'I don't want to go,' I wailed. 'I want to stay here so I never have to say goodbye. I didn't even get to stroke his face or hold his hands, so how can I think about saying goodbye?'

Ian held my hand and we walked along the corridor towards the front of the hotel. I remember drinking many cups of tea with lots of sugar as we waited in the foyer for our funeral cars. It was about 10 a.m. and the service was due to start an hour later. The men were all dressed in black, with black ties bearing Lee's name, while the women wore red ribbons on their outfits, which also carried his name. When the cars pulled into the car park, my heart sank. There was no going back now, and I inhaled a deep breath as if to will my body to carry me through this awful day. I could feel my body shaking, as I reluctantly moved towards the vehicles for a journey I should never have been making. The reality of the events hit me like a punch to my guts and face. I had to bury my son and this was going to be my last goodbye. As the car door opened, I felt paralysed, as if my feet were glued to the pavement – my heart and soul offering one last futile attempt at resistance. I started to wobble and Ian just grabbed hold of me and held me up like a bag of jelly.

We had a full police escort to the chapel, which included two police motorcycle outriders. Becky and Jack and her family got into the first car and then our family started to sit in the second.

'I'm not getting in,' I wailed. 'I'm not doing it.'

Ian and my girls didn't know what to do. They tried to comfort me as they gently persuaded me to get into the vehicle. It took about ten minutes before my mind and body allowed me to get inside and then we were on our way. I sobbed and sobbed and sobbed the whole journey, which was only a couple of miles from the church.

I remember every part of the route as if it was yesterday. Every street was lined with thousands of people who had turned out to share our sorrow and show their respects. Some had their heads bowed; others were crying and throwing flowers onto the cars, and veterans of all ages held flags up. Some had travelled long distances to be there, including from Germany and Cyprus. It was quite incredible. Even the teachers and pupils at Courtney's school came out to see us pass by, as did nursery and primary schools along the way. I'll never forget seeing all the little children standing so still. When we went through Middleton a group of bikers stood to attention. It was estimated that more than 5,000 people turned out in the streets to mark Lee's funeral.

I travelled with Ian, Sara, Chelsea and Courtney and my best friend Sandra and her daughter Natalie. There were very few words spoken but you could have filled a swimming pool with the tears we shed in that car. There was a range of different emotions from the crowds, who at times cheered and clapped but then cried along with us.

The journey was short in distance but took a long while because we drove so slowly through the crowds. When the cars pulled up and stopped outside the church, I froze for the second time. My body had become so stiff and I couldn't move from my seat. It took over five minutes before I could summon up the courage to face getting out of the car. I remember it was my daughter Courtney who eventually helped me out, and she was just twelve years old at the time.

As I emerged from the vehicle, this almighty clapping broke out from the huge crowds gathered outside the church. They recognised me as Lee's mum, and they were trying to urge me on and show their love and support. It was a wonderful display of solidarity and compassion for which I am deeply grateful.

The stairs outside the church were lined with military veterans wearing their campaign medals, and Ian and I and the girls from our car walked together in a line towards them. Ian helped me up the steps but, as I reached the foyer, my body collapsed again and I couldn't stop weeping.

'I can't do it. I won't do it. I won't go in,' I repeated.

Everyone was looking at us as I stood in that doorway, blubbering like a baby and rooted to the spot. We were the last to arrive, and everyone was already in the chapel waiting for us. It was horrendous. Courtney and Ian took hold of me on both sides and tried to keep me up as we walked gently to our seats. As I teetered down the aisle, I felt everyone was staring at me and I wanted the ground to swallow me up. I have never experienced anything so awful in my life.

Once we were seated in the front row, on the left-hand side, the service began gently with a two-minute silence in remembrance of Lee followed by the singing of hymns, but I scarcely noticed anything about the proceedings. All I could do was stare at Lee's coffin and weep.

'Why am I here?' I kept asking myself, as all around me people continued to sing their hearts out. 'This shouldn't be happening. This is too soon to bury my son.'

David Cameron and the Mayor of London, Boris Johnson, were at the funeral, although I don't remember seeing them. Aimee was there too, dressed so smartly in her Military Police uniform and proudly displaying her engagement ring from Lee, but again she was treated like a second-class citizen and forced to sit apart from our family in the back rows behind Mr Cameron and other local dignitaries. Poor Aimee. She acted with such dignity and composure, despite being made to feel like a spare part at the funeral of the man she planned to marry. It was another example of how protocol took priority over compassion, and it was shameful.

It was, without doubt, a beautiful service led by the Rev. Dr John Findon, who was truly wonderful. I didn't appreciate any of this at the time but later on I would look back and realise that a fine tribute had been paid to Lee that day. The hymns included *Who Would True Valour See*, *Lord of All Hopefulness* and *I Vow To Thee My Country*. A choir sang *Deep Peace of The Running Wave*. It was down to Lee's Commanding Officer, Lt Col. Jim Taylor of the 2nd Battalion Royal Regiment of Fusiliers, to deliver a eulogy to the congregation and he was magnificent.

He said: Lee was larger than life and was always at the centre of fun and mischief, but he was a true regimental character with real charisma and everybody fell under his spell. To be with Lee was to be where it was most fun – the centre of good times and much mischief. Whether it was in work or off duty, at a ceremonial engagement or on operations, Lee just knew how to lighten the mood.

He could brighten a room within moments and, by all accounts, clear a dancefloor in seconds if a Whitney Houston track was playing! Fusilier Rigby had a natural swagger and the confidence of someone truly comfortable in their own skin. He was always happy. His smile was infectious, as was his enthusiasm for soldiering and his passion for life. He proved himself to be a fine soldier in some of the toughest circumstances.

Lee joined the Army in 2006 on his third attempt, fulfilling his lifelong ambition. It was an early indication of how doggedly determined he was when he set his mind to achieve something. His drum training lasted six months, during which he drove everyone crazy with his incessant tapping of table, steering wheels – in fact, anything he could find to practise on while he mastered a new skill.

He arrived in the Second Fusiliers in Cyprus in 2007, having earned the much-coveted title of Drummer, and his naturally flamboyant character quickly made him popular in Fire Support Company and across the whole Battalion.

Lee was a fantastic soldier, who, despite having no musical background, became one of the best drummers in the Battalion. Known as 'Riggers' to his comrades, Lee was truly charismatic, had a wicked sense of humour and was hugely popular with his regiment.

In 2009 he put down his drum and picked up his machine gun and survived a gruelling tour of Afghanistan. Under relentless pressure from insurgents, he was dedicated, professional and incredibly brave. He took part in many firefights with the enemy and regularly had to patrol across ground strewn with Improvised Explosive Devices. His courage was tested every day and he was not found wanting. He will be remembered with pride by all who knew him.

We have a saying in our regiment: 'Once A Fusilier, Always A Fusilier'. We will all feel his loss keenly. We will remember him with pride always. Today, we, his regimental family, salute a fallen comrade. A talented soldier and musician. A larger-than-life character. A loyal friend and brother-in-arms. A gentle soul. Above all, a true Fusilier – daring in all things. So, thanks be to God for Lee Rigby. Father, son, husband, brother, friend, Fusilier. We will remember him.

The funeral was a private service inside the church, although it was being broadcast outside for the crowds and for national television. The eulogy was met with huge rounds of applause inside and outside the chapel.

Lt Col. Taylor later went out to speak to the crowds and said: 'We are here to honour Lee today and, as a regiment, support his family, stand shoulder to shoulder with them at their time of need.

'It is also a day that we, as a regiment, want to remember him for the true character he was. One of the many things about the Fusiliers is that we are a family regiment and that is not just the immediate family within the corps of drums, but much wider than that. We stand here today in Bury, which is one of our regimental heartlands, and the church behind us is the spiritual home of the Lancashire Fusiliers and has been for hundreds of years.'

The Rev. Clare Callanan, who knew many of the Fusiliers from when she served in Cyprus, spoke of the impact of the soldier's death on the hearts and minds of family, of friends and of a nation. She added it was an event which had caused outrage, horror and anger, but had also shown the courage of individuals and brought faiths together.

And throughout it all, I just continued to weep.

Two of Lee's favourite songs were played during the service – *Already There* by Westlife and *The World's Greatest* by R Kelly. Everyone was crying by this stage, as the pall-bearers lifted Lee's coffin to carry him from the church and onto his final journey. I stayed in my seat as I watched him leave, and I could hear the crowds burst into applause as his coffin came into view outside, before being placed in the hearse, still draped in the Union Jack flag and bearing his bearskin hat.

We followed out slowly, and when the bright sunshine outside hit my tired and stinging eyes, the clapping became louder. Poor little Jack, Lee's adored son, seemed bewildered by everything going on around him. He was wearing a blue T-shirt emblazoned with the words 'My Daddy – My Hero'. But, at the tender age of two, he had no idea of how huge the occasion was or even at the loss of his own dad.

We were asked by the media before the funeral how we would like Lee to be remembered. We said that while people would cry and mourn his loss, we wanted everyone to remember him with joy. We said that Lee had always been a fun-loving lad and that is how he should be thought of. We wanted people to celebrate his life and not remember him because of the shocking way in which he died.

Earlier during the day, as the funeral had begun, people across the country paid their respects to Lee. Soldiers gathered outside Woolwich Barracks, where he was killed and *The Last Post*, traditionally performed at military funerals, was played by a bugler. The regular morning summer train service between Fort William and Mallaig, hauled by the steam loco 45407, the *Lancashire Fusilier*, also paused for two minutes on the Glenfinnan Viaduct as a mark of respect.

There was one moment that really touched my heart that day. As I walked down the steps of the church, there was an old Fusilier veteran who grabbed hold of me and hugged me tightly for a minute.

'Bless your heart,' he whispered to me.

But the ordeal was far from over. The service was finished but we still had to endure the ordeal of burying Lee. As we drove through our town towards Middleton Cemetery, it was packed with people waving us on, throwing flowers and cheering like it was some sort of State occasion. A group of bikers, the Rigby Guardians, were all lined up with their bikes outside the Gardeners Arms pub in Hollin Lane and they bowed their heads as we passed. They then made their way close to the cemetery to form a solemn procession in Boarshaw Road, where the graveyard was located. From thereon in, the road was sealed off to allow close family and friends a private burial.

There were about fifty people gathered around the bleak burial plot, where I stood at the front of the grave. Planks lay across in preparation, as Lee's coffin was placed upon them. Ropes were under the coffin and, when the planks were removed, the brave Fusiliers held on. Each of them was crying his heart out.

Everything was removed from the coffin and handed to Becky, but I remember none of the words spoken at the graveside. As the drummers began to lower Lee into the ground, I lost it completely. I collapsed sobbing into Ian's arms and my legs had gone from beneath me. Had he not held me up, there is no doubt I would have been in a heap on the floor.

It was then that flashes of anger punctuated my grief. I knew that I stood at my son's grave because two scumbags had taken him away from me. I would never again have the chance to hug him or tell him that I loved him.

You bastards! I raged in my head. How could you do this to Lee and my family just to try and prove a point? Why did you take him from me?

I threw some beads into the grave and then tried to throw some earth onto the coffin but my hand wouldn't let go of it. To me, it was the final gesture of acknowledging that Lee was gone and wasn't coming back. I finally uncurled my fingers and let the earth crash onto the wooden box below. I was howling in pain as I did so.

'I love you so much, Lee,' I roared through my tears at the otherwise silent gathering. 'I want you back, sweetheart. I love you with all my heart.'

I couldn't bring myself to utter the word goodbye, and I still can't to this day. I wanted to jump in the grave and lie with my son because I couldn't stand the idea that he would be left in there, in the cold, dark ground all by himself. This was my little boy, in a box, in a horrible scary place and all alone. My heart was broken beyond repair.

The Last Post was played by a lone bugler, and I stood in despair as the melancholic music magnified my sorrow. Then the soldiers performed a gun salute across the air and into the distance. Every time they fired, I jumped out of my skin. And, with each shot, I imagined my son's killers in front of him, mocking and gloating at the brutal and fatal wounds they had inflicted on him. I was in a living hell. As the burial drew to a close, I became hysterical. It was also destroying me to see how upset my beautiful girls were. I wished I had a magic pill to make all the pain go away.

A huge military wake had been organised at the Middleton Arena, but it was the last place I wanted to go. I wanted to flee as far away from this nightmare as possible, but I knew I had to face everyone. One of the first friendly faces I saw there was Carol Valentine, who had lost her son Simon during the 2009 tour of Afghanistan. The cruel irony was not lost on us that Lee had survived fighting the Taliban but was murdered when he should have been safe, back in his own country.

I found the wake very hard to deal with, but I forced myself to go round and greet everyone and thank them for their amazing support. The drummers did a couple of performances and there was the normal food and drink on offer for mourners, as they gathered to remember. The outpouring of love and sympathy for Lee and his family was immense. But some of the Army lads found it hard to hold it together, especially as the drinks began to flow and the pent-up emotions of the previous two days began to spill over. I don't think I've ever seen so many grown men cry, but some of Lee's friends were heartbroken. During the wake, the drummers presented us with a replica of Lee's uniform and headwear and, to this day, they still proudly hang on my living room walls at home. In addition, we received a signed condolence book from the regiment. All of Lee's other possessions would later be returned to Becky.

We stayed a couple of hours but I wanted to leave after that. Ian and I and the girls then went off to meet Aimee, as she had not been invited to the gathering. En route to Bury, we stopped at Boarshaw Working Men's Club to meet with the bikers and say a huge thanks for the amazing respect they had shown for Lee. They all lined up in a row as we went in, and they hugged us and cried with us. They were amazing to us that day and have been ever since.

Our Police Liaison Officer was a huge help, but it was our Army liaison officer, Captain Paul Mitchell, who stayed with us throughout the day and night, and he was outstanding. He didn't interfere but stayed on hand to help and protect us at all times. By the time we met Aimee, I was exhausted. I could hardly see out of my eyes because I had cried so much, but I couldn't face going home yet either. We also met up with some of Lee and Aimee's friends from the Army. It was the first time all day that things began to slow down and I finally relaxed my body. We all sat together and talked about Lee. We laughed about Lee and remembered all the brilliant things about him. We raised a glass to Lee and drank way too much and eventually I was ready to go home and crash out. I was grateful for the anaesthetic of the alcohol.

The next day I woke with my head in a spin. I wanted the world to go away but I had promised some of Lee and Aimee's friends that I would take them to his grave. I was dreading it, but I didn't want to let them down. It was extremely quiet and sombre down there and it felt like a very different place from the day before. I stood and wept at the grave as they laid some flowers. There were lots of others bouquets now, and I tried to find a shred of comfort from the lovely words written about Lee, but nothing seemed to work. The one thing it did teach me, however, is that there are more good people in the world than bad – that had been made so clear to me by the thousands of ordinary people who had turned out in their masses to support us.

When I returned home I sat down in silent grief. I could hardly move, let alone function properly. I felt numb with so much sadness and sorrow and I didn't have the energy for anger or hatred. Every waking hour I felt like my heart was being ripped apart, my soul wrenched from my body. All I could think was that Lee had finally gone. His life was over and I wished mine was too.

4

Early Days

Hold him a little longer, Rock him a little more.
Tell him another story. You've only told him four. Let him
sleep on your shoulder, Rejoice in his happy smile. He is only
*a little boy, For such a short while.**

A ll I had ever wanted was to have children and be a good mum. I didn't aspire to having a fancy career or loads of money, but I wanted my family to have the kind of childhood I'd never had. My upbringing was pretty tough, because I never knew what it was like to have the safety and security of my mum and dad to look after me.

I was born on 9 December 1966 in Rochford, Essex, to Yvonne and John Seville but, when I was about six months old, we moved to Germany, where my dad had been posted because he was in the Army with the Royal Artillery Regiment. We settled into married quarters in Dortmund, and later we moved to

* Author unknown

Padeborn. Dad was away most of the time working, not that I remember too much of those early years anyhow.

My mum already had three sons from a previous relationship – John, Reginald and Ron – but they had remained in the UK with their dad. As time went by, Mum and Dad had four more children together, my baby brothers Paul, Stephen, David and, some years later, Colin. We were all fairly close in age apart from baby Colin, who was eight years younger than me.

I hardly remember a thing about my early life in Germany except for one horrible day when my mum told us all that she was leaving. I was just ten years old and I was heartbroken. She never said why; she just packed her bags and disappeared. I was later told she had met another man. As she walked out the door with her case, I remember my little brother David running after her and screaming at the front door as she closed it behind her. It was a moment I will never forget.

My dad left the Army soon after and we all returned to England with him in 1976, where we moved in with my Nanna Seville in Gorton in Manchester until we could get ourselves sorted. I was ten, Paul was eight, Stephen was seven, David was six, and baby Colin was just two years old. Dad managed to get us a home nearby until we eventually got a council house in Langley, Middleton, where we settled and grew up.

It was a pretty miserable existence for me. Dad had taken the break-up with Mum really badly and he turned to the drink for comfort. For a long time after, he didn't go to work, and just stayed in the house getting drunk before going to bed to sleep it off. It was the same pattern every day. So it fell to me to become a 'mum' to my little brothers as best as I could, even though I was only young myself.

Every morning I would get them up and dressed before doing all of our breakfasts and making sure everyone was safely delivered to school. Colin was looked after by a neighbour when we were out for the day but, as soon as I got back from school, I had to take over and sort out the dinner for everyone, including my dad. By the time I had cleaned up and looked after the kids, it was time to put them to bed.

I carried out all the normal duties of a mum, including the washing, the ironing, the cleaning and the food shopping. Each night I cried myself to sleep, exhausted and miserable, wishing I could have a normal mummy and daddy like everyone else. I felt sorry for my dad more than anything because he didn't cope after Mum left, but I preferred it when he was asleep from drinking too much because then I didn't have to listen to him talking non-sense over and again. I adored my brothers and did everything I possibly could, even though I realise my efforts weren't perfect. I didn't want any harm to come to them, so I did my very best to be a mum to them. I made myself a promise back then that one day I would have children of my own, and I would give them a wonderful childhood that was the complete opposite to mine.

It was no life for a young girl who wasn't even a teenager yet. It meant that I had no fun or happiness and no parents I could turn to for help or security. I had very few friends because I was never able to go out and play in the street like normal kids, apart from one girl, Joan Lynskey, with whom I'm still close today. She moved away from Manchester many years ago and went to live in America, but we never forgot each other and, all those years later, when Lee was murdered, she saw what had happened on the news. On the morning of Lee's funeral, she texted me to send her love and we have since been back in contact when she returned to the UK.

After we had left Germany, my mum went back to live with her mother in Southend. Dad tells me he took us all to see her there shortly after she returned. There was one other occasion, apparently, when Mum came to visit us all in Manchester, but I have no recollection of it. Apart from those two occasions, I didn't see my mother again until I was seventeen years old, and that was only because I went to visit her.

Dad eventually began to pull himself together sufficiently to get some work at a local foam factory, which at least meant there was more money coming into the house. Then, when I was about thirteen or fourteen, he met a woman called Jackie. I really loved Jackie and things got a lot better when she arrived. She already had a son of her own, but went on to have another with Dad, our baby Mark.

They were probably the only happy times I can remember as a young girl, because Jackie took care of everyone and I helped her with Mark. She was really kind and nice. She taught me how to bake and do loads of things in the home, and Mark became my little shadow. Wherever I went, he followed, and at weekends I would proudly take him down to see his grandparents and spend all my time with him. He was adorable and I loved him very much.

We had loads of laughs when Jackie was there, including the time I had a baking disaster. I had really long hair at the time, right down to my hips, and one day I thought I was the bee's knees, mixing up this cake, when my hair got caught up in the hand mixer and the cake mixture! It was a sticky mess, with my hair mangled up in the mix and the whisk, and nothing could get it out. In the end, Jackie had to cut my long hair short on one side, while the other side stayed really long! It became a long-standing family joke that we still giggle at today. They were really good times with Jackie and I was desperately sad when her relationship with my dad eventually broke down and she left our home with my lovely brother Mark. But she and I are still close today.

In spite of the difficulties I faced growing up I still managed to do quite well in school, securing five CSEs. My lonely upbringing had resulted in me being a shy and insecure young woman, but I knew there was a better life out there for me than the one I had known growing up. My qualifications helped me to gain decent office employment and, at seventeen, I began working as an admin assistant at British Vinegar in Middleton, before moving on to work in the office of a small local company called JPR Plasterers.

British Vinegar had its headquarters in Croydon and one week a manager from there was visiting our Manchester branch. He heard that I'd been trying to get in contact with my mum, so he offered to drive me all the way to her house in Southend. It was very kind of him, and he took me right to her front door and waited to make sure I got in safely.

I can't say it was a loving reunion with Mum because I had so many questions to ask about what had happened in the past. However, we were back in contact at least. I continued to visit her and it was whilst travelling home from Southend on the coach one evening that I met my first husband, Phil McClure. I was eighteen at the time and, within a year, I was married. I fell pregnant shortly afterwards and, of course, I was delighted. It was like a dream come true to be expecting a baby, but the marriage was not to prove a happy one. The relationship was already in trouble during my pregnancy but nothing was going to take away the absolute joy I felt at growing my first beautiful baby inside me. That was all that mattered to me at the time.

At precisely 11.23 a.m. on 4 July 1987, my world changed forever when my perfect baby boy burst into life at the North Manchester Hospital. I should have known even then that he was going to be a handful after putting me through the most horrendous hard labour for twenty-four hours but, as soon as I held him in my arms, all that was forgotten and I loved him with all my heart from the moment I laid eyes on him. He touched my soul in the blink of an eye and I had never felt such an all-consuming love in my entire life.

Weighing seven pounds, five ounces and measuring forty-nine centimetres, he was the most gorgeous baby I had ever seen and I felt like the luckiest woman on the planet. This tiny little child was mine and he meant everything to me. He was my flesh and blood and I vowed I was never going to let anyone hurt him or treat him badly. I was determined to give him all the love I had never had in my own life. I wrapped my arms around him and, despite being exhausted from giving birth, I couldn't take my gaze off him. He had blue eyes when just born but they quickly changed to brown. As I gently rocked him back and forth, he wriggled around and tried to open his eyes to take in the new world around him.

Lee had gorgeous, thick, dark-brown hair that was all wet and sticking up on the top of his head, and his wrinkled pink baby skin was as soft as silk against my face, as I drew him into me for a kiss. It was an incredible feeling and I knew instinctively I would always want to cherish and protect him.

'Welcome to the world, my beautiful baby boy,' I whispered in his ear. 'Happy birthday, Son. I'm your mummy.'

I remember everything about that day, even Mrs Brown the midwife and Doctor Sharp, who helped deliver Lee safely. We called our baby Lee James, and when I took him home he became the centre of my world. His nickname was Fred, because that was what I called him when he was still a growing bump in my womb, but now he was out he was a bonny, lively, loud and completely healthy baby. I was truly blessed to have been given this perfect child.

In the news at the time the sunken Zeebrugge ferry was being raised and Moors Murderers Ian Brady and Myra Hindley confessed to the killings of Pauline Reade, sixteen, and Keith Bennett, twelve. They had already been convicted in 1966 of the murders of Lesley Ann Downey, aged ten, in 1964, and Edward Evans, aged seventeen, in 1965. Brady was also convicted of the murder of twelve-year-old John Kilbride, and Hindley was found guilty of being an accessory. Now, in 1987, they admitted two more child murders and they helped police search for the bodies,

finding Pauline Reade buried on Saddleworth Moor. The body
of Keith Bennett was never discovered.

It was a huge news story and was all over the papers and
the TV, and it scared the living wits out of me as a young mum
because it reminded me of the terrifying things that could
happen to vulnerable children. It made me want to shelter my
son even more. On less frightening matters, *EastEnders*, *The
A-Team* and *The Bill* were some of the most popular shows on
television, while Rick Astley's *Never Gonna Give You Up* topped
the charts as Lee was being born. *Crocodile Dundee* and *Platoon*
packed out the cinemas.

Most of this went over my head because my life was filled
with looking after my son. I scarcely noticed much else going
on in the world. Phil and I didn't make our marriage work and,
when Lee was three months old, I left to go and live with my
mum. I had always been close to Phil's brother, Alex, known
to everyone as Gordon, and a relationship developed which
eventually led to my second marriage and the birth of our two
daughters, Sara and Chelsea. He was incredibly supportive and
caring of Lee and me and was a good father to all three children.
We enjoyed a much happier union and stayed together for five
years.

By Christmas of 1987, Lee was five months old and we went
to live with Gordon at a flat in Cheetham Hill in Manchester,
before eventually getting a council house together in Daniel
Fold in Rochdale. This would become the home where Lee, Sara
and Chelsea would grow up in their earlier years.

The first year of Lee's life was a shock to the system, to say
the least, because I was totally fatigued. He was a little bugger,
staying awake all night and then sleeping during the day,
which meant I was deprived of sleep. But no matter how hard
it was, I never complained or wished for a different life. Lee
was all I had ever wished for, so I just ploughed on and made

sure I was there to mother him around the clock, whenever he needed me.

He was completely adorable and he made my life complete. In February 1988 we christened Lee at St Anne's Catholic Church in Crescent Road, Crumpsall, and I was the proudest mummy on earth. I was completely in love with my little boy and cherished every day with him. I never got bored watching Lee and, when we hit any of the big baby milestones, I was so thrilled you would have thought I had won the Lotto!

I remember wanting to tell the whole street when he stood up on his own in his cot for the first time on 15 March 1988. I was so in awe of him, you would have thought I was the only woman to ever have a baby. It was only a couple of weeks after that Lee began to speak.

'Mamma,' he blurted out to me as his very first word.

'Oh, my lovely baby boy! You are so clever to call out for your mummy.'

He was grinning his head off as he kept muttering my name and my heart melted on the spot. Looking at Lee at this very tender, young age, I couldn't for the life of me understand how any mum could walk out on her children and leave them. I knew as sure as the sun sets each day that I would never be capable of doing that. If anything, I would be the opposite and not ever want to let them go.

Some evenings, when he went down for a nap, I would sit quietly by the side of his cot and just stare at this precious little human being who I would give my life for. I would stroke his soft cheek and smile to myself, marvelling at the miracle of life and the most wonderful gift I had been given. He was so pure and innocent and he changed my life completely.

'Sweet dreams, my gorgeous boy,' I would whisper aloud to him. 'I love you more than anything in the entire universe and I'm always going to look after you. You've made my dreams come true, precious son, and I'm never going to let you down. I'll make sure that I am the best mummy you could possibly have.'

In August of 1988, Lee began to take his first tiny steps and to me it was like he had just performed a miracle. He was such a happy, smiley baby and he was rarely grumpy or unhappy. He loved nothing better than a rough and tumble and being thrown about in the air. He was boisterous from day one and nothing would change even when he grew up.

I fell pregnant with Sara that year, so I had my hands full with Lee and a baby on the way, but it felt like this is what I had been born to do. All the money in the world couldn't have made me more content than I was at being the best mum I could be. It felt so right and comfortable and I wouldn't have swapped it for anything.

'Who's mummy's clever little boy, eh?' I would chirp at Lee, as he sat grinning at me from his high chair.

Lee would chuckle away and giggle and gurgle back at me and it would make my spirits soar just to be with him. He was a great walker once he got going, and that's when the real fun began. I had to have eyes in the back of my head to keep up with him, as he was into just about everything he could lay his hands on. He was a proper little boy, climbing all over the house and the furniture and making mischief whenever he could, but it was impossible to get cross with him because he would make me laugh so much watching his antics. He might have been a little imp at times, but he didn't have a bad bone in his body. Quite the opposite, he was very kind and loving and he showered everyone he met with affection. Everyone adored him.

I admit that I did spoil him rotten, as I did my other children, but being the first born, and the only boy, Lee seemed to get away with a touch more than the rest. He was definitely a mummy's boy and, as he grew up, he would sit on my lap and relish the cuddles. My hair was still very long, down to my lower back, and Lee would snuggle in and love to play with my hair. I recall his first Christmas like it was yesterday. I got him as many toys as I could afford but his favourite seemed to be a big dumper truck that he would race across the carpet, as he sat on the living room floor.

'Mummy, I love you so much,' he would often tell me. 'I think you're the best mummy in the whole wide world.'

'And I think you're the best son in the world too,' I'd reassure him.

Lee was as cute as a button and so comical to watch. I can still see him in my mind and hear his little voice calling out to me.

'Mummy!' he would roar across the house. 'Come and play with me!'

We had a very simple, family life – all I had ever dreamed about when I was growing up. When Sara was born, Lee had his nose put out of joint ever so slightly at first, because he had never had to share me with anyone, and now this new little baby seemed to be getting all the attention. After throwing a few 'paddies', his curiosity got the better of him and he became more interested in his baby sister.

'You were this little not so long ago, my lovely boy. And this is going to be your loving sister when she grows up. Get a nappy for Mummy so we can put it on the baby,' I would ask him.

I wanted to get him involved and the plan seemed to work because, before long, any jealousies were soon forgotten and Lee and Sara became inseparable. Apart from a short spell back at work after Lee was born, I quickly realised I wanted to be a stay-at-home mum and raise my children myself. I never regretted that decision.

Lee's first ever toy was a big fluffy elephant that he would sleep alongside at night but, as he started to get a bit older, he developed an interest in the current toys of the day. In particular, up until the age of about three, he utterly loved anything to do with Disney. You couldn't tear him away from the Disney Channel and Mickey Mouse became like his best friend. Often we would sit down together in the early evening as he watched his favourite cartoons and stroked my long hair. I remember decorating his bedroom early on in a Disney theme and Lee was flabbergasted.

'Wow, Mummy! This is amazing,' he gushed, as he rushed in for a bear hug. 'Thank you so much, Mummy. I love it. Mickey Mouse is ace!'

The one area I did struggle a little with Lee was with his eating. He was a fussy bugger and refused to eat baby food from an early age. If I tried to feed him, he would spit it out all over me. He stayed with a bottle until he was about three or four, and he would eat rusks and milk or yoghurt. I would also purée adult food for him, and he seemed to like that far more than anything from a jar.

Bath time was a riot with the kids when they were small. By the time Chelsea came along, you can imagine the chaos that a trio of lively kids and water made. But I loved it all. For me, it was part and parcel of the fun of being a mum. I laughed with them, and I just wanted to make sure they were happy and well cared for. If I could hear my children laughing, it was the best music in the world.

Lee's next obsession after Disney was the Teenage Mutant Ninja Turtles. And boy, did he love those Turtles! If it had a Turtle on it, Lee wanted it. I can remember buying him a pair of Ninja Turtle jeans when he was three and he never wanted to take them off.

'Mummy, I want to wear my Turtle jeans every day,' he announced. 'They are the best jeans ever!'

He had all the toys in the range, as well as four fluffy Ninja teddies that he would sleep alongside every night. His favourite was Raphael and it went everywhere with Lee. After the Turtles came Thunderbirds, and Lee had his very own toy Tracey Island with a little castle on it.

When he wasn't playing with his toys, he would be running riot with Sara and Chelsea, and the three of them tore around together, without a care in the world. To me, it was chaotic heaven! Fun-loving, healthy kids playing and enjoying their lives – I couldn't have asked for more.

When he was four, Lee went to a private nursery before school. A few weeks before one Christmas, the children were taught how to make plaster of Paris moulds and turn them into decorations for a Christmas tree. Lee came home as proud as Punch that day, carrying this special trinket he had made for me. It was held up by red string and, across the front, he had written: 'Merry Christmas, Mummy'. He had drawn a Christmas tree on it and coloured it in with dots. It was the first thing Lee ever made me and it was the most beautiful gift I had ever received. We hung it on our tree that year and every Christmas since. It is now held together with tape but it still comes out every year to go with all our other decorations.

I always tried to give my kids balanced and healthy meals but Lee was a total crisp junkie. He loved all shapes and flavours, but his favourites were the really strong ones like Worcester Sauce, Pickled Onion and Prawn Cocktail. All the kids loved treats like pizza, but Lee would never eat beef burgers at home, even though they all enjoyed McDonald's occasionally. It often felt like I was on a merry-go-round of cooking, cleaning and tidying up after their playing, but I was happy. My children made me that way and I will always be grateful for the joy they brought into my previously miserable life.

As far back as I can remember, Lee had always wanted to be a soldier, and I think he was about five when he made his first declaration that he was going to join the Army. I'm not even sure where the influence came from, although he did love to talk to my dad about soldiers and play with his campaign medals. Later in life, my lovely brother Mark certainly played his part as a role model for Lee because he'd been in the Army too, but that wasn't until Lee was much older.

'I'm going to be a soldier when I grow up, Mummy,' he announced with such surety at five years old. 'I'm going to wear a uniform and be in the Army.'

It was something he never grew out of and, from that day forth, his heart was set on a military career. His other big love was football and, from the age of six, he became soccer mad. He would have a lifelong passion for supporting his beloved Manchester United. He had more footballs than I could count, and Sara and Chelsea would kick along with him and form their own squads.

In those early days, although Lee was naturally flamboyant and outgoing, he didn't find it as easy as I would have thought to form friendships outside the home. He was as close as could be to his sisters, but it wasn't until we eventually moved to Langley in Middleton, where I still live, that Lee would forge some of his closest friendships – ones that stayed with him for life, even after joining up.

Gordon and I had drifted apart gradually and, when Lee was eight, we agreed to separate. I left Rochdale with the three children and moved to the house in Langley. It was an upheaval for us all, but the children quickly settled and were really happy in our new home. It was here that Lee, Sara and Chelsea made some of their best friends.

A year later, on my birthday, I had to go out and run some chores while my friend Sandra across the road looked after the children for me. When I returned, I was in for a huge surprise. Lee had asked his 'Auntie Sandra' to help him prepare a birthday party for me so when I walked through the door the table was laid with all sorts of delicious foods and decorations.

'Happy Birthday, Mum,' Lee shouted, as he ran over for a big cuddle.

'Oh, my goodness, what have you lot been up to while I've been gone?' I joked with him.

'We wanted to do something special for you to say how much we love you,' Lee answered.

'This is the best party I have ever had, my darling. Thank you so much. This will be my best ever birthday.'

There were party hats, streamers, poppers and balloons. Sandra had helped Lee and the girls to lay out a huge feast for us all with pizzas, sausage rolls, fairy cakes and sandwiches. It was amazing, and I felt so special because Lee had wanted to do it for me. He was an incredibly thoughtful and caring boy and I will never forget that afternoon. The kids were running around the house, laughing and dancing to music, and it was magic. To me, that was what family was about. Being together and being happy.

All the kids loved animals and Lee especially got really excited if we went to a local farm, where he could see all the different livestock. He loved the goats and the cows and the pigs, but he got a huge shock when we visited one place. The kids were given name badges and, as he went to pet a goat, it jumped up on him and ate his badge. Lee cried for an hour after that and it was a while before we went back to any farms. Poor little thing was petrified of the goat!

A lot of people said to me that I would regret being soft and gentle with my children, even spoiling them, but I was fiercely defensive of any criticism after the childhood I'd suffered. Lee was mine and I was the one who was going to love and protect him and make him happy, so that he didn't have to experience what I went through.

Sure enough, Lee did become a real handful as he began to get older, but I don't believe it was because he was spoilt. It was only much later in his life that we learned he was dyslexic, but this was never diagnosed at school and he went through huge frustrations and anger because he couldn't cope as well as the other kids and he didn't understand why. He was clever and smart, but his unrecognised problems with reading and writing really affected him. He became angry and abrupt, and this wasn't Lee's nature at all. He had always been kind and considerate and loving. I didn't recognise my own son, as he began to change into an adolescent who didn't seem to care about anyone or anything. His tantrums were quite frightening and, as he grew bigger and stronger, I was no match for his physical strength or mood outbursts.

There was one saving grace through it all, and that was my husband Ian. After I divorced from Gordon, I remained on my own for some while, bringing up the children alone. It was tough because I had so little money but we got by. There was always food on the table, a clean, warm house and nice clothes and, whenever possible, I would always buy the kids a treat. They never complained and I made sure that I made up for lack of cash with love and security. My kids never went without and they knew they were safe and loved.

Lee had always found it harder to warm to males than he did to women, perhaps because he had never had a permanent father figure around. With Ian, it was a different matter. He adored Ian from the very beginning and quickly came to regard him as his dad. Likewise, Ian adored all my children and embraced becoming a father to them, in particular Lee who he brought up as his own. I met Ian in 1999 and our connection was instant. Lee was eleven years old and really needed a dad in his life.

When Lee was studying at the Middleton Technology School, I was constantly being called in to see the teachers and the headmaster because of his behaviour. He would get angry and frustrated in lessons, and knock down chairs and cause a scene. Lee was finding it impossible to sit down and concentrate, and his way of deflecting from his problems was to be disruptive and make the other pupils laugh. Everyone was at a loss trying to work out why this was happening, but his dyslexia was never picked up.

He would come home from school raging, and nothing I said or did would calm him down. It was breaking my heart, but it was also putting a strain on me because I couldn't help the boy I loved most in the world. I had never known Lee to be angry or aggressive to me and I didn't know what I had done to deserve this. It wasn't as if he had got into bad company and was running with gangs or drugs – far from it. That wasn't the kind of life he had been exposed to. It was as if he was tortured internally and he was lashing out left, right and centre.

I suppose with the problems he had at school, coupled with a bucket full of growing pains and teenage hormones thrown in for good measure, it's hardly surprising that he was in meltdown. He never brought trouble to our door and didn't fall foul of the law or the police. But those temper tantrums of his were vile! The smallest thing set him off and he would start screaming and shouting in my face for all his worth. Sometimes he would storm off and hide. Panic-stricken, Ian and I would spend ages combing the streets looking for him, only to discover the little tyke had sneaked back home and was hiding out in the garden. His moods erupted if he didn't get his own way and I was tearing my hair out in despair. I never stopped loving or caring for him – I just wanted my sweet and loving child to come back to me.

Ian was amazing at dealing with Lee. When he started to kick off, shouting and raging, Ian would just talk to him and try to calm him down. If he got too unruly, Ian would bear-hug him to the ground and sit on him until he had run out of steam. Other times, he would put Lee in the car and take him for a drive and the pair of them would talk until he felt better. Ian had a real gift for being able to calm Lee's anger, possibly because Ian is a gentle and kind man too. He never flaps or loses his cool, and I think this had a soothing effect on Lee. It was also the fact that Lee trusted his dad completely. This was clearly a traumatic time for him, and he needed us to stay strong and support him.

They would also go and visit the horses in local fields and, after spending time with Ian, Lee would be fine. He was really there for my son, and stuck by him through thick and thin through his turbulent years. He really loved Lee and the feeling was returned. Their relationship grew stronger all the time. It was a mark of the love that Lee shared with Ian that, when he turned sixteen, he chose to officially change his surname by deed poll from McClure to Rigby, because he felt that Ian was his true dad. Ian was so chuffed by this and said it was a real honour that Lee wanted to take his name. They remained as close as any father and son could be, right up until Lee was killed. Later on, when they got the chance, father and son would go and have a few pints together in the pub. It was wonderful for me that my children finally had a dad who was reliable and always there for them.

Lee's teenage years were a real hell for all of us, including Lee, who was clearly out of his depth at school and unhappy as a result of that. But, despite the trauma of that period, I believed in my heart that the kind and loving boy I knew was still inside somewhere and would return one day. None of us gave up on him because we trusted and believed in him always. We dug our heels in and took the flak and waited patiently for Lee to grow up. Ian was always there for him as a sounding board and, between us, we got there in the end.

Lee was also very close to my brother Mark and he really looked up to his uncle. Mark had also been in the Army and had done well for himself. He drove a nice car and had a decent lifestyle and Lee admired him and wanted to be like him. Mark would often take Lee for a ride in his car and they would chat.

'I wanna be like you when I grow up,' he confided to Mark. 'I wanna have a nice car and do good things.'

'Well, you'd better start sorting your life out then and stop kicking off at people,' his uncle replied.

'I want to join the Army and go see the world,' Lee continued.

'You need to grow up quickly and sign up as soon as you can. If you work hard and learn then you'll go far. I know you can do it, Lee.'

It was the pep talk he needed and, when Lee left school at sixteen, everything changed almost overnight. As if he had swallowed some magic recovery pill, the anger disappeared and he began to smile again. And so did I. My beautiful son had returned to the way he had always been – fun, loving and kind. And with a wonderful future ahead of him.

5

In The Army Now

Being a mum to a soldier is one of the proudest things you can be, but it is also the most terrifying. It is such a double-edged sword. From the age of five, Lee had never wanted to do anything else but join the Army when he grew up, and it was a dream he fulfilled. I don't know where that influence came from but it had always been there – he seemed so certain his entire life that he would one day serve his country.

After leaving school at sixteen, Lee started work immediately because he knew he had to earn money and pay his way in life. From the moment he went out into the world, all the tantrums and troubles we had endured just vanished and he seemed to grow up overnight. He had a good head on his shoulders and he realised that nothing in life was handed to you on a plate. He had no real interest in the jobs he took – working in burger bars and warehouses – but they were a means to an end for him; he had his sights set firmly on one career only. As soon as he turned eighteen, Lee went straight down to the Army Recruit-ment Centre in Rochdale to join up. But it wasn't quite as plain sailing as he had hoped.

Lee should have breezed the entrance exam, because he was smart and had loads of common sense, but on two occasions he failed it and he was absolutely gutted. No one was more surprised than his recruitment sergeant, coincidentally called Phil Rigby, who knew Lee was very capable and would make an excellent soldier. He couldn't understand what had gone wrong. It was only when he sat down with Lee and talked through the exam paper that he realised Lee was dyslexic. It was the first time it had ever been recognised and finally my son's problems at school and his frustrations were beginning to make sense. He was put through two months of adult learning and Phil coaxed him through the process. Lee finally passed the exam on the third attempt and was accepted into the Royal Regiment of Fusiliers.

It was the start of the life that Lee had always wanted and we were all beside ourselves with pride and happiness. Lee loved the Army and the Army loved him. It was that simple. He was a natural soldier and he took to military life like a duck to water. He was a team player and quickly formed great friendships with the lads in his unit, who became like a second family to him. He was originally based in the barracks at Catterick in North Yorkshire, and while we all missed Lee being at home, he visited regularly and would spend hours telling tales of everything he had been up to. I was so thrilled for my son because he was living the life he had always wanted. I don't think I thought too much about him going away to fight at that early stage; I was just delighted that Lee was embracing the career he had always dreamed of.

Lee made friends very easily because people loved being around him. His easy-going nature, banter and raucous sense of humour made him a huge hit with the other lads in his unit. He was attached to the 2nd Batallion, Royal Regiment of Fusiliers, and he was so proud to wear that uniform. Army lads like to use nicknames, or abbreviations of their comrades' names, and Lee quickly became known as 'Riggers' .

It was a huge relief when Lee found his stride in the Army, because the first few weeks were a bit touch and go. I think the graft was initially a shock to his system. As with all military training, the first part was to take recruits away to camp where they have no contact back home. The first time Lee was able to make contact with a phone call home, he was in pieces.

'I want to come home, Mum,' he complained in his first call to us. 'I have to make my own bed and do my own ironing! I don't like it and I want to come back.'

I felt for my boy but I knew he had to stick at it.

'Just dig deep, Son, and get on with it,' I told him. 'You'll soon get used to it, and it'll be the best thing you've ever done. We're all behind you, Lee, and supporting you every step of the way. We know you can do this.'

'Thanks, Mum, I miss you and love you,' he replied.

It was clearly a baptism of fire for all the young recruits who had never been away from home before, but I knew Lee was capable of getting through the early wobbles. And, sure enough, within about a fortnight of his training, he was as happy as a pig in muck.

After six weeks of being in camp, Ian and I were invited to his base at Catterick, where the young recruits had a chance to show off and take us around the base, so we could see what he had been doing in training. It was a great day and we were so proud of Lee, who couldn't stop grinning the whole time we were there. He showed us the firing ranges and then all the youngsters got into camouflage in the woods and we had to try and find them. It was a lot of fun and we were brimming with pride and happiness for Lee.

The next time we saw him was on week thirteen, when he and the recruits he had joined up with were to pass out at the end of their training. It was the most bitterly cold day in November and everyone suffered from the low temperature, including Lee. There were military and local dignitaries in attendance and all the loved ones of the soldiers passing out but, as the ceremony wore on, the cold had a real impact on everyone. As all the lads lined up on the parade ground, the drill sergeant had to discreetly take Lee's weapon from him, so he could warm his hands up and, when he had done so, he handed back his rifle. His hands had become so cold he couldn't hold the weapon any longer. No one else noticed apart from me and Ian, because we had eyes only for Lee, but it was a great show of support from his boss, who wanted to stand by all his lads on passing-out day. It was an immensely proud day and everyone was relieved when we could go inside and warm up!

Ian and I couldn't stop giggling at Lee and the amazing transformation the Army had made in him. There is no question they took on a boy and made him into a man. But Lee, being a li'l devil, never totally lost his sense of mischief, even though he had clearly had to learn some hardcore discipline. He now had the most pristine room, and an immaculately made bed with perfect hospital corners. As for his cupboard in barracks, no one was allowed to touch it because it was so neat and orderly, and his ironing was impeccable. That didn't stop the fun though.

The lads were always playing pranks on each other, Lee more than most, as he was the natural-born joker. I remember one tale about how all the lads would wait for their senior officers to go to bed at night and then take loads of bottles of washing up liquid and squirt them all down the corridors before the lads began sliding all over the place, as if they were on a skating rink. How they never got caught, I don't know, but each time they did this they would clean up before morning, as if nothing had ever happened. It was just lads being lads, having a daft few hours of fun to let off steam and enjoy themselves.

Lee had four days at home after his pass out and then he got his first posting as part of the 2RRF to Cyprus. As far as he and a lot of the lads were concerned, their first posting was one big adventure. For a young man, Cyprus seemed like a holiday camp – but it was not to remain that way. When Lee got there, his mentor and hero, Corporal Simon Valentine, was already there. Simon would move up the ranks eventually and become sergeant but, at that stage, he took all the new recruits under his wing. Among Lee's closest friends out there was Simon Annis, nicknamed 'Treacle', as they had done their basic training together and Simon Valentine, 'Val', got hold of them both and showed them the ropes. From the very start, he was the man they looked up to and saw as someone they could trust. Val looked after all the recruits and saw they stayed on the right path.

After the relatively simple induction of Cyprus, Lee was posted to Jordan in the Middle East with his section. They had been tasked to work with the Jordanian Army. As the army there didn't know how to use the latest new weapons, Lee and his comrades were despatched to help train them, having just completed their own training on the most efficient weapons in the market. I remember Lee phoning home on his first arrival in Jordan.

'Oh my God, Mum, you won't believe where I am. I'm in a hotel with gold taps and luxury everywhere! It's unbelievable!'

I laughed but his luxury was short-lived. When he arrived in Jordan he had the pleasure of plush surroundings for about two days and then Army life kicked back in. He was sent with his troop into the desert, where there were no further niceties and he had to train hard with the men he was stationed with. He spoke about how they were run ragged all over the desert as they carried out weapons training. It was far from five-star luxury, but Lee was an exceptional soldier and blended well into his environment.

There was one thing that Lee remained exceptionally proud of and that was his success at shooting. In early Army life he had struggled but, as ever, Lee would set his bar high and strive to become the best. He certainly achieved that because he went on to win his course at target practice. This was when the riflemen had to shoot at moving targets and Lee ended up being the highest scorer in his unit and won the 'Top Gun' prize. Lee lived on that for a long while and, when he came home, he was so chuffed that he joked about getting a leather jacket and sunglasses like Tom Cruise in the film of the same name. His mates took the mickey out of him, but it remained a sense of real pride for Lee to have achieved something brilliant when the odds had seemed stacked against him. He never let us forget: 'I am Top Gun, don't you know!'

We always laughed with him because he wasn't a big head or an idiot – he was the first to take the rise out of himself – but his success was important to him because he had to fight for everything. It was wonderful to see him enjoying a real sense of achievement.

On his return to the UK, he decided to become a drummer for the regiment and returned to Catterick for another thirteen weeks of training. He had no musical training at all, but was determined to give it all he had. After he qualified for that, he went onto ceremonial duties with the Drummer Corps of the Fusiliers. His mentor, Val, was already a drummer, and I think that held a lot of sway with Lee. Where Simon went, Lee followed. The duties of the Drummers involved playing at some of the most prestigious Royal postings, such as Windsor Castle, Buckingham Palace and the Tower of London. Lee's unit of drummers became known as one of the best the regiment had ever produced. He was the proudest and happiest soldier you could have met.

It wasn't until 2009 that he was deployed to Afghanistan, at the height of some of the bloodiest fighting our troops faced during the war. I was devastated when he broke the news to us but I knew it was part of the job.

'It's what I signed up for, Mum,' he told me. 'Don't worry about me. I'm a part of the best army in the world!' he chided confidently.

I tried my best to hide my fears from Lee but, in private, I was heartbroken. Like all parents, I didn't want my baby boy to go to war and face the terrible dangers out there. Our troops had been hit by so many fatalities and devastating injuries, the number one threat being from IEDs (improvised explosive devices) that were littered across Afghanistan. The list of dead soldiers was growing and I prayed that Lee would not join them. That sounds incredibly selfish, but I wasn't being heartless towards the families that had lost loved ones; I just didn't want to lose my son.

'I don't want him to go,' I sobbed to Ian. 'I just want to keep him safe here with me.'

'We have to let him go,' Ian reasoned. 'The best thing we can do is show our love and support and not let him see how worried we are. He needs to keep focussed on his job and not be worrying about his family back home.'

'I know, but what if he's killed or maimed?' I argued.

'You can't think like that. We have to stay positive for Lee and see him through this tour.'

Saying goodbye was horrendous. He was back home in Middleton and he was in great spirits. It was me that was struggling to hide my emotions but I did my best to keep smiling throughout his leave. When it was time, I held him close and didn't want to let go.

'I love you, Lee. Be safe and come home soon,' I told him.

'I love you too, Mum. I promise I will be safe.'

That was the start of some very dark days and nights. I was too scared to watch the news or listen to the radio. Everything was just such bad news and there were some terrible casualties out on the frontline. I knew very little about army work, so I won't pretend to know much about what Lee was going through. I just wanted to know that he survived each day. Ian knew much more about the nitty-gritty of soldiering than I did because they would spend hours chatting together over a few pints when Lee was home on leave.

There were some lighter moments during his tour that we all laughed at later on. I spent a lot of time making up parcels to send out to Lee and there was one particular package that had him in fits of laughter. I wracked my brains to come up with something different to send him and I hit on the 'brainwave' of sending him some delicious pots of jelly. I thought he would be so thirsty out there, because of the heat, that the jelly would be refreshing. Well, my plan didn't work because, by the time it arrived, the jelly had all melted and he was left with just pots of water! Lee laughed his head off and thought it was hilarious. I would send out other bits and pieces too: Haribo sweets, bags of crisps and biscuits. The lads were all living off ration packs, so they loved to get little luxuries from back home and it always boosted morale to get letters and gifts.

When Lee was able to phone home, it made my heart soar just to hear his voice. He would always try to ring when a soldier had been killed to let us know he was safe. I'm not a religious person, but I prayed every single night to God to bring him back safely to me. I plea-bargained and begged for some unknown force to protect him from danger.

'Please God, bring my boy back home to me. I will do anything in return. Just let him survive,' I would mutter in the dark at night.

I would lie awake petrified of what perils my son was facing. I accepted that soldiers sign up to fight in wars but, however proud I was of Lee, at that time I just wished he was anything but a part of the military. I know I am not alone in this. Many mums have gone through the same thing because all you want to do is protect your young and keep them from harm. My son was in one of the most dangerous places on earth and there was nothing I could do to look after him. Being so out of control in that way was like a form of torture and I hated every moment of every day that Lee was in Afghanistan. I felt like a nervous wreck and I jumped out of my skin every time there was a knock on the door or the phone rang. I was just living for the day I knew he was coming home.

That year saw some of the worst fighting and British fatalities of the entire thirteen-year war against the Taliban. During the whole conflict 454 servicemen and women lost their lives and more than a hundred of those were in 2009. The Royal Marines and the Rifles bore the heaviest losses in brutal combat, but a whole list of other regiments suffered fatalities too, including the Parachute Regiment, the Welsh Guards, the Light Dragoons, the Grenadier Guards, the Coldstream Guards, the Mercian Regiment and the Royal Military Police.

The Fusiliers lost seven men, including two of Lee's closest friends and mentor, Sgt Simon Valentine and his recruitment pal Simon 'Treacle' Annis. Those brave young men would become known as the Magnificent Seven. It was truly devastating for everyone but Lee took the deaths badly, especially those of the two Simons, who were killed one day apart on 15 and 16 August. Val was killed first and it broke Lee in two but then, the following day, his world was shattered again when his closest buddy 'Treacle' also lost his life. The two young men had signed up together and were posted to Cyprus and Jordan together and had become inseparable pals.

Simon Annis was killed along with another comrade, Fusilier Louis Carter, aged eighteen, as they tried to save their severely wounded commander, Lance Corporal James Fullarton, who was twenty-four. The soldiers had been advancing into Sangin, a Taliban outpost dubbed the most dangerous place on earth. During the mission, L/Cpl Fullarton triggered a bomb, badly injuring himself and others. Fusiliers Annis and Carter rushed forward to help the wounded but, as they carried their commander away on a stretcher, they set off a second blast – killing them both. L/Cpl Fullarton later died of his wounds.

Lee would never be the same man again after that tour. For all his exuberance and boisterousness, those who knew him well recognised that he was changed forever by the things he saw and the loss of his brothers-in-arms, like so many other thousands of soldiers before and since. He would later confide to Ian that being out in Afghanistan was a living hell and here he describes what Lee went through.

Before he was deployed to war, Lee didn't seem to have a bother in the world. He loved his Army life and, as far as he was concerned, he couldn't wait to get out to Afghanistan and get stuck into a job that he had been trained to do. He wasn't frightened or anxious – just keen to do his bit to serve his country. This was probably because he had no idea of just how ferocious things would be out there and maybe that was a good thing. Once soldiers had been to Afghanistan, they always dreaded going back because they were more aware of what they would be facing.

As part of his role in the Fusiliers, Lee was a drummer but he was also a trained machine-gunner, a role he fulfilled when he was on the frontline. It's heavy-duty stuff and not the kind of job that allows you to sit in the background. You are up there fighting hard, as well as trying to save your life and the lives of your comrades around you.

Lee hadn't been 'in country' very long before the full horrors of war came crashing down on him. He absolutely hated it out there and couldn't wait to come home. This is how Lee described it to me: 'It's the biggest s***hole I have ever been to in my life. It's like walking into hell. We spent one week in Camp Bastion acclimatising and then we went out on a mission into the middle of nowhere. We were being fired on all the time by the Taliban and there were massive gunfights all around.

'We were living rough in tents in makeshift camps and there were insurgents in the caves and the mountains all around us. I had no idea it would be like this but you have to be in a war zone to truly understand.

'The routine patrols were rough enough, but being isolated in the wilderness was dreadful and our unit had only each other to depend on. The mission was to chase the Taliban into the mountains of Pakistan, and it was working, but it came at a heavy price. It was a massive push and, in total, 10,000 troops were involved. Nothing can train you for the scale of that.

'There were artillery planes destroying Taliban land, as well as desert tanks and ground troops, and I have never seen anything like it before. You just didn't realise the extent of the missions.

'We were in our own unit with our own task to perform and we just watched each other's backs the whole time. I knew these were my friends for life and that I would have taken a bullet for any one of them and they would have done the same for me. The camaraderie was amazing and we were bonded together for life. But it changes you. No one can be the same person again after going through such experiences. Lads were getting shot and blown up everywhere. Some of them we knew of, others we didn't, but we were all in it together.

'You just keep going until the job is done. You can't think too hard out there or else you lose your focus and put everyone's lives at risk. It's when you get back home that your head goes into overdrive.

'You would see bits of human remains hanging from trees and limbs of soldiers scattered on the dirt tracks. It made me feel physically sick but you have to carry on regardless. If you crack up, you're vulnerable and open to mistakes, but all the images are stored in your mind forever and they are always waiting to trip you up.

'Some of the landscape in Afghanistan was really beautiful and spectacular and the light was something out of this world. Night-time was really special because the skies were so clear and I've never seen so many bright and sparkling stars in my entire life. It was like a magical light show. But the conditions and lifestyles in the villages and towns were horrific. It was like stepping back in time a few centuries. It was a completely different world to the sophistication of the UK. Lack of sanitation and all the facilities we take for granted made for some really basic living conditions and, to me, it looked so ancient that it felt like I was walking through the pages of the Bible.

'And then there were the local village kids caught in the middle. I hated that part most of all. It felt alien to me that kids would be scared of me or didn't want to talk to me because I was wearing a soldier's uniform. I would give the kids Haribo lollies or sweets to try and show them I wasn't going to hurt them. I wanted to make friends with them and win their trust. Some of these children had never known anything but war and fighting in their lives and it was heartbreaking. It was a desperate situation and all of us who served there were affected.

In the end, Lee served only half of his six-month tour after being taken seriously ill with gallstones. He was flown back to the UK and straight to hospital for treatment and it was a relief to know he was back on home soil.

It was less of a relief for Lee, for although he hated

Afghanistan, he didn't want to leave his mates in the unit before the tour was over but he had absolutely no choice. He wasn't well enough to continue. Typical of Lee, he made a joke of it when he returned and said that at least he would get half a medal for completing half a tour, but I think he felt he had let the lads down by not being able to stick it out for the entire six months.

We all noticed the difference in him when he returned. He had always been happy-go-lucky and the first one to crack a joke, but now he seemed more serious. He still smiled and laughed but he had done real service with real action and the horrors stayed with him. He had gone out there as a young lad and came back as a grown man with demons that none of us could comprehend. He had been on the frontline and survived, thank God, but it was a sobering experience, and he never got over it. The tour had certainly knocked the youth out of him.

Sadly there was much worse to come. It wasn't long after Lee returned that Sgt Simon Valentine was killed in action. He was the man all the lads looked up to in their unit. He was a born leader and a soldier who made it his business to look after everyone else. He was a man who inspired confidence in others and a soldier that all his men wanted to be. He was known to be kind and compassionate but at the same time strong and courageous. If the lads were in trouble or needed any help, Simon was the one they turned to. From the moment Lee joined the Fusiliers as a teenager, Simon, or 'Val' as he was known, took him under his wing and guided him throughout his career.

Simon was twenty-nine when he died from catastrophic injuries following an explosion on foot patrol in Sangin, Helmand Province. His death completely broke Lee and none of us could console him.

*   *   *

Ian was brilliant at talking to Lee about Army life, but even he wasn't able to reach him or help with his sorrow over Simon's death. I think most of the lads felt that if Simon was killed there was no hope for anyone. They thought he was invincible because he looked after so many lads and the shock at his loss was profound.

The Magnificent Seven fusiliers who died that year and who passed into regimental legend will never be forgotten. They were Fusilier Petero 'Pat' Suesue, Cpl Joseph Etchells, Sgt Simon Valentine, Fusilier Simon Annis, Fusilier Louis Carter, L/cpl James Fullarton and Fusilier Shaun Bush.

It was Simon Valentine's mum, Carol, who was one of the few who saw just how badly her son's death affected Lee and all the other lads in their unit. Carol is the most phenomenal woman I know. Just like her son was the man all the soldiers turned to in crisis, Carol is the one that all the other bereaved mums turn to when they need help or advice. She is strong, dependable and trustworthy and one of the kindest people I have ever met. Clearly the apple didn't fall far from the tree with her lovely son. Despite the fact that Carol has to live her life without her adored son, she never gives up or stops battling for the underdog or for justice. She still hurts as much as the rest of us but she won't often let it show.

Her best friend Jo Cleary describes Carol perfectly:

Let me tell you about my BFF Carol. This woman is amazing and, yes, I know I am biased, but those who know her will agree with me. Those who don't agree, well, you're obviously jealous of her strength, compassion, her ability to drink most men under the table, her laughter, commitment to military causes, her loyalty and many costume changes to entertain whatever the occasion. I am in awe of her unconditional love for her three beautiful children, Kelly, Simon and Zak. My heart is with Carol, Kelly and Zak because, on 15 August 2009, Sgt Simon Valentine was killed in Afghanistan.

I watch my best friend six years on, still raw with heartbreak. I watch in awe how she carries on. I watch her unconditional love for her two surviving children, always putting their needs before her own. I watch with pride as she recalls memories of her Simon and she has me in tears of laughter with tales of what he got up to. Her stories are so real, you believe Simon's actually in the room with you. I watched her with tears in my eyes as she almost burst with pride when she showed me his name on the memorial wall at the National Arboretum. I could go on but, as I said, I am biased.

Carol, I love you. I'm proud to be your friend. You truly are a woman to aspire to. Sgt Simon Valentine: OAFAAF. R.I.P.

Jo's words really hit the nail on the head because Carol is very, very special to those who know her and are privileged and lucky enough to be able to call her a friend. She is a battler like Simon was, and everyone I know is so proud of her. Simon might have been a Superman soldier but Carol is our superhero mum – the mum of all mums! She knew Lee long before he died and she adored him. She has some very special memories of him and Simon and their wonderful friendship. She has agreed to share them below and reveals how her son's death rocked Lee and his whole battalion.

Carol: Lee was one of those lads that once you had met him, you never forgot him! He stood out from the crowd because he was loud and funny and everyone fell for his cheeky charm. I used to say he was a loveable rogue but he was also one of the kindest and most genuine lads I had the privilege to meet.

He and my son Simon had been close mates and colleagues for years and they shared a lot in common. They were both jokers, even though Lee was definitely the loudest, and they were both passionate about being part of the drummers within the Fusiliers. This certainly strengthened their bond because the drummers would often go away on trips to perform public ceremonial duties. This meant long hours and coach trips there and back, during which all the lads entertained themselves and became close mates. Sometimes they wouldn't finish until 3 a.m. but the banter never stopped and they all loved Army life. Having the craic with each other was one of the best bits of it!

There was another thing the two men had in common, and it was something that tickled all the lads who took the mickey out of them mercilessly – they were both huge fans of Westlife. The bigger and soppier the ballad, the more Lee and Simon loved it! They would croon away together and make everyone laugh. They didn't give a hoot that their mates thought it was hilarious. I genuinely think it shows that neither of them was afraid to show his feelings, which was something to be proud of. They were a great complement to each other and I know that because Lee was a lot younger and less experienced than Simon, that he looked up to him and admired him greatly. Everyone looked up to Simon and I couldn't have been prouder of my son. He was my hero too.

He was an exceptional soldier with great talent and wisdom and he gave his job his all. He always put his troops before himself and he saw it as his duty to protect them and keep them safe. He had done so many different and varying tours of duty, including Kosovo, Northern Ireland and Iraq, and it was his second tour of Afghanistan when he was killed on 15 August 2009. His experience, combined with a sackful of charm and a genuine concern for his men, meant that his mere presence made his troops feel safe and confident, even when the chips were down. Everyone trusted him and loved him. But he was more than just a great soldier and a friend. He was a character who was fun and full of life. His big passion in life was the Marvel comic superheroes, especially Superman, and even his quarters on tour were decorated with a big 'S' sign. But all the lads saw him as their superhero.

Simon and Lee were deployed to Afghanistan with the regiment in April for Operation Herrick 10 and it turned out to be the bloodiest and most horrific tour any of them had ever experienced. Regiments across the board were suffering colossal losses including members of what would become the Magnificent Seven from the Fusiliers. The first to die was Fijian soldier 'Pat' Suesue and Simon carried him on his back to try to reach safety and save him. He rang home after that to reassure me he was alive and well and asked me to keep any cuttings about Pat in the press so he could read them when he got back.

Halfway through the tour, Simon flew home for a short R&R (rest and recuperation) and I've never seen him so shaken. There was just something different this time and it shocked me. He didn't go into too much detail with me about the tour because he never wanted to alarm or upset me, but when I asked him how it was going, his reply was: 'It's the worst one ever.'

I don't know if he had a premonition or just a bad feeling about the tour because it was so horrific and the body count was rising, but there were certain things he insisted he wanted to do before he returned to Afghanistan. He wanted to spend as much time as possible with his family and he wanted to do things away from Army life. He took his wife Gemma and their daughters Chantelle and Niamh to Alton Towers for a day out and he was adamant that he was taking

Niamh to my dad Tom's grave. Simon knew this as 'grandad's patch' and for some reason he really wanted to share this with his daughter. Perhaps the scale of the bloodshed had frightened him for the future of his family but it was as if he was preparing for the worst and knew that he may never be coming back.

With nine tours of duty under his belt, it wasn't as if Simon had never experienced the savagery of battle before but, even for a hardened soldier like him, this was not like all the rest. There was something very different about him – his eyes didn't seem to sparkle anymore. Instead there was a haunted look in his face. I felt like he was putting his house in order because he feared he was about to die in combat. When he left me before returning, he was clinging on like never before. He was holding me and didn't want to let go. I had never known my son like this before. I can only imagine the terrible horrors he and the lads must have endured in theatre.

I always maintain that when a young man signs up to serve his country, so does his mum! You are at the end of the phone when everything is kicking off, you are stressed out when they are on tour, and you take the mood swings, flak and dirty washing when they return. Simon had been in the Army a long time, so I was accustomed to him going away but still, I spent most of my life watching Sky News when he was on the frontline. It's a mother thing. Not all the mums can do it and some prefer not to know what's going on, but I was the opposite. I was almost obsessed with knowing as much as possible. Nothing could have prepared me for the devastation of being told my son was dead. It felt like my world had ended. And it was the same for a lot of people who had served with him.

Lee was in the UK when it happened, having already returned due to ill health, and he was utterly beside himself.

The first thing he did was ask his mum Lyn to send some flowers for me, and without a second thought he got in his car and drove to see me in Bedworth, near Coventry. This was in total contradiction to Battalion instructions not to disturb Simon's family in their grief, but it was very typically Lee, who just followed his heart. I am so very glad that he broke the rules on that occasion because he was one of the soldiers I would have wanted to see and his visit meant a great deal. Simon loved the bones of Lee.

As soon as he heard the news, Lee just took off and landed on my doorstep. This caused quite a scare for his mum and dad because they knew how distraught he was at hearing Simon had died, and they didn't know where he had gone. Their heads were racing with worry for hours until they knew he was safe. When he came in he was just in pieces. Gone was the cocky livewire I had always known, and instead a broken man stood before me like he was a ten-year-old schoolboy. One look at him and I knew his heart was broken like mine.

'I'm so sorry to just turn up like this, Mrs Valentine, but I had to come and see you,' he spluttered, as he gave me a desperate, tear-jerking hug. 'I can't believe he's gone. I can't believe it's true, which is why I had to come here and find out for myself.'

'It's true, Lee,' I replied. 'I only wish it wasn't, but it is.'

Lee continued: 'If this can happen to Simon, it can happen to anyone. We all believed he was invincible. He was our leader and our hero. It can't end this way for Simon. The whole battalion is rocked off its hinges. I just keep thinking I'll wake up at some point and find it's all been a nightmare.'

I realised that Lee was in as much shock as me. I made us some tea and Lee sat in the chair opposite me looking completely bewildered and lost.

'He looked after every one of us before himself and he was the finest soldier I have ever met,' Lee whispered. 'He showed no fear and every soldier I know wanted to be like him. Everyone in his platoon idolised him, including me. He would say to us: "Don't worry about me, just look after yourselves first. I will be fine because I am awesome."

'We would all laugh but we really believed him. He made us feel as if we could survive any situation. He was our hero and we all called him Mr Awesome. I can't believe this great man is gone and is never coming back.'

Lee and I chatted for an hour before he finally left to go back home. He was really choked up and emotional and kept thinking that he should 'man up' and deal with it but he couldn't. He was utterly grief-stricken and I just wanted to mother him, even though I had lost my son.

We laughed at some of the antics they got up to and he told me all about the giggles they had shared over the years. Most of all, I just think Lee wanted to share his sorrow with me. I will always cherish the fact that he was the one who came to see me. He was so very special to all of us.

It was obvious that Simon's death had scared a lot of the lads. His officers always said that if you have Val on your unit, you are on the winning side, but even superheroes can't beat the odds all the time. His last act of valour had been trying to clear landmines to keep his troops safe when he stepped on an IED, which blew his arms and legs off. He never recovered from his injuries.

I have other happier memories of Riggers, like the time he rode a pushbike round camp while still wearing his drummer's uniform because he needed to sneak off to get some ciggies. He was always very polite and courteous but he was also a cheeky li'l bugger. I saw Lee often after Simon died. I would be invited to functions with the battalion and I would go to as many as possible to stay in touch with everyone. If Lee knew I was attending any 'do's, he would always make sure he put himself on for duty so he could see me.

I remember one such occasion, not long after his son Jack was born, and he had him with him. He brought him over to show him off and Jack was wearing a little Manchester United football shirt. Lee was as proud as punch of his boy and he was a wonderful father. He also came to me to chat when he was thinking of coming out of the Army. He was just a lovely, sweet-natured lad who thrived on making other people happy. I last saw him at a big service in Warwick, shortly before he was murdered and, as ever, I was delighted to catch up with him.

The next thing I knew, I was watching the news and saw that he had been killed in Woolwich and my blood ran cold. I could hardly bear to watch what was unfolding before my eyes. I thought of Lee's infectious laughter and his fooling around and I thought about his poor family. But Lee's murder was also a huge shock for people around the world. We had all witnessed the terrible fighting and the deaths in Afghanistan, but that was in a war zone in a foreign country. Lee met a barbaric death on the streets of his own country where he should have been free and safe from danger. His murder changed everything.

Carol and I have become such close friends since the loss of our sons, and she has always had my back. In some of my darkest hours, she has been the one who has helped pick me up and try to put me back together again. She has a certain way about her that makes you sit up and take notice. We have attended many military functions together since the loss of our sons and I always find them highly emotional but Carol has always been by my side to catch me before I fall. If ever I started to crack up or cry in public, she would always have the right words to help me.

Typically, she would say: 'Lyn, you can stop that crying right now. It's heads up and tits out. You're a Fusilier's mum, so start acting like one!'

It was the brilliant, hilarious and no-nonsense approach that I needed to carry me through public events, but she was always there afterwards to hold me when I wept. There was another occasion when Carol pulled me through with her daft sense of humour: the very first television interview I did after Lee's murder, on *This Morning* with Philip Schofield and Holly Willoughby. I was so frightened of doing it that I nearly backed out at the last minute but Carol was having none of it. She gave me the most rib-tickling pep talk I've ever had.

She has a huge crush on Philip Schofield, so she told me that if I felt nervous during the interview, all I had to do was imagine her in her living room, watching the show live while licking the TV screen every time the camera shot to Philip! It was so daft but it worked because Carol gave me the strength and courage to press on and do the interview. Philip and Holly were wonderful. They put me at ease and were so warm and caring that I got through it, all the while imagining Carol on her hands and knees in her house licking the telly! She has never lived the TV-licking saga down and it remains a favourite joke of ours to this day.

There is a certain bond between mums who have lost military sons because they never need to explain anything to each other. There's just an unspoken understanding of what it's like to suffer such paralysing, emotional pain. Carol and Simon and so many others will always be a part of my 'military family' and, like Jo, I admire and love Carol very much. I will always be in her debt for looking after me, as well as looking out for my son Lee when he was still alive. He thought the world of her and trusted her as much as he had trusted Simon. I have been grieving Lee for more than two and a half years now and Carol knows every step of the rocky road I'm travelling, because she has been there several years before me. Our sorrow and grief will never end but at least we can draw comfort from one another, as well as share our pride and love for our sons. We only ever intended to loan the Army our boys but, sadly, we never got them back.

6

Tortured By My Grief

There's no easy way to come back after your son has been murdered in such a savage and public arena. I will never again be the woman who was so happy just to be a mum and care for her children. That has been stolen from me forever because my beloved son and first-born child has gone and I could do nothing to protect him. I often ask myself why this happened to my family. To me. Am I being punished for something? Did my son or I deserve this cruel battering in life? Why was it Lee who was picked out and murdered that terrible day? And then I have to remind myself that I'm not the only one who has suffered a devastating loss.

As a mum, nothing can be worse than losing a child, no matter what the circumstances. But it remains the loneliest place on earth because part of your being has been taken away. It feels like your heart and soul have been violently yanked from your body and you are left with the most enormous vacuum that can never be filled. You yearn to see and hear the child that forms part of you. It's an 'inside job'. No one can fix you from the outside – no pills, no doctors or therapists. It hurts constantly, not just emotionally, but with physical pain too. There are days when my bones are aching and creaking and I feel a constant weight on my chest, as if my heart is going to give out. I have consulted with doctors and hospitals and had every test in the land, but each time they tell me it's stress and grief. It is, quite literally, heartache.

I rarely sleep for more than a few hours a night now, and even then it isn't real respite. My sleep is peppered with violent nightmares about Lee being murdered. Most nights, I still wake up shaking and crying, bathed in sweat from the horrors of the images of my son's suffering that play out in my mind. Some nights I dream about how Lee's killers tried to chop off his head in broad daylight. Other nights I see myself standing alone at Lee's grave and the tombstone is splattered with his blood or I see Lee's body, as a child, lying covered in blood in the road at Woolwich where he was murdered. I am either running fast to try and save him or I'm stuck, unable to reach him to protect him from danger.

During these nightmares, I let out bloodcurdling screams and wake up with cold sweats, my heart thumping. I have sat up in bed so many nights and begged for someone or something to take the suffering away, but it is always there. I have forgotten what normal feels like. Sorrow has become my default human setting and it haunts me round the clock. Every day on opening my eyes, it's like re-entering the pits of hell because I can never shake away the violence and bloodshed indelibly seared onto my mind. I don't want to think about the ghastly, monstrous acts of evil that were inflicted on my beautiful son, but they are so vivid that they won't leave me alone. It's as if my brain has become stuck on the same scenes of a horror DVD and won't stop play-ing them over and over in a loop.

After the funeral, life fell apart spectacularly for a long time because I was drenched in the detestable and grim reality that my precious boy had been slain in public in a bloodthirsty murder that was witnessed around the world. The pain of losing a child is hideous enough, but then trying to grapple with the enormity that millions of people watched it happen is beyond comprehension. A few months earlier, I had been an ordinary, anonymous mum who loved her family and now everyone knew our names. If I went to the supermarket or the local shops, people stared and nudged each other because they recognised our faces from pictures in the newspapers or footage from the television. That was so hard to cope with and, when it happened, I just wanted to run home and bolt the door behind me so no one could see me or get to me.

At night-time, I would wait until my two younger daughters were in bed, then I would light some candles, play sad music and drink to try and numb the pain. It was melancholy and maudlin, self-indulgent mourning, but I didn't know any other way of dealing with it. Just as there is no handbook for life, there is no idiot's guide for dealing with death or grief. I had all these feelings festering inside me and I didn't know what to do with them. I genuinely thought the pain of losing Lee was going to kill me and I would find myself talking out loud to him.

'Hello, my beautiful son. I hope you are being cared for in heaven and that you've managed to make lots of new friends and had some fun in the Heroes' Bar up there. I'm sure you'll have met up with both Simons and the rest of the lads for a pint or few. It's comforting to know you are in superb company and that you won't, at least, be lonely. It's me that's lonely without you.

'I miss you more than words can say, Lee, and I would do anything to have you back here where you belong. But at least nothing can hurt you now because you are safe forever from any harm. You didn't deserve to die so young and in such a grisly way and I will never forgive myself for not being able to protect you or take your pain away. When you were a little boy, I would wash your grazed knees and put plasters on them when you fell down. I would hold your little hand and kiss your forehead and make you feel better when you cried in pain. But I couldn't save you when you needed me the most and I am so, so sorry, my darling boy.

'If I could swap my life for yours, I'd do it in a heartbeat, so you could carry on living life to the max, as you always did. I love you dearly, Son, and, until next time, night night, sweetheart and sleep tight.'

It sounds weird, but these conversations with Lee made me feel connected to him because my heart was sending him all my love. But it wasn't the answer to my misery. Inevitably the alcohol I was pouring down my neck at night started to compound my suffering and I would end up in a heap, night after night, sobbing until the early hours. Often I would just crash out on the couch in the living room, not even making it to bed, and I would rise at first light before my children woke up. The self-destruct fuse had been well and truly lit and this would continue for a long time, until I was ready to step out from behind the fog of the bottle.

There was no escaping Lee's murder because it was such an abhorrent and significant crime and it featured in news bulletins across the globe. Even more than two years on, rarely a day goes past without the name Lee Rigby being mentioned in the news somehow. We had obviously lost a lot of men in the Afghanistan war, but this was the first time a soldier had been run over, attacked, mutilated and murdered in this country by home-grown terrorists. It was also a crime of its time because, in the age of modern technology, people who witnessed it recorded it on their mobile phones and, consequently, footage was captured of Lee's brutalised dead body as one of his killers gloried in his own cold-blooded atrocity. Few can erase the detestable images of Michael Adebolajo bragging about butchering Lee in the name of Allah, as he stood in the street spewing his twisted religious venom. My son lay dead in the road just a few yards from where this monster stood, brandishing a meat cleaver, with his hands still dripping in my boy's blood. As he continued to spout and rant his jihadist bile, he encouraged passers-by to film and deliver his hideous and nauseating 'justifications' for the ferocious attack on an innocent man.

Lee's murder was a crime that marked uncharted military history and prompted certain phrases to enter everyday usage, which I refer to as 'Rigby-isms.' For example, the most commonly used phrase was when journalists compared other similar and subsequent crimes to Lee's murder. They reported on 'Lee Rigby-style' attacks where individuals, not necessarily part of a large terrorist cell, would go out and commit so-called jihadi crimes of violence on their own. These are also still referred to as 'lone wolf' attacks, almost always with a reference to the first crime of its kind, which was Lee's murder. With such notoriety, there was never any escaping publicity about Lee and, in the end, I stopped reading the papers or watching the news. I even turned off the radio, which I always listened to during the day, because if an unexpected bulletin came on the news about Lee, it left me felling queasy and unnerved.

It was hard for me to tell the difference between the days any more. I felt like I was stuck in *Groundhog Day*. I would walk about like a zombie in the day, and by night I would attempt to obliterate my feelings by sinking alcohol to drown them out. It was the only way I could get any respite from the unbearable, toxic emotions that were persecuting me twenty-four hours a day. In the long term, it didn't ease the pain one bit. It merely drowned it out for a short window in time until I could find alternative ways to try and cope with my grief.

Not long after Lee died, I asked the Army if I could have one of his T-shirts to keep, but they refused because his belongings from

Woolwich Barracks were to be returned to Becky as next of kin. This really hurt me because I wanted something personal that had belonged to my son, but the Army is not an organisation that bends the rules for anyone. In the end, Aimee gave me one of Lee's shirts that she had at her house, and I still sleep with it under my pillow to this day. It's just one tiny thing I can do to feel closer to Lee.

I hit one of my 'rock bottoms' about nine months after the murder. I had become a slave to my grief and it was all-consuming. I felt as if I was going insane, out of my mind, and I couldn't think about anything other than the loathsome killing spree that had ended my boy's life. One Saturday evening I drank too much and flipped out completely. It was a very cold and dark winter's night in February and I simply stood up and walked out the front door shortly before midnight. I began marching up the road, in freezing temperatures, towards Middleton Cemetery, but my mind was so frenzied that I scarcely noticed the harsh conditions. I just wanted to be with my son.

When I reached the cemetery, I cut across the darkness to Lee's grave. It was the most wicked night but, as I sat on the stone bench we had put by Lee's plot, I felt more at ease than I did sitting at home in the warmth and comfort of my living room. The cemetery is on high ground, so the weather was even worse up there. It was biting cold and throwing it down with icy sheets of rain. Typical Manchester weather in the winter, but not something I would normally be sitting out in at midnight. My hair was soaked and the sharp sting of the rain lashed my face, but I didn't care a damn. My soul felt as dark as the wretched blackness that now surrounded me. It felt like the right place to be.

I had tried to be so strong for Lee and my daughters but, at that moment, I couldn't cope any more. I was drowning in despair and I didn't know how to ask for help. I needed to be near my son and the only way I knew how was to sit at his grave in the middle of the night. It was terrifyingly bleak and desolate and I have never felt so alone in my life. If someone had come along right at that moment and asked me if I wanted to go inside Lee's grave with him, I would have said yes.

Somewhere inside I knew that wasn't right because I had four beautiful daughters that still loved me and needed me, but my judgement and thought processes were not balanced at the time. I find it hard to forgive myself for being so absent from my girls during that period of intense grief. My private agony had eclipsed my love for all those that remained living and I feel so ashamed of that.

That night, as I sat at the grave, my thoughts were only with Lee. It didn't cross my mind that this was abnormal behaviour – I no longer knew what rational thinking was. I knew one thing only and that was that I wanted my son back with me. I somehow believed that by sitting in the cemetery it might bring him physically closer to me, but it was a pretty desperate measure, whatever I had been thinking. It was heartbreaking and lonely, but that's how I felt every day inside. If someone had told me a year earlier that I would feel safe sitting in the dark in a graveyard, I would have said they were insane. Normally, I would have been petrified under circumstances like that, but grief really works a number on your thinking. As I sobbed in the pouring rain, I was completely blasé to any dangers I might be putting myself in.

Lee's headstone had not yet been installed because it had been commissioned by the Army, as this was an official military grave. It takes a while to get the right memorial stone but, even so, it made the site look even more forlorn, without even bearing my son's name. Right then, it was just a slab of dreary grass commemorating an anonymous soldier who died for his country. Surveying the godforsaken spectacle before me, I dropped to my knees onto the sodden, waterlogged ground and lay flat along-side my son's grave and began wailing into the night.

'Please God, let me have my son back again,' I begged. 'I can't live without him. I love you so much, Lee, but I can't cope with this pain any more. I don't want to live without you.'

I wanted to claw away at the grass and get into the grave to hold and cuddle my son to bring him some comfort. My drunken ramblings continued into the night for at least an hour as I became more saturated by the minute. It was tipping it out of the dark, eerie skies and I was soaked through to my bones.

'I hope you're looking after yourself up there, Lee, eating lots of nice food and cracking jokes with your mates. You were the best son a mum could ever have and I was blessed to have you for twenty-five years. I just don't know that I can go on without you. It feels wrong to be alive when you are dead. I'm so sorry that you're lying in the cold, dark ground on your own. I just want to tell you that your mummy is here with you now, to keep you company and give you some comfort.'

That was one of the worst issues for me to deal with – the thought that my gorgeous, handsome lad was buried in a hole in the ground beneath me. It was hard to accept that Lee was truly gone and that only his decaying corpse remained on earth. My soul was completely derelict.

'I wish I could stay here with you all night, Son, but mum's going home shortly,' I spoke out loud to Lee. 'I want to take you with me, back to the warmth and safety of our home, but I can't. I'm distraught at having to leave you here all alone but you will always be with me in my heart. Goodnight and God bless, Son. I love you so much.'

I pulled myself together and got up from the soaking floor and sat down on a bench next to the grave. I was wringing wet and in a real mess, but there was some kind of strange comfort for me, sitting in the quiet night with my son. I picked up my mobile phone and I rang a close friend and explained where I was. That friend was Rosie, the trusted confidante who was writing my book, but also someone who had become a person I looked to in times of trouble. She was very calm and gentle and talked me down from my hysteria. It was then, as the madness began to subside, I suddenly felt the cold and wet that was assaulting my body. I knew it was time to go home. Rosie guided me back there and stayed on the phone until I was through the front door and returned to my family. I was in very safe hands.

I realised something had to change because I was on the road to disaster. My daughters needed me, my husband needed me, and I had to step out from the shadows to start loving them and caring for them all again. I began to have trauma counselling that was arranged through the Victim Support agency. It was very hard to face because I didn't want to talk about the things that hurt the most, but it was a huge help for me. It didn't take the pain away at all – instead it gave me some tools for dealing with it better and some basic survival tips. I stopped drinking as much, so I began to feel marginally better physically. I also began to engage with my family more, letting them know how I was feeling and sharing some of that pent-up burden that previously stayed trapped inside me.

All my girls were fantastic at doing their bit to help me. Courtney would help in the house and talk to me and Amy would give me the biggest hugs ever when I was feeling low. She became chief hugger and she always brings a smile to my face when she embraces me. My grief didn't vanish but I had faced it head on and answered back. I was not going to let it beat me because I had four more children who needed my love too. I owed it to Lee to fight back because I vowed I would create a fitting legacy for his life. It still felt like I had to climb a mountain some days, just to get my head off the pillow, but it was a journey I had to make.

The last time I saw Lee alive was Easter Sunday, before he returned to barracks for work. We had enjoyed a wonderful weekend with Lee and Jack, who was the spitting image of his dad. Lee adored his baby boy and loved spending time with him. It was a beautiful thing to see – my son holding his own little boy, and he was a truly fantastic dad. He was committed and devoted to Jack and I know he was looking forward to being there for him as he grew up. Jack was a giggler like Lee – a real chip off the old block and even looked exactly as Lee had at the same age. It was like rolling back time twenty years and no one could have imagined that fate was about to deal the cruellest hand of all to Lee and his family.

It was the joyous times when Lee was home that my therapist tried to encourage me to remember – replacing the horror movies with loving and happy scenes. He never failed to charm anyone and a weekend in his company always made you feel so alive and invigorated. You always felt better in his company, even if he was like a human hurricane, blowing in with such force and energy before swirling out again leaving us all gasping for breath!

His laugh was contagious and he constantly had us in stitches with his wind-ups and tales of mischief in the Army. He had such hope and vigour for the future but every dream he held dear was smashed to pieces just a few weeks later on that dreadful day in London. I had been a nervous wreck when Lee was in Afghanistan. It felt like I was holding my breath the entire time he was away on tour of duty, and the relief when he touched down in the UK again was enormous. I could get on with my life again and breathe easy, knowing my son was home safe and sound. When Lee left us after that Easter weekend, I had none of the fears I'd harboured when he went to war. Not in a million years could anyone have predicted that Lee was in graver danger in his own country. It's almost like someone played a sick joke on us – allowing Lee to survive Afghanistan only to snatch him away from us on a summer's day in London.

I will never forget those incredible last hours we shared and I can still hear him laughing raucously, playing around with his younger sisters and making us all fall about with hilarity. When he left us, he gave me a big hug and kiss as usual.

'I love you, Mum. Look after yourself and I'll see you soon,' Lee said, neither of us knowing it would be the last time we spoke in person.

'I love you too, Son,' I replied. 'Stay safe and come home as soon as you can.'

As he walked out the door, he turned around and flashed me the biggest smile ever. I never saw him again. If I had known of the peril he was heading into, I never would have let him go that day, but Lee proved to be right about one thing and that was to live each day as if it's your last, for one day you'll be right. He packed more into his twenty-five years than most do in a lifetime. I will never get over losing Lee but I have to try to keep moving forwards and not backwards. I base most daily decisions now on trying to second guess what Lee would have wanted and what he would have done in certain circumstances. I have to live a life for both of us now and make sure that Lee is never forgotten. That, and my family, is what drives me on to do Lee proud and make sure his legacy is protected. More than two years on, I still stupidly keep thinking he is going to burst through my living-room door with that giant smile on his face. If only that could be the case.

I still have the text Lee sent a few weeks earlier on Mother's Day. He was working and couldn't make it home at the time, so he sent flowers and chocolates but it's his last text to me that I will treasure forever. He didn't send many texts, because his dyslexia made it difficult for him, but it's why this message is so precious, because of the effort he made to write it.

Goodnight Mamma. Hope you had a fantastic day today because you're the most fantastic one-in-a-million *mum anyone could ever wish for. Thanks for supporting me all these years. You're not just my mum, you're my best friend. So goodnight and love you loads. Xxx*

That is how I will always remember my son – emotional, kind, affectionate and loving. He was my shining star but now for evermore he is out of my reach.

7

Facing The First Anniversaries

People tell you that the first year of grieving is the most savage, not just because the loss of a loved one is still so raw but because you have to face so many milestones and anniversaries for the very first time. Going through Christmas, birthdays and family holidays when one of your clan is missing is horrific because everyone knows the circle is not complete. The first anniversary of Lee's murder was particularly painful because it felt like only yesterday that he'd been killed, and the horrors of that day came flooding back like a tsunami.

I considered making a pilgrimage to Woolwich to mark the day and pay our respects, but in the end I couldn't face going to the actual road where he lost his life. The only time I had been there was several days after his murder and virtually the entire street had been turned into a shrine of flowers, cards, pictures and condolence messages. The response was quite amazing from such kind and caring people, but it was far too distressing for me to be at the precise spot where Lee had been killed. I had been there once and I knew I didn't want to return in a hurry.

Instead of travelling to Woolwich, my family opted to stay at home and spend the day together. We began the morning by going with Sara to a place that carried out special 3D baby scans, as she was now expecting her fourth child. There were about fifteen of us in all who traipsed into the centre with her and, despite the sorrow of the day, we did have a laugh between us. What I hadn't realised was that Sara had also arranged for a surprise get-together with family and close friends to mark the anniversary. I got told to go home after the scan pictures were finished and then Sara revealed her big surprise.

My eldest daughter had secretly organised a private room in a local pub where we could all have a meal together and remember our lovely Lee. There was all of my family, my best friend Sandra and her family, and my baby brother Mark and his family. It was a lovely gathering but still deeply emotional. It was the perfect way to spend the day because we were away from the gaze of the public and the media. Some heartfelt toasts were made to Lee and many tears flowed. I still felt bereft without him, but I had the safety net of my wonderful family and friends around me.

When the meal ended in the afternoon we all went up to Lee's grave to spend some time with him and lay fresh flowers. The adults each had a red rose with a personal message attached to it, while the children had a balloon each to let off into the sky. It was an extremely hard day to get through, as I kept reminding myself it was a whole year since I had lost my son.

The next milestone was Lee's birthday on 4 July, when he would have turned twenty-seven. Technically, it was the second birthday we had endured without him, but the first year had been so close to the funeral, and my grief still so raw, that it passed in a blur of grieving. This year I was staying away from home at my friend and co-author Rosie Dunn's home in Exmouth in Devon. It was a beautiful summer and I had taken Courtney and Amy with me for a break for the first time since Lee was murdered. We really needed the respite and, as it was right by the sea, we had the joy of waking up each day to sit in the sunshine and watch the ocean. It was the perfect tonic for all of us.

Being away from our own house made us all relax more and, for the first time in over a year, we all managed to smile again and even laugh amongst ourselves. The difficulty I faced was feeling guilty for daring to laugh, and I was so worried that if anyone saw me with a smile on my face they would think that my grief had disappeared, and that I was no longer hurting inside. Nothing was further from the truth. I had simply learned how to camouflage my emotions.

During the trip I was lucky enough to meet some Royal Marines, past and present, who live in the town and work at nearby Lympstone, the next village along from Exmouth, where the commandos have their training centre. I was desperate to do something to mark the occasion. We had considered laying a wreath at the war memorial in Exmouth town centre when one of Rosie's friends, a former Royal Marine of twenty-two years and Afghanistan veteran, Paul 'Dixie' Dean, stepped in to help us. Dixie phoned an old comrade, who was by now in a senior role within the Marines, and lined up a very special treat for Lee's birthday. The Regimental Sergeant Major, Phil Gilby, who was in charge at the Commando Training Centre (CTC) at the time, invited us all to the centre for a special afternoon to mark Lee's birthday. It turned out to be such a memorable tribute to Lee because he had pulled out all the stops to make sure my son wasn't forgotten. Myself and the two girls and Rosie arrived at the camp where we met Phil, and he couldn't have been more welcoming. He looked so smart in his combat uniform and green beret.

'We are honoured to have you here with us today, Lyn,' he said, as he gave me a big hug.

'Thank you. It means a lot for us to be here. Lee would be very proud.'

I could feel myself welling up because it seemed like I had been given the chance to do something really exceptional for Lee with some really kind people. Lee may have been a Fusilier but, as I discovered, the Marines are also a huge family regiment and everyone I met that day embraced me as if I was one of their own. They considered Lee part of their extended military family, as did so many other regiments.

We were given VIP treatment from start to finish. It was a boiling hot summer's day and the King's Squad, the most senior troop in training, were performing their final practice and drills on the parade ground before their passing-out ceremony the following day. We were invited to watch as the Royal Marine Band played and it was really spectacular. It took me right back to when Lee passed out and a lump caught in my throat as I watched these proud young men being put through their paces. In a matter of weeks, some of them would be despatched to Afghanistan as fully fledged Marines, and I remember hoping they would all return home safely. I was privileged to watch them.

As they came to the end of their drill, the troop and the band began to march towards the end of the parade ground. A few yards away stood the Royal Marines' wall of remembrance, which has honoured all the fallen commandos since 2000. Phil invited us to the memorial wall to lay a floral wreath we had made in red, white and blue flowers. It was extremely solemn and, as I walked over with Courtney and Amy, my legs felt like jelly.

The three of us lay the wreath at the foot of the wall and a lone bugler played *The Last Post*. No matter how many times I hear it, it never fails to choke me up, and the tears began to fall. I stood between my two girls and we linked arms, listening in silence as the song played to the end. I had my head bowed in the scorching summer sun, just thinking about my son. It was a truly brilliant tribute and I felt honoured to have been given the chance to remember Lee on his birthday in such a beautiful and fitting manner. Inevitably, the sadness was overwhelming for all of us and I wished with all my heart that I didn't have to remember a dead son.

'Happy birthday, Lee,' I whispered softly to him. 'I would give anything to have you here with us now so we could give you a hug and kiss and celebrate your special day in the way we should. You should be with your family, laughing and joking and enjoying a pint with your dad.'

We stayed for a while to read the memorial wall, and it brought into sharp focus for me just how many young men have lost their lives in recent conflicts. I thought about the families of these wretched souls who never came back from war and I was filled with sadness. Phil stood proudly with us and asked if we were OK. He couldn't have looked after us any better and I think he realised how much the day meant to us.

'Lee would be very proud of you all,' he told us. 'We're privileged to be able to pay our respects to him today.'

The mood lightened a little as we left the memorial and were given a tour of the camp, which is the size of a small town. It was extremely impressive, with state-of-the-art gym and training facilities for the thousands of Royal Marine recruits who are put through their paces before earning their green berets and being sent out to fight for and protect their country.

The afternoon ended with us being invited to the sergeants' mess for drinks. As we sat outside for an hour, a stream of marines came up to us to say hello and pay their respects. Word had got around the camp that we were visiting and unprompted they made it their business to come and greet us. It was a wonderful gesture from all of them and it made us feel so welcome. I was so proud of our Armed Forces that day.

Among the well-wishers were two experienced training instructors who wanted to speak to us.

'Welcome to the camp, Mrs Rigby,' one of them piped up. 'We heard you were here and we wanted to say how sorry we are for your loss and to pay our respects to you. Everyone was appalled at what happened to your son.'

The second man joined in: 'We are privileged to have you here today and we hope the day has gone well for you. You will always be supported by the Royal Marines.'

It was a jaw-trembling moment because I felt so humbled that these fine young men should care enough to seek us out and say such kind and heartfelt words. I struggled to reply, apart from thanking them for their support. Shortly after, we were presented with some lovely gifts and beautiful framed photographs that a naval cameraman had taken of us with the troop earlier in the day. I will treasure them always.

As we left, Phil told us: 'You are welcome to the camp any time you want, Lyn. Come and see us and, if you need anything, if we can do anything for you here, call me and it will be sorted out. It is a proud military tradition of the Corps to look after bereaved families and we regard you as part of our extended family.'

It had been a wonderful day with all sorts of emotions: pride, sorrow, heartache and gratitude. Most importantly, we had been given an opportunity to honour Lee and say a very special Happy Birthday to him. I will never be able to thank Phil and Dixie enough for organising such a memorable day. Some weeks later, I commissioned a steel dog tag for Phil engraved with a hologram of Lee. Very few people have them, just members of my family, but I wanted to show how much his kindness had meant to us.

There have been other very special occasions where we have been able to honour Lee, not least when his name was engraved onto Britain's largest military memorial. In June 2014, I travelled to the National Memorial Arboretum near Lichfield, in Staffordshire. I was joined by my husband Ian, daughter Sara and her partner and fellow Royal Fusilier, Rob Sarjeant, who is now her husband. It has to be one of the most serene and peaceful places I have ever visited, which is quite extraordinary when you consider the purpose of the arboretum. The arboretum is the UK's year-round Centre of Remembrance and Armed Forces Memorial, where you can celebrate and honour the men and women who have served our country in many different ways. It recognises service and sacrifice and honours those who have been killed on duty or as a result of terrorism, from the end of the Second World War to the present day.

There are over 300 unique memorials within the 150 acres of woodland and gardens, including a memorial to the Fusiliers, but the huge wall that bears all the names of the fallen is the most spectacular sight of all. Sadly, each year, new names are added and this time Lee was about to join that list, immortalised in stone for his sacrifice.

It is a very spiritual place and somewhere that allows you the tranquillity for deep reflection. At the time, Lee's name was added to those of 16,000 fellow comrades previously killed in action. Our first trip to the arboretum that summer was to be the first to view the tribute to Lee just moments after scaffolding was removed to show stonemason Nick Hindle's painstaking work. It was a difficult and moving occasion but it was also a pilgrimage we all wanted to make.

When the scaffolding and covers were removed, I was almost lost for words to see my son's name, Rigby, L J, alongside so many others who have lost their lives in service. I felt a desperate mixture of acute grief and sorrow to see so much loss, including that for my own son, but it was also a moment of extreme pride to see that he had been honoured in such a beautiful piece of work. But the sheer scale of the loss of men and women will stay with me forever. It really makes you question war and conflict and the plight of mankind that we are still stuck in violent struggles.

Despite the backdrop of immense and catastrophic bereavement, there remained this quiet and peaceful monument of pride that seemed to wrap itself around you to bring you comfort. There was a sense of real beauty in the tributes to the warriors who had made the ultimate sacrifice.

'Oh Lee,' I sighed out loud. 'I'm so proud of you, son. You served your country well and now it's time for us to honour you.'

I know that Lee would have been so proud to be remembered alongside such brave and fearless soldiers. His Army career meant so much to him and the unveiling of his name amongst some of the greatest military men and women would have made him puff his chest out with honour. He was now immortalised with his comrades.

The stonework was amazing and I was deeply moved by the symbolic significance of my son's inclusion to this great wall of courage. I almost felt numb with emotion but I didn't regret that we stood there united as a family to witness the occasion.

I stepped forward, towards the markings where Lee's name peered out, and it took my breath away. It was a huge moment and quite overwhelming. I knelt down, almost in prayer, to reach out and touch my son's name, and I burst into tears. It was like a dam had burst and I couldn't stop crying. It touched me deep in my soul. I was so proud of Lee but also profoundly saddened.

The names of sixteen other soldiers who had been killed in the line of duty in 2013 were also unveiled, and it was clear that a lot of love and devotion had been shown to remember those soldiers. I felt some relief that at least our fallen men and women were honoured in such a dignified and proper manner, despite the obvious sorrow. It's sad that such a memorial has to exist at all, but it is a fitting tribute to those who have given so much. This is our nation's tribute to those who have died on duty.

The hugely talented stonemason Nick Hindle described his work: 'It's painstaking work, but given the scale of sacrifice it represents, it's a job I'm hugely honoured to do.

'I carve around ten letters per hour and visitors are always moved at seeing me add so many names. I'll regularly stop and answer their questions about the process. I have always done military work, but this is the biggest monument in the country. I have to really concentrate on what I'm doing, but at the same time I cannot help but think of the stories behind each and every name. Everything has to be double-checked, cross-checked and signed off to make sure there are no mistakes; it's all measured out very carefully. It's a job I am privileged to do.'

We spent two hours at the arboretum that day and I drew some comfort in realising that Lee will never be forgotten, not just by me or his family, but by a nation that he pledged to protect. We spent some time at other smaller memorials, including the Fusiliers' wall, where we paid our respects to comrades from Lee's regiment. It was gut-wrenching to see the names of soldiers Lee had served alongside in Afghanistan and who had died before he had. We naively thought his life had been spared when he returned to England safely but his name, now finely chiselled into the wall of remembrance, was a stark reminder how mistaken we were. Seeing that name cut us all really deeply and Sara was particularly distressed when she tried to explain her feelings.

She said: 'Just over a year ago, me and my big brother were horsing around like kids on a night out together. Lee gave me a piggy-back and we were laughing our heads off. Now all I have are my memories and Lee's name imprinted on a wall. It's something that's very hard to accept and it's a very strange sensation to see my brother's name on the wall. I'm so proud of him but it's beyond sad. It's changed my life forever.'

It was a solemn journey home that day but I tried hard to hold onto the sense of peace the visit had instilled in me. I thought about all the other families who had been through the grief that I was now struggling through and I realised it would become my mission to create a lasting and fitting legacy for Lee.

Of all the big occasions, I think Christmas has to be the worst. There are such high expectations across the country that it has to be the happiest time of the year but, if you've lost a loved one, no matter what the circumstances, it's totally unbearable. You see joyful life going on around you but inside you feel dead. You do not want to celebrate.

I still got out of bed and tended to my daily chores. I got my children to school; I cleaned the house, hoovered the floor and cooked the meals. I put on the laundry and answered the telephone. I forced myself into the supermarket to buy food for my family and I tried to smile at times to please other people. But it was a mere existence and I certainly didn't feel alive for most of the time. I had known a better life. I knew what it felt to experience huge joy, watching my children grow and flourish and it was food for my soul. Now that nourishment had been stolen from me and I was permanently depleted of the basic needs for survival. I was constantly lugging a ten-ton sack of emotional rubble on my back. It was torture. Would I ever feel happiness again? Would I ever allow myself to feel anything but misery? I knew it was down to me to try and reclaim a purposeful life without my son, but putting it into practice was far harder than anything I had attempted before in my life. It was so hard to shake off the gnawing fear that I had become part of the hopeless community of the living dead.

*

The Christmas before Lee died was a riot! It was always crazy with Lee around and 25 December 2012 will stay in my happy memory bank forever. It still makes me smile when I think about it. We organised to have the big family dinner at Sara's house, and she and Lee insisted they were going to do the cooking to spoil me. Happy days, I thought, mentally putting my feet up amid the merriment as I waited for my Christmas dinner to be served up.

It wasn't quite as straightforward as planned, though, and that was where the hilarity began. For a start, Lee didn't even like Christmas dinner or Sunday roast, so he had never cooked a meal like it before. Sara wasn't much better either. She had bought a gammon and a chicken and I could hear all this noise and laughter in the kitchen as the pair of them grappled with cooking the meat.

'Do I put cling film all over the chicken to cook it, Mum?' Lee shouted from the kitchen.

I burst out laughing and knew it was going to be one of those special 'Lee' days. I went in to see what they were up to and there was this poor bird encased in cling film as they were about to put it in the oven!

'You daft sods!' I giggled. 'What do you think is going to happen to the cling film if you put it in the oven?'

'I dunno,' he chuckled. 'Just thought we needed to wrap it up first.'

I rolled up my sleeves and rescued the chicken before shoving it in the oven, this time in tin foil. The next laugh was with the gammon and it's a joke we have never let Sara live down. It was one of those 'cook in the bag' meats and, when it said on the wrapper that it doubled in size, Sara thought the meat was going to be twice the size once it had been roasted instead of the *bag* growing to twice the size. We were crying with laughter by now.

Eventually the dynamic duo in the kitchen managed to pull a decent meal out of the hat, although I swear I have no idea how they managed it. Lee ended up eating sausages and chips while we tucked into the meat and trimmings and laughed all afternoon long. We had drinks and sat around in our Christmas cracker party hats, as Lee entertained us and made us giggle for hours on end. It was a Christmas Day I will never forget – nothing fancy or posh, just a big meal and everyone together. There was a buzz about the place and a warmth and love among us that I will never again experience.

'Happy Christmas, Mum, you're the best,' Lee bellowed, as he wrapped me in a big bear hug. 'I love you with all my heart.'

'Ah, that's lovely, Son. I love you more,' I replied, feeling truly loved in that moment.

I was very blessed to have a son who constantly told me how much he loved me.

The music channel was playing in the background all day and it was a brilliant, happy family occasion. The following year couldn't have been in starker contrast, seven months after Lee was murdered. As the Christmas songs sparked up about two months before the day itself, I just wanted to scream out loud and tell the world to shut up. The closer it got to the day, I felt like running away and never coming back. It was unthinkable to celebrate Christmas when my son had been butchered to death. I loathed Christmas at that moment and I felt angry that people were going out shopping, buying presents and food. How could this be happening when Lee lay dead in the ground? As everyone ran around like crazy in a demented state of ho-ho-ho, I just wanted to go to bed and sleep until it was all over.

'Don't you know my son was murdered in cold blood?' I wanted to shout, as people bustled about their business, laughing and joking and looking forward to the kind of fabulous day I had enjoyed the year before. It was the time of year that you should be with your family and mine was never going to be complete again.

It didn't help that just six days before Christmas, Lee's killers had been found guilty of his murder when their trial ended at the Old Bailey on 19 December. I obviously welcomed the verdicts, but we had spent almost three weeks in London attending the trial and I was thoroughly exhausted and drained. This was not a year for any sort of celebrations.

On Christmas Day, I put on a brave face for my girls but no one was in the mood for festivities. Again we went to Sara's, and we all wore Christmas-themed jumpers to make an effort for the day, especially as my daughter's children were still very young and looking forward to it. I just went through the motions, trying to hold back the well of tears that was blinding me. The void left by Lee was horrendous and I kept thinking back to the year before, when life had seemed so ordinarily perfect. My appetite since Lee's death was awful and it was all I could do to push my food around my plate as the family tried to eat their dinners. We made a toast to Lee during the meal and then later had some drinks and managed to share some stories about him, but the day was a trial in itself for me. Much of it passed over me, as I found myself drifting off into thoughts of Lee and the memory of him hugging me and wishing me Happy Christmas the year before. I would have given anything to return to that day.

That night, before I went to bed, I stared up at the stars and wished with all my might for someone to lift the pain that was crushing the life out of me.

'Merry Christmas, Lee,' I murmured. 'I love you with all my heart.'

8

Trial and Verdict

The trial of Lee's killers started on 29 November 2013 and would last three weeks, during which my family and the jury would hear the most shocking details of the attack and murder of my son. It would prove to be the most testing time I had endured since Lee was killed.

There had never been any doubt that my family and I would attend the hearing, despite knowing that we would learn horrific truths that would stay imprinted on our minds forever. Our Police Liaison Officers and senior police from the New Scotland Yard briefed us in full beforehand, warning that some of the evidence was extremely graphic and that the jury would be shown video footage including the moment Lee was mown down by a car and killed. I didn't want to go to court but I had to. This was my son who had died and I had no option but to form part of the judicial process that sought retribution for his murder. I had to witness the punishment of the monsters who stole Lee from me.

The men on trial were Michael Adebolajo, twenty-eight at the time, and Michael Adebowale, the younger of the pair, who was twenty-two. They are two British-born men of Nigerian descent who were brought up in this country as Christians but later converted to Islam. After declaring their allegiance to Allah, they became radicalised extremists and willing cold-blooded killers. After their arrest in May, the pair had been held on remand in Belmarsh, a Category A prison in Thamesmead, south-east London, not far from where Lee was stationed and killed in Woolwich. Huge security surrounded the trial, which was being held at Britain's top criminal court, the Old Bailey, located in the City of London, near St Paul's Cathedral. That first morning saw Adebolajo and Adebowale arrive at court in separate prison vans escorted by heavily armed police to protect against any reprisal terrorist attacks or attempts to spring the jihadis from custody.

I knew this was going to take me away from home for a while, so I arranged for Courtney and Amy to stay with Chelsea back in Middleton, as she wanted to attend court only on the first and last days. It was with Ian, Sara, Chelsea and Lee's fiancée Aimee that I stood in solidarity that morning, and we walked with our heads held high into court to face the gruesome details of how my son died. I knew I would be facing Lee's killers for the very first time and I had no idea how I would react. I had a knot in my stomach that seemed to tighten with every step I made towards the courtroom.

Please God, give me the strength to get through this day and I beg you for justice for my son, I prayed silently. I had no idea how much I would need those prayers to be answered, as the evidence unfurled into a stunned courthouse. I had steeled myself for my first glimpse of the killers but it was initially far less dramatic than I had anticipated because the judge had ordered for the glass barriers around the dock to be partially covered in brown paper to spare my family having to look at them throughout the trial. It wouldn't be until a little while into the hearing that I would get a chance to see the killers in detail.

I don't mind admitting that I was terrified sitting in that court.

It was way beyond my comfort zone, and so sombre and stern I was convinced it would unnerve the cockiest of defendants who stood trial there. Anyone who has ever been inside the Old Bailey will know how magnificent and grand the building is, and it almost commands respect. The courtroom was completely packed out with legal teams, members of the press and public, who occupied every available seat. Family members were seated along the front benches and I was in the middle of them all, protected and surrounded by loved ones.

I could sense all eyes were on us as people waited for our reactions to Adebolajo and Adebowale, but the reality was, in those early days, we couldn't see them. It wouldn't be long, however, before our emotions were well and truly laid bare for all to witness, as we began to hear the gruesome evidence.

Mr Justice Sweeney was the trial judge and, as he strode into court that day, I felt the knot grip even tighter in my belly and my hands began to sweat with nerves. The tension in the room was palpable and you could almost touch the adrenaline coursing through the air. As the judge sat down everyone else followed suit and you could have heard a pin drop.

The accused men had already pleaded not guilty to the murder of Lee on 22 May 2013 and had entered a further not guilty plea of attempting to kill police officers. It was now down to the prosecution to prove otherwise and convince the jury to send them down.

Prosecuting barrister Richard Whittam QC opened the case by outlining Lee's murder, and you could hear men and women gasp out loud as the details emerged. I grabbed hold of Ian's arm and listened in agony.

'The details of this case, which took place on May 22nd 2013, are truly shocking,' he warned the jury. 'The two accused almost decapitated the body of the young soldier after Mr Adebolajo and Mr Adebowale drove their Vauxhall Tigra straight into Rigby as he crossed the road, shortly after 2 p.m. that day. The men got out and attacked Rigby's body with knives and a meat cleaver, then dragged the body into the middle of the road.

'The defendants continued to attack the body until his head was almost decapitated. They wanted members of the public to see the consequence of what can only be described as their barbarous acts.

'One witness has described that Mr Adebolajo was like a butcher attacking a joint of meat as he continued his assault on Lee. They had committed, you may think, a cowardly and callous murder by deliberately attacking an unarmed man in plain clothes from behind, using a vehicle as a weapon, and then they murdered him and mutilated his body with that meat cleaver and knives.

'Adebolajo tried to decapitate the soldier while Adebowale stabbed and cut him. As a police vehicle arrived on the scene, both men moved towards it, one aiming an unloaded gun at the police. Both were shot and detained.'

The jury then heard that they conspired to kill a police officer when they arrived on the scene. Mr Whittam went on to contrast the 'bravery and decency' of passers-by after the alleged event with the scene on the Woolwich street.

He said: 'Despite the abhorrence of the scene, one woman went to the lifeless body of Lee Rigby and stroked him to provide some comfort and humanity to what had unfolded. Others went to see if they could provide first aid. Another woman engaged Michael Adebolajo in conversation, despite the fact that he was still holding the meat cleaver and his hands were covered in blood.'

Mr Whittam also told the jury a little about what had happened in the days before Lee's murder. He said that Adebolajo had bought a set of five kitchen knives and a sharpener from the Argos store in Lewisham the day before, showing the court a CCTV image of the defendant in the shop. Whittam claimed that the two men had come together four and a half hours before the alleged murder. They drove and parked near barracks and waited twenty minutes.

It was a shocking rundown of how brutal and calculated my son's murder had been, and I must have looked like a ghost as the details were read out. I felt sick at the very description of how Lee ended his life and I wasn't sure how much more I could take. The decision to leave the court was made for me when the prosecutor warned the jury he was about to show footage of my son being hit by the car. I couldn't watch that, so Ian and I adjourned from the room while this was going on. As I went to stand up, I felt my knees buckle and Ian grabbed my arms to hold me up. I was almost gasping for air by the time I got out the courtroom door.

'I can't believe what we just heard in there,' I choked. 'Those evil bastards treated my son like a slab of meat and chopped him up. How could they do it a living human being? I thought I was going to pass out when I heard what they had done.'

'Yep, they are pure evil,' Ian agreed. 'Let's just hope that the jury agrees and sends them to prison for a very long time. This is all about justice for Lee now. If you don't want to go back in there, I will stay in court for all of us,' he added.

I didn't want to go back to court but I didn't see that as an option.

'I hate it in there, but I have to go in so that these cowardly monsters don't win. My son suffered so much worse than us, and so I'll have to find the courage to go through with it.'

We had a short break as the hearing continued, and we bought some teas and coffees as we tried to take in the full magnitude of what we had already heard in such a short space of time. We returned to our seats after the video was over but later learned that it showed CCTV footage of the car seen swerving across the road, hitting Lee from behind, lifting him onto the bonnet before crashing into a road sign.

The court heard from several eyewitness called by the prosecution about what happened next. One, a shopkeeper, said he saw the driver with a 'chopper' and the passenger with a knife both attack an unconscious soldier then drag his body into the road. Another told the court that Adebolajo's actions in the attack were 'like a butcher attacking a joint of meat'. Mr Whittam told the jury that Adebolajo held Lee by his hair before swinging the meat cleaver and repeatedly hacking at the right side of his neck just below the jawline with 'considerable force'.

And so the horrific details continued to tumble out and I remember feeling real sorrow and pity for the eight women and four men of the jury who had been selected to sit on this trial. They were just normal everyday folk who were being subjected to one of the worst murder trials ever. The jury then heard how, as my son's body lay on the road, the two killers stayed at the scene, talking to people who passed by. Some of those conversations were caught on camera and relayed to the court, showing Adebolajo with the cleaver in his bloodied hands as he ranted: 'Your soldiers go to our land and kill our people – so an eye for an eye.'

The jury was also shown a piece of paper Adebolajo handed to a bystander. The hand-written note spoke of 'international armed robbery' and referenced the Qur'an and jihad. It said: 'Fighting Allah's enemies is an obligation', and went on: 'Do not spend your days in endless discussion with the cowardly and foolish. It means that it will delay your meeting Allah's enemies on the battlefield. Sometimes the cowardly and foolish can be those dearest to you. So be prepared to turn away from them.'

The handwritten note suggested 'carnage reaching your town' was 'simply retaliation for your oppression in our towns'. Mr Whittam argued clearly to the jury that Adebolajo's justification – on film and in the letter – was not a defence.

'To seek out and to kill political opponents on the grounds that you say that they have oppressed your countrymen, or people of your religion, is still murder. Disputes have to be settled by lawful means, not retaliation.'

Adebolajo was described as a Muslim extremist but that he was not acting as part of a group when he killed Lee. We also saw footage of Adebolajo and Adebowale being gunned down by police, before being given first aid and then detained by the officers. Adebolajo told paramedics at the scene: 'I did it for my God. I wish the bullets had killed me so I can join my friends and family.'

The court heard from so many witnesses who had been unfortunate enough to be in the wrong place at the wrong time that day. Several described how Lee's head was almost sliced off when his motionless body was attacked in a 'cowardly and callous execution'. One bystander said that Adebolajo had 'pure evil' in his eyes as he hacked away at Lee, while another described how the men behaved like 'animals' as they mutilated their victim. A further gruesome account said that Adebolajo had held up Lee's head by his hair and hacked at his neck like it was a tree. Adebowale, meanwhile, acted like a savage and continually stabbed and cut Lee's body in a frenzied assault, until even his accomplice had to pull him off.

One particularly grisly account came from witness Cheralee Armstrong, who told the police the attack was so ferocious, '... it was like they were trying to remove the person's organs from his body.' She also said, 'I first saw a rocking movement. At first I thought they were resuscitating a man on the floor after a car crash. I then saw the feet of the man. They were jolting in rhythm with the two men standing over him. He kept ramming the two knives into the man with so much force. When the knives came up I could see the whole length of the blades, which were covered in blood. It was like they were mutilating the man's body, trying to remove his organs from his torso. I shouted, "They are stabbing him. They are killing him." I got out my car and shouted, "Stop, stop." The man in the hat was staring at me. His expression was blank, but pure evil, and his eyes were bulging. They threw the soldier's body into the road like it was a rubbish bag.'

The court also heard about the outstanding bravery of several women on the day who were popularly dubbed the 'Angels of Woolwich', after doing everything in their power to help and soothe Lee in his dying moments. The accounts of two of those amazing women are included in detail later in my story.

Police officers also gave evidence throughout the trial and recounted some of the conversations they had with Adebolajo while he was held and interviewed by detectives in custody.

He would tell them: 'I am a Muslim extremist. This may be the only chance you meet one. Your people have gone to Afghanistan and raped and killed our women. I am seeking retribution. I wouldn't stoop so low as to rape and kill women. I thank the person who shot me, because it is what Allah would have wanted. I love Allah more than my children. Believe me, I am not a man who gets enjoyment in horror movies, seeing blood and gore across the camera lens.'

I watched the jurors leave at the end of every day of the trial and they looked shocked and drained. I just hoped that for their sakes that they wouldn't be left with lasting visions of bloodshed in their minds. They were awful days, listening to what can only be summed up as grotesque acts of evil. When I returned to our hotel room, I often went straight to bed with painkillers because my head was pounding from the stress and tension of the events of the day. I tried to close my eyes but all I could conjure up were the frightful images of how Lee had been murdered without mercy on a sunny London street. It was horrific and I must have lain awake for hours replaying the same appalling snapshots of my son's last moments alive. I later learned that I was not alone. Members of the public and the jury were so sickened by the horrors of what they had heard that many of them too were unable to sleep properly for days on end. The barbarity refused to let their minds rest.

Our room at the Premier Inn at Blackfriars became our home for the next three weeks, as we had to suffer the callous and indifferent attempts of justification and defence from Lee's killers. I hated them with a passion and wished I could be as far away from them as possible, but I had to stick it out. I knew the worst part of all would be listening to them spouting radical nonsense because I was powerless to stop it. But, inevitably, the time came for their defence.

The first time I had been given the chance to take a proper look at the men who killed Lee was when they stepped forward in the dock. I had waited a long time for this moment, to see if these cowards could look me in the eye and face the reality of what they had done. I wanted to see if there was the slightest hint of remorse or strain of humanity but, as I stared at them, they refused to look at me, instead staring down at their Qur'an. It was hugely frustrating because I had wanted the opportunity to stand up for my son, and his killers wouldn't even pay me the respect of acknowledging me. I was sickened and I felt real anger rise up from the pit of my being. I just kept thinking of my beautiful child, the baby I had carried and given life to. I nurtured and cherished him every day for twenty-five years and here I was in a heartless courtroom looking at two twisted individuals who cared nothing about the infinite sorrow they had inflicted on my family.

I wanted to scream out at them, 'How dare you ignore me,' but the words never left my mouth. All I knew as I looked at their miserable faces was that they had to pay for stealing my son's life. They had proved themselves to be cowards as well as evil.

Adebolajo was clearly the ringleader and the mouthpiece of the pair, and he wasn't backwards in coming forwards with his warped mantra of Muslim religion. One afternoon he took the stand for four hours and it was hell having to listen to his poisonous preaching of how he justified murdering my son. I hate him with a passion. He openly admitted that he killed and tried to decapitate Lee, but then tried to insist he had done so because he had been 'obeying the command of Allah'.

He said: 'Allah commands that I fight those militaries that attack the Muslims. I don't feel that I have any choice. I obey Allah and I commit my affairs into his hands. We planned a military attack which obviously involved – sadly, it's not something enjoyable – the death of a soldier,' he said.

His barrister, David Gottlieb, went on to ask him what his defence to murder was. Adebolajo replied: 'I am a soldier. I am a soldier. I am a soldier of Allah. I understand that some people might not recognise this because we do not wear fatigues and we do not go to the Brecon Beacons to train. But we are still soldiers in the sight of Allah, and to me this is all that matters. If Allah considers me a soldier then I am a soldier.

'Basically it's a war between Islam and those militaries that invade Muslim lands. One of them just happens to be the British military and therefore the war continues even to this day. I love al-Qaeda because they are my brothers. I've never met them but I love them. I consider them my brothers in Islam.

'I have no animosity or bad feeling towards the soldier's family, because every soldier has family, and his family love him just like me. My family did not stop loving me the moment I became a soldier, so I don't blame them. I killed somebody who they love and who is dear to them. At the same time, people who I love who are dear to me are killed as well. We are not the only ones who feel pain in this country. Muslims feel pain too. We love people too.'

The whole thing was a sickening charade – sheer excuses for

My beautiful baby Lee at six months old – he was the light of my life, the centre of my world, and that gorgeous smile will stay with me forever

Lee and his devoted sister Sara at ages four and three. This pair went everywhere together and adored each other

The gang all together for a school photo – what a lucky mum I was to have such wonderful healthy and happy kids (ages nine, eight and five)

One of my favourite photos. Just me and my baby boy and a whole heap of love. Lee loved to play with my long hair and he was such a loving child. I was the luckiest mum in the world

How could I forget this day, when Lee and Sara organised a surprise birthday party for me. Lee couldn't be any happier and neither could I!

Nearly a complete family. This group shot was taken in 2001 when Courtney was just a baby. All we needed was Amy, who was yet to be born

Ian and Lee share a pint together on Christmas Day 2012 – Lee's last Christmas

e proud day of Lee's homecoming
rade in Rochdale after his tour of
ghanistan in 2009

My brave son in his Army fatigues. He
loved his regiment and I am forever
proud of him

Boy, did Lee adore his
drums! They were as
loud as he was

In the Army together. Lee and his fiancée Aimee were simpl made for each other

Horsing around together. Aimee and Lee loved to have fun together and I'm so glad he found true love and happiness before he died

The handsome couple cuddle in for a snap

A sight I never thought I would see: my son's funeral cortege in Bury – one of the worst days of my life

Too heartbreaking for words. Lee being carried by his regiment pals with full military honours

The carpet of flowers, cards and messages for Lee and our family left at the murder scene in Woolwich

Private tributes from our family at the murder scene a few days after Lee was killed. Sara left a bottle of HP sauce – a private joke, as it was Lee's favourite and he put it on everything

United together. Ian, myself, Sara and Chelse. walking into the Old Bailey on the day Lee's killers were sentenced to life in jail. We wore our Justice For Lee Rigby T-shirts with pride

Celebrating Lee's 27th birthday in 2014 at the Royal Marines Commando Training Centre in Lympstone, Devon. Me, Courtney and Amy are with RSM Phil Gilby and the RM band on their parade ground. After the photo was taken, we laid a wreath for Lee at their memorial wall to the sound of the *Last Post*

My beautiful girl Amy in 2014 with her Child of Courage award, presented to her by her school for her outstanding attitude following her beloved brother's murder. I am so proud of her and all my other children who have faced this trauma with real bravery

truly tender moment for mum and daughter on Sara's wedding day in August
15

very precious picture that I shall cherish forever: me, Sara and my best friend
ndra – possibly the bravest lady I have ever met. I love her dearly

The last photo taken of Lee on the day before he was killed. I have never seen him so handsome and happy, as he modelled at a wedding fair. It is how I will always remember him. R.I.P., my darling son cold-blooded murder. This was a man who killed in hatred and not in the name of any God. Apart from listening to the tragic and hateful acts of violence committed on my son, this was probably one of the worst days of the trial for me. I was forced to listen to the diatribe that came from the man who murdered my beautiful son and it was nauseating.

When it came to his cross-examination, Adebolajo became quite heated and refused to answer some of the questions put to him, repeating over and again: 'I remain a soldier of Allah.' He told the courtroom that he and Adebowale had wanted to achieve 'shahada' – become martyrs – and the two men argued about who would hold the one pistol they had between them, as the person with the gun was most likely to be killed when the police arrived. Adebowale did not testify in his own defence throughout the trial and his police interviews were not heard in court.

Finally, on 19 December, the trial came to an end after three weeks of intense and difficult times for us as a family. At 11 a.m. the jurors were sent out to consider their verdicts and it remained a tense time for all, even though we couldn't imagine they would be found not guilty. Just 90 minutes later we were called back into court number two, because the jurors were already decided on their outcome. I was shaking like a leaf when they returned, but that fear turned to relief when they delivered unanimous verdicts of guilty to the charges of murdering Lee. They were found not guilty of attempting to kill police officers, as the jury accepted their argument that they had wanted to become martyrs and had wanted the police to shoot them dead.

We all burst into tears, including Ian, who wiped away his tears before whispering to me: 'It's justice for Lee. Thank God.'

Ian kept his arm tightly around me as I sobbed into his chest, relieved, exhausted and broken after what had been three weeks of torment to remain in the same room as the men who had slaughtered my child. We had been warned not to expect an immediate sentence because Mr Justice Sweeney had made it clear he wanted to wait for a key ruling by the Court of Appeal in January on the legal use of whole-life jail terms. This was good news for us because it meant he was considering sentencing the men to die in jail without ever being released on parole.

We returned home as a family, battered, bruised and somewhat bewildered. We were incredibly grateful that the magnificent jury had found these two killers guilty of murdering Lee, but it felt far from being a conquest or a victory. Lee was still gone and he was never coming back. It was less than a week before Christmas and I have never felt sadder in my life.

9

Sentencing and Appeals

O n 26 February 2014 it was time to return to court again. This time it was for the sentencing. I dreaded the trip down to London. I was still in the grip of intense grief and nothing seemed to shift it, but as a family we were all determined to be present when sentences were handed down.

Ian, Sara, Chelsea and I walked into court that day all wearing the same T-shirts that had been printed for us by a supporter in our home town. The black tops were emblazoned on the front with a picture of Lee in Army uniform with bold white letters that read 'Justice For Lee Rigby'.

We weren't trying to be confrontational or anti-establishment. As a family, we have the highest regard for the law, but it was a gesture that gave us solidarity and sent a message out to the world that we wanted to see the right sentence handed to Lee's killers. As we got into the Old Bailey, we were politely told that we wouldn't be allowed into the courtroom wearing our shirts, as they would be seen as political, so we hastily did as we were told and turned them inside out. The last thing we had intended to do was be disrespectful in a court of law. We met up with

Aimee once inside and we all walked into the courtroom together and took our places in the family benches reserved for us. What happened next completely floored us.

The proceedings began with the legal teams addressing the judge, starting with prosecutor Richard Whittam QC, who outlined the impact of the murder of Lee on his family. He said: 'The lives of the family of Lee Rigby have been devastated. The scale of the impact on them is too obvious to set out in detail. Lee Rigby had a young son and all the lives of his family have been irreparably changed for the worse.'

He also read out some of the victim impact statements that we had put before the court, including Ian's sorrow and confusion.

'After all that our son Lee had been through in Afghanistan, all he was doing was walking through London. Seeing everything on the television and the scale of the violence is something none of us can comprehend. You see it all but it doesn't quite click in your head. It is like being somewhere else, as if you are watching it as someone else.'

Defence lawyers for the killers argued that if the court sentenced Adebolajo to life without parole, it would make him a martyr, while Adebowale's team said that a whole-life term would be inhuman for a man of that age.

Then it was time for the judge to start his deliberations. He began by saying that the two men had been convicted on overwhelming evidence of the murder of Lee, and that their actions were a betrayal of Islam. The judge said they had been radicalised and had betrayed their religion, and their murder of Lee had been sickening and pitiless.

'You each converted to Islam some years ago. Thereafter you were radicalised and each became an extremist, espousing views which, as has been said elsewhere, are a betrayal of Islam,' Mr Justice Sweeney said.

At that point, the proceedings descended into mayhem, as

Michael Adebolajo jumped from his seat and started shouting at the judge. 'Allahu Akbar (God is great),' he hollered, as his sidekick Adebowale began screaming as security guards tried to wrestle him to the ground.

'It's a lie,' shouted Adebowale. 'It's not a betrayal of Islam,' he ranted, as he continued to scream abuse. 'Britain and America will never be safe.'

The noise in the courtroom was horrific and it was sheer pandemonium. My heart was pounding as if it was going to burst out of my chest and there was all-out fighting in the dock between the two killers and nine guards who tried to restrain them and put them down to the floor. It was utter chaos and petrifying. As the fight continued, Lee's killers continued to hurl abuse at the judge, and the guards fought hard to regain control. The men were dragged from the dock head first and jostled down into the cells, as everyone in the court sat aghast at what had happened. Even as they were put into the cells beneath the court, we could hear them screaming and banging on the walls and the ceilings as the judge tried to restore order to his court.

The whole uproar had been terrifying for me and my family. We were sitting just a few feet away from the dock when the violence erupted and I feared for my life. We ran from our seats in the melee, Ian gripping my hand and pulling me to the corner of the courtroom for safety. I was sobbing and trembling from head to foot. I remember the court staff being so kind and lovely, handing us tissues and trying to comfort us as this madness exploded all around us.

Hearing the racket and commotion of the killers shouting and fighting in the dock took me back to the day Lee was murdered. They had been relatively quiet through the trial, but now, on the day they were to be sentenced, they kicked off big style. I could easily imagine them ranting in the street in Woolwich over my dead son's body, with his blood on their hands. Everything I had heard in that courtroom came back to haunt me as reality. I saw for myself the true violence and horror these men were capable of. I had dreaded going back into that courtroom but I had never imagined I would be faced with the venom that my son had encountered. It was out of control chaos and the noise was excruciating. I thought I was going to have a heart attack from fright.

As I heard the violence and shouting from below, I knew these must have been the voices that Lee heard as he lay dying. I tried to block out the noise from the cells by covering my ears, but nothing could silence it. I had screamed out loud in the courtroom as the killers began fighting and police officers rushed to surround and protect me and my family as we fled for cover. I was terrified that the glass screen around the dock was going to smash and I was struggling for breath in my terror. I don't think I have ever felt so frightened and I didn't think I was going to survive it.

The judge was really stoic and amazing. Despite all of the commotion, he remained calm and dignified and, even as the hooligans continued their scrapping, he turned to my family and apologised that we had witnessed such terrible scenes. He asked us if we were happy for him to continue his sentencing in the killers' absence and we agreed. He made the point that the murder of Lee had also betrayed the peaceful Muslim communities who gave so much to our country. I was still shaken, but we sat back in our seats. I had so much admiration and respect for this judge, who was determined not to have his sentencing disrupted. As he continued with his words, I knew that Lee's murderers had ended this terrible crime in the way they had begun it – with violence and hatred in their hearts. It was their final insult to my son and I would never forgive them. They were jumping all over my son's grave with cruelty and barbarity, just as they had ended his life.

After scenes of undignified brawling on a level that has rarely been witnessed in the Central Criminal Court, the sentences were finally delivered, and the judge spoke for a long while about the crime and the punishment he was to give out. Michael Adebolajo was given a whole-life term, while Michael Adebowale was jailed for life with a minimum of forty-five years – meaning he could be back on the streets by the age of sixty-seven. The judge had decided that Adebolajo should never be free again and would serve his entire life in jail without parole.

It should have been a triumphant moment. Instead, the trauma of the events in court number two had left me ill. As I tried to stand up, I didn't just feel woozy from nerves or emotion, I collapsed. My legs went from beneath me and I fell to the floor. Ian and Sara were there for me and tried to get me up, but I had gone completely. Someone passed me a bottle of water, but I couldn't even hold it because I was shaking so much. The court staff were so concerned that they called an ambulance and I was carried to a private room in the Old Bailey to be looked after.

I remember sitting in that room, thinking I was about to die. I couldn't see straight and my entire nervous system had gone into meltdown. I remember very little until a paramedic was by my side. I was shaking and sweating and crying. I was laid down on a bed in a side room and all I could see in my mind was Lee's killers hacking away at my son.

I remember saying to Ian: 'If I die, make sure you look after our girls. Tell them how much I love them and how much we love Lee.'

'Don't be bloody stupid,' Ian responded. 'You're not going anywhere. Not without me, anyway!' he retorted.

I was wired up to all sorts of machines by the paramedics and they told me that my blood pressure was sky high but I hadn't suffered a heart attack. That was a relief, at least, because I thought I was on the way out that day. I was given a hot cup of tea for shock but I still felt so ill, and I stayed in that room for about two hours. I had no concept of the world outside and yet the press was going crazy for the story that had unfolded in court. I learned later that the killers were taken away in separate vans and television helicopters traced them to where they would spend their first night, sentenced to life imprisonment. There was no sense of euphoria for us. What should have been a day of relief for us had turned into a sideshow of horror. After a good rest, and a thorough check by the medics, we finally left court by a side door into a car with our Police Liaison Officers. We hadn't had to face the media but earlier we had issued a statement to the press.

It read: 'The Rigby family welcomes the whole-life and significant sentences that have been passed down on Lee's killers. We feel that no other sentence would have been acceptable, and we would like to thank the judge and the courts for handing down what we believe to be the right prison terms. We would also like to thank everyone who has supported us in the last nine months. It has brought us a lot of comfort and we feel satisfied that justice has been served for Lee. It just remains to be said: "Rest In Peace, Lee."'

The way these men behaved in court was a travesty. They wanted one final stab at defiance, the final word in a frightful and needless crime. It was disgraceful, but I like to think that the judge and justice had the last say in the matter. Despite their shocking behaviour, the judge carried on and handed down a whole-life sentence to Adebolajo. He will have plenty of time now to reflect on the brutality he dished out to my son. They showed no respect or dignity to my family after we were forced to sit and hear some of the worst things a mother could learn about how her child was treated, and still they thought it was acceptable to behave like that in front of us. I can never forgive them for that. The whole process was traumatic enough without this added drama that made things a whole lot more painful and distressing.

The paramedic crew diagnosed that I had suffered a giant panic attack as the men kicked off in the dock. It felt more like I was dying, as I struggled to catch my breath and get oxygen into my body. The adrenalin had kicked in hard and fast but, as that began to subside, my body ached from top to toe. When I finally got back to Middleton, my head was pounding and my body felt as if it had been kicked all over by a horse. Every bone and muscle throbbed with pain, but I was so relieved that I had managed to stay in the courtroom until the end of sentencing and that I was now a long way from the madness. I even allowed myself to feel proud of sticking it out to the end. I was never going to let those butchers deprive me of the satisfaction of watching them being sent to jail for life.

Senior police at Scotland Yard also gave their response to the sentences, which were a tremendous result for our family. Assistant Commissioner, Cressida Dick, had this to say:

'Our thoughts remain with Lee's loved ones, who have shown dignity and strength throughout the judicial process. Today's sentencing reflects the true horror of their actions in taking this young man's life in such a barbaric way.'

Sue Hemming, head of special crime and counter terrorism at the Crown Prosecution Service, added: 'Lee's family has found the whole court process distressing, while Michael Adebolajo and Michael Adebowale revelled in one of the most appalling terrorist murders I have seen whilst head of counter terrorism at the CPS.

'Not only was the attack brutal and calculated, it was also designed to advance extremist views. As a soldier, Fusilier

Lee Rigby was targeted in a clear act of revenge, deliberately carried out in full view of members of the public for maximum impact.'

My family welcomed the support and recognition of our suffering from all those who had looked after us and I agreed wholeheartedly with the judge. I don't have a wicked bone in my body, but I want those two to suffer every day for the rest of their lives in prison. Only a life for a life is acceptable. They deserve to have to live with what they inflicted on my poor, defenceless boy – a young man with his whole life ahead of him. They deserve the harshest of punishment until their dying breath.

They behaved worse than frenzied pack animals when they butchered Lee in the street, and then they showed their true colours, yet again, as they resorted to violence in the dock. We no longer have capital punishment in this country but, if we did, it would be too good for them. They wanted to become martyrs, to be killed by the state, yet I'm glad they survived and were deprived of the luxury of death. It would have been too quick to end their misery and now they are stuck in cells, caged like the rabid dogs they are. Their explosive behaviour was the clearest indication that they feel no remorse or shame and that their only concerns are for themselves.

Justice has been served for Lee and I am so grateful to Mr Justice Sweeney for the exceptional way he conducted the trial and, ultimately, handed down the most severe sentences in his power. It's a huge relief to know that they will never walk free again and will never have the chance to hurt any more innocent people. They didn't just take Lee's life and destroy the lives of his loved ones; they also affected the lives of those who were unfortunate to be there on the day that Lee was killed. What they witnessed may traumatise those people for the rest of their days and that should also be on the consciences of the murderers.

When the drama of the courtroom was finally over and I began to recover from the fright, I was finally able to reflect on the sentences. It was then I sent a silent prayer of thanks to God and whispered to my son: 'It's time for you to finally rest in peace, my beautiful son. Justice has been served and so I want you to rest easy and sleep well, until we meet again. With all my love, your devoted mum.'

I knew our pain wasn't over but I was relieved to know for sure that Lee was suffering no longer. He had endured enough during his attack and now we, his family, have to share the life sentence that was meted out to his killers. A light went out the day they ripped my son from me. It left us all in a very dark place and our grief and misery will last a lifetime.

It was momentous for us to hear the judge's wise words and to know that he recognised the magnitude of the crime. He showed Lee the ultimate respect by choosing full-life sentences. The images of how they butchered Lee like a slab of meat will remain in my head forever, but I'm never going to give up because that would be like letting my son's killers win. I have to keep going for Lee's sake because it's my duty to ensure the world never forgets him. He was loved by everyone who met him and he was the complete opposite to the maniacs who took his life. How they can have inflicted such slaughter on a man they had never met before, is truly beyond me.

I hate these men so much it burns into my soul, but despite that I still couldn't inflict such savagery on anyone. I have always lived a quiet and simple life. I am naturally gentle but I have never hated like this before. I have never been vindictive or vengeful, but it brings me the smallest of comfort to know they will have a long life ahead of them behind bars. I want them to live in fear and I hope their hearts and minds remain tortured for the terrible things they did. They hurt my son so badly that I will never be able to bring myself to forgive them. Maybe that makes me a bad person but I believe in justice. These men had murder in their hearts and evil on their minds when they targeted Lee as he walked along a London street. Now they will pay for that for the rest of their miserable lives. They deserve to die in prison after a very long time.

We are still so proud of Lee. I just wish with all my heart I could change places with him so I could give him back his life.

Mr Justice Sweeney's sentencing speech says so much about the trial. I have included the full text below. I have read it many times. It reaffirms my belief in our criminal justice system and I believe it deserves to be read in its entirety.

Michael Adebolajo (also known as Mujaahid Abu Hamza) and Michael Adebowale (also known as Ismail Ibn Abdullah), you have both been convicted, on overwhelming evidence, of the barbaric murder of Fusilier Lee Rigby in Artillery Place in Woolwich in the early afternoon of Wednesday 22nd May last year. You are British citizens, aged twenty-nine and twenty-two respectively. Adebolajo, you are married with four step-children and two children of your own.

The judge went on to outline the details of the case, which to me was very important because it is an historical record of the crime as recorded at the trial. He was extremely thorough in his details and I think it is important to have his account in this book.

He continued: Having presided over your trial, I am sure of the following facts. You each converted to Islam some years ago. Thereafter you were radicalised and each became an extremist – espousing a cause and views which, as has been said elsewhere, are a betrayal of Islam and of the peaceful Muslim communities who give so much to our country.

You decided between you, and in order to advance your extremist cause, to murder a soldier in public in broad daylight and to do so in a way that would generate maximum media coverage, including getting yourselves killed by armed officers who would be bound to attend the scene in the aftermath of the murder – thereby expecting that you would become martyrs and each gain a place in paradise.

The planning took place over a period of time. You, Adebolajo, acquired an old handgun which, although it did not work, was to be used at the scene to keep the public at bay and to threaten the armed officers with when they arrived. The day before the murder you, Adebolajo, bought five knives and a knife sharpener, which you used to sharpen some of the knives in preparation for their use in the murder.

On the day of the murder the two of you met up some hours in advance. Eventually Adebolajo drove you both to Woolwich in his car, where you parked up in Wellington Street and waited to spot a soldier to murder. You had with you a total of eight knives and the gun. It was whilst you were waiting that Lee Rigby walked past. He was instantly recognisable as being a soldier as he was wearing a 'HELP *for* HEROES' top and carrying his Army day sack.

He was twenty-five years old, had joined the Army in 2006, and amongst other postings had seen active service in Afghanistan in 2009. An outgoing and popular personality, he was by the time you saw him in a recruiting post dealing with young people and involved in other duties at his Regimental HQ at the Tower of London. Indeed, he was on his way from his HQ to the Woolwich Barracks when you saw him.

He had done absolutely nothing to deserve what you went on to do to him. You stalked him in the car as he walked along Wellington Street, crossed the South Circular Road and went into Artillery Place where he crossed the road in front of you. Seizing your opportunity, Adebolajo, and once he was no longer looking in your direction, you accelerated hard to 30–40 mph and ran him down from behind. The impact carried him up onto the bonnet of the car breaking five vertebrae in his back and five ribs. The speed of the car was such that it carried up onto the pavement and crashed into the support of a road sign and stopped, depositing Lee Rigby in the area between the front of the car and an adjacent wall. He was unconscious and certainly unable to defend himself.

You both exited the car armed with knives and, over a period of around two to three minutes, you butchered Lee Rigby – going, as you were well aware, far beyond what was needed to murder him. You, Adebolajo, concentrated on his neck, hacking at it repeatedly with first a substantial cleaver-type knife and then another knife, all in an attempt to decapitate him for maximum horrific effect. In the end you failed, but in the process you caused horrendous injuries as shown in the materials before the court.

You, Adebowale, concentrated on Lee Rigby's torso, stabbing him a number of times in the chest in frenzied fashion and with severe force. It is no exaggeration to say that what the two of you did resulted in a bloodbath. Aspects of all this were seen, as they were intended to be, by members of the public.

Once you had finished, and again in order to achieve maximum effect, you then carried and dragged Lee Rigby's body into the road in Artillery Place and dumped it there – thus eventually bringing the traffic to a halt.

In the thirteen minutes that passed between then and the arrival of the armed officers, the number of members of the public at the scene grew. You both gloried in what you had done. Each of you had the gun at one point or another and it was used to warn off any male member of the public who looked as though he might intervene.

My family has nothing but respect for this very wise and clever man who presided over the trial because he clearly based his summing up on facts and not on the emotions that had been so apparent throughout the three weeks of the hearing. It takes someone like him to be able to separate feelings, that were inevitably running high, from fact, and we are very grateful to him for that. We know these two men had a fair trial within the British legal system, of which we remain very proud. After dealing in the facts of Lee's murder, the judge went on to talk about the men's behaviour after Lee died. He reiterated how they had gloried in their actions, seeking to justify their murder of my son, and welcomed people to film and photograph them as they made political statements in the street. But he also made sure to compare their behaviour to the courageous people who had acted so differently on the day.

He said: Your sickening and pitiless conduct was in stark contrast to the compassion and bravery shown by the various women at the scene who tended to Lee Rigby's body and who challenged what you had done and said.

The armed police officers arrived in a marked police vehicle. At that time, you, Adebolajo, were still armed with the cleaver and the other knife, and you, Adebowale, (by agreement between the two of you) were armed with the gun and a knife. You, Adebolajo, sprinted towards the officers jettisoning the knife and carrying the cleaver above your head as if intent on attacking one or more of them, whilst you, Adebowale, went down the adjacent pavement and pointed the gun at the officers.

The officers shot you both. They were clearly entitled to do so. It is thanks to their professionalism, including the speed with which they rendered First Aid, that neither of you was killed – especially in your case, Adebowale, given that you pointed the gun at them again even after you had been shot for the first time.

As is clear from their moving Victim Personal Statements and, unsurprisingly, the consequences of the murder, its brutality and the publicity, have had a severe and lasting impact on those close to Lee Rigby.

That said, neither of you, I am sure, has any real insight into the enormity of what you did, nor any genuine remorse for it either – [your] only regret [being] that you did not succeed in your plan to be shot dead, which has resulted in you being brought to justice before the courts.

Interestingly, Mr Justice Sweeney was in no doubt that Adebolajo was the more dominant of the pair and he was certain there was no real prospect of him being rehabilitated, as he went on to discuss jail terms. Having outlined that the sentence for murder is mandatory life imprisonment, his next role was to make a judgement on how long each killer should serve before being eligible for parole. And that's when he declared his first bombshell on the killers.

Adebolajo, he decreed, must serve a whole-life term with no option for parole. In other words, life really would mean life in his case, and he would never be free to leave jail. Adebowale also received a life sentence with a recommended tariff of forty-five years. The judge had claimed the final words in a horrific three-week period of our lives.

He said: In your case, Adebolajo, there is no mitigation, and whilst to state the obvious, that this is not a case of mass or repeated murder, it is nevertheless one of those rare cases where not only is the seriousness exceptionally high but the requirements of just punishment and retribution make such an order the just penalty. Accordingly in your case I propose to impose a whole-life term.

In your case, Adebowale, I am persuaded that the combination of your lesser role, your age and your pre-existing and continuing mental condition mean that it is not appropriate in your case to impose a whole-life term. Nevertheless, in your case there must still be a very substantial minimum term. The term that I propose to impose is one of forty-five years, less 272 days spent on remand.

Michael Adebolajo, I sentence you to life imprisonment with a whole-life order. Michael Adebowale, I sentence you to life imprisonment with a minimum term of 45 years less 272 days spent on remand.

In both your cases I make a Notification Order for the maximum of thirty years. In each of your cases there will be an appropriate victim surcharge.

On 8 April 2014, Adebolajo launched an appeal against his whole-life term. On 29 July the same year he was refused permission to appeal and the case was heard by a panel of Court of Appeal judges. Almost a year after their first conviction, the two killers lost legal challenges to their sentences when they were rejected at the Court of Appeal on 3 December 2014.

Since they were convicted for Lee's murder, the men have been held in a number of Category A, maximum security prisons. Adebolajo began his sentence in Belmarsh but, in September 2014, he was moved to Frankland jail in County Durham after it was feared he was radicalising inmates in London. He was placed in an isolation unit, segregated from other prisoners. It has not been an easy ride for him in jail. He has been the subject of numerous beatings and knife attacks and, in one incident, some of his teeth were knocked out.

In July 2014 Adebowale was also transferred out of Belmarsh but he was taken to Broadmoor Secure Hospital in Berkshire after claiming to hear voices in his head. He insisted he was experiencing psychotic episodes and was taken to the mental health unit for assessment and care. There had been some talk of Adebowale suffering mental health issues during his trial but, after seeing the way he behaved, I was always suspicious that he was trying it on to get himself a cushier life outside of a top-security prison.

In total, the murder trial was delayed for more than two weeks because Adebowale claimed to be mentally ill. He said he was hearing Nigerian voices in his cell and that he had paranoid fears about being attacked and walking through doorways. He also said he was being influenced by 'djinns,' or spirits, and would tell prison officers that he believed he was possessed and thought about committing suicide.

When was on remand for Lee's murder, he was extremely disruptive and violent during earlier court hearings and, on his first appearance at Westminster Magistrates' Court, he attacked three police officers during a twenty-four hour spell. He had to be handcuffed in the dock after punching the first officer in the face, spat in the face of the second, and threw a glass of water over the third policeman.

When he was transferred to the prison's mental health wing at Belmarsh, he went on a hunger strike in protest. The prison psychiatrist, Dr Ian Cumming, approved Adebowale's transfer to Broadmoor on 14 November – just four days before the trial was listed at the Old Bailey. He was then assessed by a series of psychiatrists while at court to check whether he was fit to stand trial. All four – Dr Neil Boast from Broadmoor, Professor Nigel Eastman, Dr Philip Joseph and Dr Cumming – found he was fit under the 'Pritchard criteria', meaning he could give instructions to his barrister and was able to give evidence. However, Dr Boast and Professor Eastman advised delaying the trial for up to two months. Adebowale is reported to have had a history of mental illness going back to 2008, when he was stabbed and witnessed a friend being murdered.

On 26 November, Mr Justice Sweeney ruled that the trial could go ahead, and the case finally opened on 29 November. It ground to a halt again on 10 December just as Adebowale was due to give his evidence. Representing him, Abba Lakha QC, told the court he had concerns for his client's wellbeing and asked for time for him to be reassessed by psychiatrists. Adebowale himself insisted he had been shown a statement from his co-accused that stated he did not need to give evidence.

Dr Joseph added: 'His position was that he wants to give evidence but he is not going to because he has been advised not to.'

The trial was delayed by more than twelve court days as a result of the mental health issue. I had always been sceptical about the whole thing and thought his claims to be unwell were little more than a pantomime being used by Adebowale to worm out of giving evidence or going to prison. When I heard he had been transferred to Broadmoor after his sentencing, I was fuming because I didn't believe he was ill. He had been assessed by psychiatrists at the trial, who found him fit to plead and able to stand trial for murder.

He spent over a year in hospital but, at the end of September 2015, I was delighted to get a phone call to tell me that Adebowale has now been declared fit and well and sent back to a mainstream prison. Not only was he transferred to a prison, but was sent to what is known as one of the harshest jails in the country.

His new home is now at Wakefield Prison in Yorkshire, dubbed as Monster Mansion because it houses some of the most violent criminals in the UK. It was a long overdue move and I was thrilled to know he was back in a prison where he deserves to be punished. A soft and cushy hospital is not the sort of regime I expect for a man who has been declared mentally sound. He had a fair trial, and to try and duck out of the sentence by faking mental illness is not justice in my eyes. This turnaround signified that the authorities agreed with me – Adebowale was bad, not mad. A prison is the only place he should be punished and anything less would be an insult to Lee.

Criminals at secure hospitals, like mass killers Peter Sutcliffe and Ian Brady, have a very different and gentler life from prison inmates. It's no picnic inside these jails but Adebowale deserves to be locked up with all the other violent offenders. He knew what he was doing when he and Adebolajo murdered Lee. It was a deliberate and calculated attack and his punishment has to fit his crime. I'm sure he will find it extremely tough in Wakefield but it's nothing less than he deserves. My son doesn't have the luxury of living any more because of him. Now Adebowale and Adebolajo have to pay the price for that.

10

Angels and Demons – Part One

E arlier in the book, I spoke about the incredible people who helped my darling son in his dying hour of need. There were many people who played a part that day in trying to help Lee, some of whom I will never know. To those people I would like to send my heartfelt thanks, even if I never get to know your names. Then there were the very special few who stepped up with courage and humanity to try and save Lee, putting their own lives and safety at risk.

They were dubbed the 'Angels of Woolwich' in the media and I can't think of a more fitting title for them. Two of them have kindly agreed to tell their stories and how Lee's murder affected them in the long term. Mum Tina Nimmo, who in 2013 ran the Melbourne Arms pub in Woolwich, and her daughter, Michelle, were two of the first people on the scene that day and they witnessed the true horror of what happened to Lee. Here is Tina's story.

It was just a normal day on May 22nd, 2013, when Michelle and I set off in the car towards the local council offices, where we had to drop off some paperwork. For some reason we had decided to take an alternative route to the one we would usually have driven and, as we turned into Artillery Place, it all kicked off.

Michelle spotted it first and just shouted out at me, 'Mum, someone's been shot. Over there.'

Michelle pulled the car to a halt and saw that a vehicle had crashed into a pole on the pavement. I then saw two men shouting and waving weapons about and there was a body on the floor.

'Stay in the car, Michelle. Don't get out,' I told my daughter. 'Ring the police quickly.'

I went towards the mayhem and spoke to a few people nearby and a man told me that he had been threatened by one of the men with a gun. I can't really say what was going on in my head at that moment, but your natural instinct kicks in, and I just ran towards the body lying on the floor. I wasn't thinking about the danger I might face. I just saw someone in trouble and I went to help.

As I got close to Lee, one of his attackers approached me and told me to leave. I felt really threatened by him and I could see a gun, two knives and a meat cleaver. The next thing is almost too hard to describe. Here, in broad daylight, in the middle of London, the two men started hacking at the body on the floor. I could see butchers' knives and cleavers that they were using to chop and cut into him all over his body. They were stabbing him too. It was like a scene from the worst horror movie ever.

I wanted to get closer, to save the unconscious victim on the floor, but I couldn't. I was completely helpless and I just remember screaming at them in despair: 'You have to stop. Please, please stop. Leave him alone.'

They shouted back at me: 'Please don't come any closer. Keep back.'

When I looked at their faces, it struck me very clearly that these two didn't look deranged, mad or out of their heads on drugs. It was sheer madness on the street that day but there was not a police officer in sight at that point.

There was blood everywhere but these two men were not finished with their victim yet. They stopped chopping momentarily and then got hold of Lee by his arms and pulled him into the middle of the road, in front of a car. There was a huge trail of blood being left behind him. With Lee's head down, they dropped him on his face onto the road with a thud. I can still hear the sound of his face smashing onto the tarmac. It was utterly horrific. I knew I couldn't save Lee by then, but I did rush to stop the vehicle to prevent him being run over. That was something I could do.

Lee was completely covered in blood to the point that his face or features were no longer visible. At first I thought he was a black man, because his face was so dark with the amount of blood covering him. It was only when I saw his white back as his top rode up that I realised that wasn't the case.

The men then started to saw and hack indiscriminately at his neck and body. Lee didn't make a move or a sound. Not a murmur or a flicker from his body. I knew then that he was dead. There was absolutely nothing from him. It was a scene of absolute carnage but still these two animals continued to kick Lee like a football.

I couldn't get to Lee to save him but in my mind I thought his attackers were trying to get him run over, and so I was running around everywhere, screaming at people for help. I was trying to stop all the traffic from travelling down the road and still there was no help from paramedics or the police.

Michelle was still on the phone to the police and it was real panic stations. I got on my phone to the police as well and told them they needed armed response to the scene immediately.

Meanwhile, Lee's killers were going nowhere. It was

bizarre and really sick. They started parading around the street looking very happy and proud of themselves. They seemed to be gloating about their actions and began spouting off to people passing by. There was, by now, thick red blood from the pavement to the middle of the road and there was not a flicker of remorse or emotion from the killers to recognise that this was a human being lying dead. They had no intention of leaving and clearly didn't care about being caught.

Further up the road a bus had stopped and everyone was getting off. I remember shouting at everyone to stay put, trying to look after their safety.

'Stop! Stop! Don't come down here. They have a gun,' I roared out.

It was at that point that a woman approached one of the killers, Michael Adebolajo, as we would later know him. She tried to ask him why he had carried out such a terrible crime, and he began to rant about Muslim ideology and Jihad. Another woman and her daughter had now been allowed near to Lee and one of them was holding his dead body. It was a truly devastating scene. Totally screwed up. You couldn't have made it up in your worst nightmares.

Finally we could hear the wailing of sirens in the distance, then getting closer and closer, and I heard Michelle yelling at me to come back and get out of the way, but I didn't feel as if I had a choice. I had to stay to the end.

Eventually the police arrived and started shouting at everyone to back off and move out the way. I stayed put and, as far as I can remember, four shots were fired at the two killers by armed officers.

Adebolajo went down first and then his sidekick, Michael Adebowale. My reaction was simple.

'Fucking good job,' I shouted out, before telling the armed police they were brilliant.

Neither of the men were killed, just wounded, and were taken away to a hospital under heavy police guard. Michelle and I were taken to nearby Plumstead Police Station and separated so we could be interviewed independently. I still had no idea that Lee was a soldier but things soon became a lot clearer. We were told that this had been the terrorist killing of a soldier and there were Army officers everywhere.

We stayed in the station until about 10.30 p.m. that night and we were interviewed on camera, on tape and by a written statement. I must have still been in shock and it was one of the worst days of my entire life.

When Michelle and I returned home to the pub we were both in a terrible state. I remember pouring a large Bacardi and chucking it down my neck. All the adrenaline that had been pumping through my body earlier in the day had drained away and I felt awful. There were still some people in the bar who were asking what had happened, but I couldn't bring myself to speak. And I think it was then that I realised for the first time how dangerous the situation had been, but at the time you don't think about those things. All I had known was that a young man was in trouble and I had wanted to help, foolishly or not. You can't help the way you react in extreme circumstances. It's fight or flight and, clearly, my mind and body chose fight that day.

As I sat down at home I felt truly stunned and, for the first time, I began to feel real fear. I was very scared. These are terrorists who have killed in cold blood, I thought. Am I a target now? 'What have I got myself involved in?' I asked myself aloud.

I couldn't fathom what had gone on. It was beyond my comprehension that I had witnessed the slaying of a Queen's serving officer on a bright afternoon in London. I stayed up all that night playing the scene over and over again in my mind. I looked grey and drawn, and felt like I had aged ten years. The following morning I turned on the telly to watch the news coverage of events. There were all sorts of stories coming out, theories and guesswork, many of which were just not true. It kept coming back to me that I was actually there and had seen it all. It was a hard one to get my head around because I had seen with my own eyes the truth of what went on and it didn't seem to click with some of the news stories I was hearing.

And then I started to hear about Lee's family. When I first saw the attack the previous day, my first assumption was that it was something to do with a turf war over drugs. That's normally what violent crimes in the city boil down to. But even if the victim had have been a drugs dealer, he still wouldn't have deserved the savagery dealt out.

To discover he was a soldier who had a two-year-old son broke my heart. And then I thought about the young man's mum. As a mother myself I couldn't imagine what she was going through, especially as I had seen how brutal the murder had been.

For about three days I stayed indoors, refusing to go out and face the world. I didn't eat, sleep or wash and I cried constantly. I felt as if I was losing my mind and I felt sick all the time. The trauma was really having a huge impact on me.

'What's happening to me?' I sobbed to my husband Pete. 'Why do I feel this way? I just want it to go away so I can go back to my normal life before this happened.'

Until this point, I had always been a confident and forthright person. I would always speak my mind and not back down from an argument, but all that fighting spirit seemed to have drained out of me. I was just a shell of my old self and it didn't get any better with the passing of time. If anything, it got worse. I felt emotional and tearful all the time.

We had been advised by the police not to talk to the press or anyone about the events of Lee's murder, but I didn't have the courage to do so anyway. I would never have done anything to jeopardise the case the police were building against Lee's killers, but there was no escaping coverage of the murder in the media.

I remember watching Lee's funeral on the television and I couldn't stop sobbing and I couldn't explain to anyone why. And I still had to face giving evidence at the trial. My moods became horrendous and I started having gory flashbacks to the day Lee was murdered. I didn't invite them in; they just arrived out of nowhere. I could be sitting in front of my mirror, brushing my hair, and out of nowhere I could see all the bloodshed and violence playing out in my mind and there was no 'off switch' to get rid of the images. I could often lose up to ten minutes just transported to this horrible place in my head.

I couldn't get rid of the faces of the men who had done this terrible thing. I saw them chopping Lee up over and over again, lifting their arms up above their heads and hacking at Lee with great force. Their faces were contorted with pure hatred and venom. The vision of the young soldier being dragged into the road, covered in blood, has never left me.

As the weeks passed, the flashbacks kept coming. The nightmares would wake me up and I would be bathed in sweat. Other times, I couldn't sleep at all. I was so exhausted and distressed, I could hardly string a sentence together and my life felt like it was falling apart. I was wandering around like a zombie with these terrible pictures dominating my mind. I couldn't talk to Michelle about it because I was trying to protect her. I knew she had been there too, but I didn't want to worry her by saying how ill I was becoming.

Working in the pub business became almost too much to bear, having to put on a brave face and smile at people. I didn't want to do my job because I just wanted some peace in my head. I felt so guilty too. Guilty that I couldn't save Lee and that I wasn't able to do more for him. I no longer have peace of mind. I'm not the outgoing, happy person I had once been – I'm just a shell of a person as a result of what I saw.

I hate going out and, when I do, I can't walk the streets without fear. I have developed all sorts of avoidance issues, like not being able to go into a supermarket because they sell knives in there. I can't even drive my car any more because my confidence is shot to pieces. Instead of socialising, I prefer to stay in my bedroom and cut myself off. It is a very lonely existence and has even affected my marriage because I find it hard to be close to anyone.

At my lowest point I felt suicidal because the trauma in my head was so awful. I actually considered downing a load of pills just so I could escape from the misery. But the overwhelming pain was that of guilt for not being able to save Lee, and guilt that my daughter was there that day too. My faith in humanity was completely destroyed and I couldn't make sense of anything. But I knew it was my life and I had to deal with it and sort it out somehow.

A year ago I finally got some treatment after struggling alone for a year. I was officially diagnosed with Post Traumatic Stress Disorder and I started a course of cognitive behavioural therapy, as well as medication, including anti-depressants. It's not a quick fix. You never fully get rid of PTSD, just as I will never completely get rid of the nightmares and the flashbacks, but I do think I am starting to improve slightly. Through counselling I have been able to say how low, lonely, isolated and afraid I feel. That makes a big difference.

I'm still scared and I know I've been left with a lasting legacy of the violence I witnessed. But I'm learning how to manage my feelings a lot better. Two years on, I have never been able to go back into the centre of Woolwich, even though this is the town where I live. I can't go swimming or be in public places because the fear still hasn't left me.

I am also left with a burning anger inside that I have to come to terms with. My counsellors have taught me that Lee's killers did not see him as a son or a father or even a human being – they just considered him as a uniform they wanted to destroy. I don't know if that has helped me or not, but I know I'm still angry with them for taking Lee's life. I am even more furious at the radicalisation of young men and women in this country who carry out such terrible acts of violence. It is all so senseless and inhuman and I fear every day that there will be more attacks and murders like the killing of Lee Rigby. We must be stronger and bring the radicals into line to prevent this happening again.

Lee's family are the ones who have suffered the worst. My pain is nothing compared to what they have been through, but no one should have to live in a world where this sort of violence and hatred is tolerated. I have to start rebuilding my life now but it's not always easy. I have some terrible dark days still but I'm trying hard to recover from that dreadful day. I know it will never fully leave me. How could it? You cannot watch a young, innocent man being butchered to death and walk away unscathed. I still don't know what took me over that day, but I knew I couldn't just walk away. Despite what I've suffered, I believe I would still do the same again. As hard as it has all been, I don't think it would have been easier if I had turned my back on that young man and walked the other way.

When I finally went to the Old Bailey to give evidence against Lee's killers, it was an important day for me to know they were facing justice, but at the same time I was petrified. For the first day I wasn't called but went into the witness box on day two of the hearing. I saw those two bastards sat behind glass screens. As I looked at their evil faces, I knew I was starting to take back some control.

The prosecutors read out my witness statements and there was a big screen up on the wall. I didn't have to say too much, as they were comparing my account of what happened to the diagrams being shown to the court. Throughout the hearing I couldn't take my eyes off the killers. I stared at them intently, hoping they would look at me and show some kind of emotion, but not once did they look my way.

Then I saw Lyn and her family in the court and my heart went out to them. They looked broken and destroyed. If there is anything I am grateful for, it is that Lee's mum, dad and sisters didn't have to see what I witnessed that day. They live with that loss constantly and I don't know how they get through each day. I'm not sure how I would cope if that was my daughter.

When they were finally jailed for life, I knew justice had been served. They deserved nothing less than to spend the rest of their days behind bars but, if I am really truthful, I wouldn't have been sorry if they were dead. I still don't understand how two human beings could act that way, but I'm glad I don't possess the kind of evil that lurks within them. Watching Lee being murdered that day changed my life forever but I vow not to be beaten by it. I don't know what the future holds, but I will try to keep getting stronger for the sake of my family who have supported me so well. I hope that I can also be there in some way for Lyn.

11

Angels and Demons – Part Two

The second 'angel' is another very special lady who also risked her own life to help Lee. I will never be able to repay the love, kindness and compassion she showed my son that day. Amanda Donnelly lives with her grown-up children in Woolwich and, like Tina, had no idea what was about to confront her when she left home that day. Here is Amanda's story.

I remember it being a lovely warm day in May and my daughter Gemini asked me if I would give her a lift into Woolwich town. I needed to run some chores, so said I would drop her off at the same time. It was afternoon and the sun had put us all in a good mood. It wasn't a very long drive from home – just a few minutes to reach town. We were driving along and, just before we got to Artillery Place, Gemini started screaming. It was a really piercing scream that made me jump, and I slammed on my brakes and pulled the car up.

'What the hell is it?' I yelled.

'I need to get out, Mum. Quick,' she blurted back.

It was then that I saw for the first time what had made

her so upset. The very first thing I saw was two men holding another man down on the floor and both of them had either side of his head and they were hacking away around his neck. At first I just froze. My blood ran cold and I didn't know what the hell was going on. I grabbed for my mobile phone and tried to ring the police but I couldn't do it. My hands were shaking so badly, I couldn't even press the numbers on the keypad.

Both Gem and I jumped out the car and I was still trying to ring the police. I got through and told them that a man was being hacked to death. The men were still attacking the body on the ground and I just ran over and started pleading with them.

'What are you doing to him?' I blurted out. 'Leave him be. Leave him alone.'

I was shaking from head to foot but they kept saying to us: 'Go away. Just leave now.'

The next thing they started saying was that they were soldiers of Allah and that British soldiers are killing children all the time. I couldn't believe what was happening in front of me. From driving my daughter to the town centre, I felt that someone had picked me up and dropped me on the film set of a horror movie. I was completely petrified.

Me and Gemini tried to talk to them and we just kept asking why they were doing this. They carried on with their rant about Muslim religion and kept saying that British soldiers do this to their people every day. They kept saying they didn't want to hurt us but we had to leave.

They were standing just in front of us, covered in the blood of the young man who lay on the floor. They didn't seem at all deranged. They were very calm and matter-of-fact and, the more we spoke with them, the less threatened I felt, because instinct told me I was not their target. I was determined to try and reason with them, to try and get to the man lying in the road behind me. I didn't know for sure whether their victim was alive or dead at this point, even though I had a pretty good idea that he had not survived such a brutal attack. But I still had to try, so I carried on talking to them.

'I know your religion respects women and children and so, as a mother, will you let me go to this man?' I pleaded with them.

'No, go away. This is not your fight. We are not here to harm women and children, even though your soldiers hurt ours all the time.'

'Please,' I begged. 'As a mother will you let me go to him? I am not religious but no man should die in the street alone.'

I didn't think I was getting through to them but, all of a sudden, one of the men, Adebolajo, as I now know, seemed to relent.

'You two can go,' he gestured to me and Gemini. 'But no man is allowed to approach the body. Just you and her.'

It was a mad moment but something in him responded to me as a mother. I took a few slow steps over to where Lee was lying lifeless on the road and I gently sat beside him. I knew in an instant he was dead but it made no difference to me. I still wanted to comfort him. I started to rub his back and whispered gently to him, 'No one's gonna hurt you any more, son. It's all over now.'

My heart felt broken in pieces at the sight of the stranger I held in my arms. He was literally covered in blood at the top. I knew nothing about him except that his life had ended in the most terrible way possible. His injuries were so bad and the blood so thick, I couldn't even tell what age or ethnic background he was from. It was truly awful and, even though he was clearly dead, I still wanted to protect him from even more damage.

I placed my arms around him and began to cradle him to me. I was wet with his blood but that was of no concern to me. All I could think was that this was some mother's son and he was dead in my arms.

'I'm so sorry I couldn't save you, whoever you are,' I told him. 'I'm not gonna let anyone hurt you anymore. Your suffering is over.'

I must have lain on the hard floor with Lee for about twenty minutes. I held him, patted him and spoke to him, even though I have no idea to this day why I carried on speaking to him, knowing he was gone. I kept looking around me. Lee's killers were still prowling around, ranting at passers-by, and I felt like I was not in the real world, as if somehow I had been yanked out of reality and thrown into a nightmare. I was aware that these men had been trying to hack Lee's head off, and it seemed they came very close to achieving that. If it hadn't been fully chopped off, it wasn't held on by much. I didn't move Lee's body; I just lay with him and held him.

In the distance I could hear sirens getting closer and I knew that I couldn't lie on the floor forever, but I didn't want to leave this poor man in the middle of the street. I never once felt in danger for myself. I didn't even think about it when I went to Lee. I come from the streets and, by that I don't mean I lived on them ... I just knew what it was like to live in a tough, inner city place where violence and murder are happening all around you. You have to learn to be a bit tough to survive in some communities, but that doesn't mean getting involved in crime. You just have to have a sense of right and wrong. I'm not the sort of woman who would ever look for trouble but I'm no Superwoman either. This was simply an act of compassion and humanity in Lee's hour of need.

I'm not a religious person but I would say I'm spiritual – a bit of an old hippie – and I care about people. I have a son and two daughters, and when I'm out there I'm everyone's mother. That's how I felt about Lee. I know how I would want people to react if that was one of my children lying hacked to death on the floor in broad daylight. I wouldn't leave any dying person alone in the street. I think my first instinct that day was as a mother. When you have children of your own, you can't help yourself – instinct kicks in.

I knew that, however bad it already was, I had to protect this man from any further mutilation. For a long time, as I sat on that road with Lee, I wasn't aware of too much else going on around me. It felt like the rest of the world had almost zoomed out. I remember seeing so much blood running down the road, the kerb and the pavement, but I just stayed put. I felt this huge and terrible sadness at such a terrible loss of life in a savage manner.

I knew I would have to leave this man soon, as the sirens were drawing closer, and the one thing I did fear was being caught in the crossfire of a shootout between the killers and armed police. I didn't want to take my arms away from him and, as I got up to go, I hugged Lee and leant over him to speak to him one last time.

'I'm so sorry I couldn't have done more for you. You didn't deserve this. Rest in Peace, whoever you are.'

I felt distraught leaving this body in the road. It was a scene of carnage and bloodshed. I returned to my car, and to meet up with my daughter. It was then that I heard the gunshots and I knew everything was getting really crazy. I drove home in a daze and, when we got through the front door, I just stood there and burst into tears.

It was then that I looked down and realized I was caked in blood all over my hands and my jacket. It was shocking. My neighbour sat with me, and I had a strong cup of coffee, but I could hardly speak a word. I was in utter meltdown.

I can't say I remember much about the next forty-eight hours. Friends came round to see me and check I was OK but all I recall is talking total gibberish, just random nonsense. I didn't sleep that night and I stayed in the same clothes for two days, unable to function at even the most basic level.

Lots of news had filtered through about the man who died that day and, of course, I learned he was a soldier. And then the flashbacks started. I had loads of recall about the attack and the blood and Lee lying there on the road, but the most vivid flashback was quite weird. I remember on the day seeing Adebolajo with an orange Sainsbury's supermarket carrier bag. At the time I had the notion that it was the bag these men had intended to put Lee's head in and take it away as a trophy. I tried really hard, but I couldn't get rid of the image of this orange bag flashing through my mind. Pictures of the attack also ran through my head, including the killers' faces, and it was a terrifying experience.

The day after the murder, the press started to arrive at my door. Loads of people had taken mobile phone pictures and video footage as I lay with Lee, and this had ended up with the media. My picture was everywhere and everyone wanted to talk to me, but I couldn't face it. My street was filled with press cars and there were long lenses from cameras pointing from every direction. It was really daunting and upsetting. There were cards and letters from reporters and editors, pleading with me to talk to them, but I couldn't do it.

I was being dubbed a hero and an 'Angel of Woolwich', but that wasn't what it had been about for me. I didn't want glory or praise or a pat on the back. I just kept thinking of Lee's mum, and the fact she had lost her son. For me, I just did what came naturally and what a lot of other mums would have done in my place. It wasn't heroic. I didn't choose to be there, or witness what I saw. I had no choice but to act out of compassion.

First came the press and then, the following day, I received a card through the door from the anti-terrorism police, asking me to ring them urgently. I phoned them back and four officers came round to my home. They asked me what seemed like hundreds of questions, and I felt completely bombarded by it all, even though I knew they were just doing their job. It was really daunting. They then took me to the police station, where they took my clothes and shoes and phone for analysis, before taking my fingerprints and a DNA swab. I accept that police have to be thorough, but I almost felt like I was a criminal when all I had done was try to help someone.

We worked with the police for a few weeks, and I went to the police station three times to try and help as much as I could. But it was hard because all I had wanted to do was help Lee. I had to get into all sorts of role play with officers to try and bring out every last detail of what had been said and what had gone on. It was exhausting and quite disturbing, although there was never any hint of accusation that I had done anything wrong. When it was all over I told police I was happy for them to use my statement for prosecution, but I didn't want to go to trial. I still had to protect my own family and I was aware that there are a lot of crazy people in the world.

Despite everything, I never once regretted my actions that day. I understand why some people step back and won't get involved in situations because they fear they'll be hurt. It's natural. But what I did was in my make-up. Regardless of the danger, I took a risk and I would do it all again tomorrow.

If it has changed me at all as a person, it has made me ever more aware that the world is becoming more and more dangerous. You have to be on your guard twenty-four hours a day, and this makes me particularly sad for young people and children, because it is a much tougher place for them than it ever was for me at that age. I know not everyone wants to watch the news, because it is so alarming sometimes, but I do think we should all be aware of our civilization and how it is being eroded with mindless violence.

Lee's murder dominated the news and I learnt a lot about him and his family, and I often thought about them all, especially if something came on the news. I saw how Lyn looked and the sorrow she went through, and all I could think about was how she had lost her little boy. My children are grown up now, but they are still my babies and always will be. I wouldn't wish that on any parent.

I also feel so sad for the future, in that Lee's killers felt it was the right thing to attack and kill him in such an atrocious way. How can normal and caring human beings feel that way? Maybe one day they'll realise how wrong they have been and repent in some way.

In the first year after Lee was killed, we were offered so many opportunities to talk publicly and were even offered a Pride of Britain award, but I refused it all because I don't feel like a hero or that I have done anything amazing. I didn't go to help Lee to be recognised. I don't like the attention and found a lot of it embarrassing. I don't want an award for helping a man who was so cruelly killed. It doesn't feel right. I'm just a normal woman who was living a normal life when this terrible thing happened. I was even offered an award from Greenwich Council but, again, it didn't seem right to go and collect it. It's not heroic to get caught up in something you don't plan. We all react differently in times of crisis, but my maternal instinct was what drove me on that day. The idea that someone could leave my son or daughter lying in a road in that state without comfort fills me with dread.

I have only one regret, and it's that I wasn't able to rescue or save Lee before it was too late.

12

Angels and Demons – Part Three

Hearing the stories of the women who were there when Lee died was overwhelming, and it taught me many things about the human spirit. These were total strangers who didn't think twice about their own safety but rushed in to help my son. I will never be able to thank them enough for their courage and compassion. It also showed me that many people were affected by the horrific events of that day, not just those who lost a loved one to a senseless murder.

Tina, in particular, has suffered really badly, and her emotional torment goes on. Her act of bravery has cost her dearly and she may have to live with those emotional demons for the rest of her life. It's a price I wouldn't wish on anyone, and she doesn't deserve the pain that she now suffers daily. She tried to do so much that day by halting traffic to prevent further injuries to Lee, and to protect other people from harm. She acted without thought for herself and, as a result, had the terrible tragedy of seeing just how savage the attack on my boy was. I still play the imaginary images of that day through my mind but Tina knows the full truth and I wish I could take that away from her.

As for Amanda, she acted like any loving mother would at seeing a young man in his dying moments. Like many mums, we understand that natural maternal instinct to protect and shelter people in trouble. I wish with all my heart that I had been the one to hold and cradle my son but, that day, Amanda acted as if Lee was one of her own children and rushed to his aid. She stood up to blood-soaked men wielding knives and guns and pleaded to be allowed to tend to Lee. She responded to my precious son in the way I would have done myself.

Knowing that a loving mother like Amanda stepped up and did that for Lee leaves me forever indebted to her. She was fearless and brave, but she was also full of kindness and grace, as she lay on the floor and embraced my dead child. I am still overwhelmed at what she did under such extreme circumstances and my emotions towards her run very deep.

For a number of reasons, it was a long time before I had the opportunity to meet these two fabulous ladies in person. There was huge publicity over Lee's murder that never seemed to go away but, in the first year, we were preparing for the trial. The Scotland Yard investigation continued for months and we were advised by our Police Liaison Officers not to contact any potential witnesses, and this included Tina and Amanda. If we had done, it could have prejudiced the forthcoming trial, and there was no way we would put that in jeopardy. One top of that, I wasn't even capable of looking after myself at that time because I was so grief-stricken. I never intended to be selfish or rude by not getting in touch, but I always knew that I would when the time was right.

Despite this, I was still attacked in one venomous newspaper column by a female journalist who took the high moral ground without even checking her facts. On the first anniversary of Lee's murder, Ingrid Loyau-Kennett gave an interview in one of the papers about how, a year on, she returned to the scene of the crime. She was asked if I had ever phoned her or spoken to her and she correctly said no. Ingrid had been in Woolwich that day, as had Tina and Amanda. She got off a bus when she saw the chaos. Without hesitation, she walked straight up to killers Adebolajo and Adebowale and starting having a go at them for what they had done. It was an incredibly brave decision, and her remonstrations with the armed men were captured as phone footage and video. She too was dubbed one of the Angels of Woolwich, and rightly so. She was amazing in her defiance and fearlessness of these men who had carried out such a cowardly attack.

Ingrid was the only one of the 'Angels' who has ever fully spoken about her experience, and her story is well documented. She spoke eloquently on television news channels and in the papers about what happened to Lee and how she had spoken to the killers. She was clearly a hero, and I remember seeing some of the footage in the early days after Lee died. I simply wasn't well enough to talk to anyone in the first few months afterwards, so it was extremely hurtful when this high-profile columnist publicly slated me for not getting in touch with Ingrid. She judged it poor that I hadn't seen fit to thank Ingrid that it was:

Sad that, a year on from Drummer Lee Rigby's murder, she has never been contacted by his family. She may not have lost a son, but the horror of that day will live with her forever, too.

It was a cruel and unnecessary dig at a time when I was facing the first anniversary of the killing. And if that writer had walked just a mile in my shoes she would have known how I felt.

Ingrid is an exceptional woman but has since suffered problems of her own, which have also been well documented. I often wondered whether the mental health issues she endured were related to the trauma of what she saw that day. And for that reason, I didn't want to drag it all back up for her again by talking about it in this book. However, this is an opportunity for me to publicly thank Ingrid for the outstanding way she behaved that day, and I am forever thankful and proud of her. I also wish to thank her for the care she showed in the moment of such crisis and I wish her well always.

I had always wanted to meet the women who helped Lee and so, after the first anniversary, I made plans to do so. It was in January 2015 on a cold wintry afternoon that I finally had the privilege to see them for the first time. It was a daunting prospect to be meeting these incredible people, and I was filled with nerves and fear when I set off for London on a Friday afternoon with my husband Ian and our two youngest children. I had waited a long time to do this and I knew that I was finally ready to face whatever lay ahead. We had arranged to meet the following afternoon in Woolwich, where Amanda lived, but this filled me with trepidation and sadness because it is was where Lee died. At this point I had never returned to the precise spot where he was killed because it was just too much for me. Not even on Lee's first anniversary did I go there, because I couldn't cope with the horrors that had taken place there. And so I was terrified for two reasons that day: returning to Woolwich and meeting Amanda for the first time.

I didn't know what to expect and I played over and over in my mind what I might say to her, and how she would react to me. All I really knew was that I wanted to thank her with all my heart. I went to a florist and had a bouquet of flowers made up for her. It seemed inadequate as a symbol of gratitude but it was well intended. We had organised a private room in a restaurant, so we could talk uninterrupted. I was a bag of nerves when I sat in that room, watching the door, not knowing who was going to come through it. All of a sudden Amanda breezed in, and I jumped up to give her a giant hug. My nerves vanished and I was over-whelmed with emotion when I saw this amazing woman for the first time. We had never spoken before, but we just stood there, hugging each other for ages. No words were necessary. The warmth and love I felt in that moment were unbelievable. Tears welled up and rolled down my cheeks. It was hugely emotional, and it's hard to explain why, but she made me feel safe. Perhaps it's because I had seen the natural way in which she had been so loving and kind to Lee.

'I don't know how to thank you,' I sobbed on her shoulder. 'What you did for my son was the most beautiful thing ever. I am so grateful you were there to hold him at the end.'

Amanda squeezed me tighter as she responded: 'You have nothing to thank me for, Lyn. Any loving mum would do the same and that could have been one of my children out there.'

All my fears were gone for good and I was elated to be in the company of this exceptional woman who had done so much for me. For the next couple of hours, over coffee and biscuits, we talked non-stop. Amanda was relaxed and kind. She had this abundance of long black curls framing her face and the biggest and loveliest smile you could imagine. Just like my Lee.

'My son had a huge smile, just like yours,' I told her.

'I wish I had met him while he was still alive,' she replied. 'You've told me so many lovely things about your son that it makes me realise how my instincts to help that day were right. I have a grown-up son myself, and I understand how much we worry as mums that they will be safe when they go out into the world.'

We talked about our children a lot that day and we bonded so closely. Amanda is the kind of woman you would choose as a good friend because you know she will never let you down. She is the kind of person who will always have your back, no matter what happens. And she gave me something else very precious that day: I had lost so much faith in human nature after Lee was killed that I trusted no one, but Amanda showed me the goodness in people again. And we laughed! We allowed ourselves to laugh at some of the daft things we spoke about and it felt good and natural.

From the moment I met her, I knew I could trust Amanda because she has a heart of gold and a rare honesty. That day we struck up a bond that I believe will remain between us forever. How do you thank a woman who cradles your murdered son, covered in his blood and oblivious to any danger to herself? Amanda has never wanted any recognition for what she did but, for the rest of my life, I will never forget her heroism. It makes her very special to me and words don't come close to my feelings. She has good, old-fashioned family values about looking after loved ones and being there for people in need. If only the world had more people like her.

I enjoyed talking to Amanda about Lee. I told her all about how cheeky and boisterous he was and she laughed loudly when I shared some of his antics. I felt I owed her the chance to learn a little about the stranger to whom she had given so much love. By the end of our time together, we both felt we had been gifted with an amazing friendship that will grow from strength to strength. It doesn't matter how old your children get, they will always be your babies. Amanda understood that on the day she went to my son. She knew that was some mother's baby and she dived in to help. I think that showed true love, compassion and courage. She is a true angel.

Amanda on Lyn: I had always wanted to meet Lyn and I was pretty certain that, when the time was right, she would get in touch with me if she wanted to. As a mum, I understood that she must be paralysed with grief at the loss of her son in such a repulsive manner, and so I just got on with my life, even though I often thought about Lyn and her family. I wasn't exactly waiting for contact with her, but I was thrilled when last winter I received a letter out of the blue from a friend of Lyn's asking if I would consider speaking to Lyn and meeting with her.

It was a Saturday morning when the post arrived and it was the last thing I had been expecting but it was a nice surprise to read that Lyn wanted to chat. It felt wrong to not have that link with his mum and family, and unresolved and inappropriate that I couldn't reach out to Lee's mum and tell her how much I cared. I think I also needed to know a little about the man who lay on that street covered in blood. I had cradled him in his final moments on earth because he was a human being and, from my heart, I believe no man should lie in the street alone as Lee was left.

I was a bit nervous going to the meeting, because you never know how things will go, but I needn't have panicked. From the second we met, I felt a natural affinity with Lyn. I gave her the biggest cuddle and I knew everything was going to be OK. She couldn't stop saying thank you to me.

'You have nothing to thank me for,' I kept telling her.

'Yes I do,' she said. 'You were the one who treated him with respect and dignity and kindness at the moment he needed it the most. You treated my son as if he were your own. You are a very special person.'

'No,' I stressed. 'I'm a very ordinary woman who just happened to be there that day. I don't want thanks from you. I just wanted to meet you to show you how much I cared and to say how sorry I am for your loss. No one deserved to die like that, and I only wish I had been able to get to him earlier, to save him. I'm so sorry I couldn't do more for Lee.'

Lyn grabbed my hand. 'You did everything you could,' she reassured me. 'If you hadn't gone to my son, he would have lain alone, covered in blood, dead in the middle of a street. It was horrific enough, but I know he was not on his own. I wish I had been there to comfort him myself but you did it for me.'

They were emotional words between us, but Lyn and I were completely at ease with each other. I could see, just by looking into her eyes, how broken she had become by this terrible tragedy, and it made me full of sorrow for her. I tried to imagine how I would feel if I was in her shoes, but it was impossible to imagine the hurt she must go through continually. And all for nothing.

I found it hard to leave Lyn that day. I just wanted to keep talking, because it felt right. She has the wickedest sense of humour, something she told me she shared with Lee, and I could see what a devoted mother she is. She loved her son with all her heart, and I know this will torment her for the rest of her life, but she has good people around her and I will always be there to support her.

I first met Tina almost by accident. We share mutual friends and, in 2014, I went down to London to join a march in honour of Lee through Woolwich with some Fusilier veterans. I was staying with my dear friend Lorna Taylor, who has been hugely instrumental in drumming up support for a permanent memorial for Lee. That evening, after the march, Ian and I went out with Lorna to a pub in Woolwich run by one of Lorna's friends – Tina. I was aware who Tina was, but she had largely shied away from the media so, while I knew she had helped Lee on the day he was killed, I didn't know her full story. I certainly had no inkling of how much she had suffered as a result.

It was a social occasion, and not the right time for hugely emotional meetings, but, as the night wore on, I was introduced to Tina and that was it! By the end of the evening I was staggered to learn her journey, as we talked into the early hours, long after her customers had left. It was heartbreaking to hear how her life had fallen apart as a direct result of the murder.

'I'm so sorry you've suffered in such a terrible way because you tried to help Lee. It's horrific,' I told her, but she was quick to sweep away her own problems to try and comfort me.

'No, don't you ever be sorry, Lyn. I feel so guilty that I fell apart this way when it wasn't *my* son who was murdered. What gives me the right to be in bits when you're the one who lost her child?'

I felt an instant bond with Tina and she taught me how so many had been traumatised by Lee's murder. It's terrible to see how something so violent can bring people to their knees. I could also see that she was a strong woman who had been decimated by this experience. That night, we both pledged to help each other and we have remained friends ever since.

I think, when you meet people, you often get a sixth sense about the kind of person they are. I knew that Tina had integrity and honesty about her, which is probably why she acted on impulse to help Lee. She told me she desperately tried to reach Lee, but she couldn't get to him and that lives with her all the time.

'I felt so helpless, Lyn,' she cried to me. 'All I wanted to do was to go and help but they wouldn't let me through at that point. I wish I could have done more.'

'You did what you could, Tina, and I will always be grateful for you. So many ran away that day in fear. I don't blame them, but you stayed put and laid your own life on the line to help a stranger. I can never repay that.'

Tina on Lyn: The first time Lyn and Ian walked into my pub, I froze. I knew instantly who she was and I was all flustered because I was terrified of saying the wrong thing to her. The last thing I wanted to do was offend or hurt her in any way.

Not long after she arrived, friends brought us together and it was as if I had known her all my life. Lyn is a very generous and giving woman who still wants to help others even though she has been through so much. She picked up very quickly that the events of that day had played havoc with my health and she couldn't have been more compassionate. But I felt awful to feel so bad when she was the mum who lost her son.

'It's not your fault you have been ill,' Lyn said. 'What you saw and did would disturb the strongest person on the planet and you tried to do so much for Lee,' she added.

'I wish I could have done more,' I said. 'It was the most horrific day ever and I know it will stay with me always. But I will never experience the pain you have been through. I'm not sure I would still be standing if that was my son.'

Her reply was simple, as it said so much about her love for all her children.

'I have to carry on. I have to live for Lee and look after all my other children. It is what Lee would have wanted me to do. It's harder than anyone will ever know, but I'll never give up, for Lee's sake.'

That evening was one of the first of many meetings Lyn and I have now shared and our friendship is stronger than ever. It's incredible that something so bad can produce the most wonderful of friendships and I'm blessed to have Lyn in my life. I just wish it wasn't because she had lost her son.

13

Devoted Sisters

I know that in many ways I'm still a very lucky woman. I've lost my precious son, and I know I'll never get over that, but I am still blessed by having four beautiful daughters who are my world. They are all very different and unique but they were all totally devoted to their big brother Lee. Each one of them had their own special relationship with him and their own very precious memories they will keep forever.

My girls have been absolutely amazing to me over the past two and a half years and it is because of them that I'm still standing. The sadness they have endured has been huge but, in many ways, they didn't just lose their brother, they lost a huge part of their mum too. I know I will never be the same person as before Lee died but I don't want to inflict further pain on my other children, so I have to make sure I am strong for them and that they all have happy and healthy lives in the future. All the girls have dealt with losing Lee in different ways, unsurprisingly, as they are all different ages and personalities, so I have to adapt and help them in ways best suited to each daughter. They are all vulnerable, although Amy is still so young and I have had to protect her from so much that went on. She's still only ten now, and was just eight years old when Lee was murdered.

She knows Lee was killed by bad men but Ian and I have tried our hardest to shield her from the more grisly details of the murder. I know she hears things at school, and when she gets older she'll discover more about what happened, but for now it's vital for me to treat her like the little girl she still is. The murder had a huge impact on Amy because it has left her very frightened of the world in general. She is very much like me – quiet and sensitive and doesn't like the limelight – but she has a heart of gold, just like her big brother.

She takes things to heart very easily, so I'm very gentle with her and try to build her confidence as much as possible. All my daughters have had trauma counselling following the murder, and they all think it helped them greatly to deal with the issues they have been left with. For Amy, the big one is fear. She remains petrified that the men who killed Lee are going to break out of prison and come to our house and murder us all. It broke my heart when she confided this, and she became so scared that she would return home from school and refuse to go out again because she thought something bad was going to happen to her. No child that young should be living in fear like that and I worry it will have a lasting impact on her as she grows up.

Even the mention of Lee's killers terrifies Amy, and one incident had her fearing for her life. In September 2014 one of the convicted murderers, Michael Adebolajo, was moved from Belmarsh maximum security jail in south-east London to Frankland Prison in County Durham. Even though he was still locked up in a Category A prison, Amy was sobbing because she believed he was being moved closer to our home in Manchester, which would make it easier for him to escape and come and get us.

It may seem irrational to most people, but to a little girl

these men are monsters who stole her brother away. It took a long time to convince Amy that she was safe, but she is still frightened of a lot of things. The authorities say they moved Adebolajo to Frankland because they feared he was radicalising fellow Muslim inmates at Belmarsh. That may be the case, but a ten-year-old girl only understands that he now lives much closer to us. A ten-year-old should be playing with her friends without a care in the world, not hiding away in her house because she thinks she's going to be murdered. It just feels so cruel for her.

Amy is a completely adorable girl and everyone loves her. She is polite and kind and caring and loves going to school, despite everything that has happened. I am so proud of how she has tried to deal with such huge trauma in her young life. Her teachers and her friends have also recognised that she is a special little girl and, in July 2014, just over a year after Lee had died, she was given a special Child of Courage award at a school assembly for her outstanding attitude. She deserved it so much because she is sweet and loving to everyone. She even comforts me, even though I am the parent and she is my child. If I have a weepy moment or get upset, she is the first to rush to my side and cuddle me.

'Don't cry, Mum,' she always tells me. 'Lee doesn't want us to be unhappy. He wants to see you smiling again.'

'I know, sweetheart, but I just miss him and love him so much.'

'Me too, Mum, but he's safe now and up in the stars looking down on us. He hasn't really left us at all. I will look after you always.'

Her words always pick me up and remind me that I have to move forward, not just for Lee, or for my own sake, but for all my children, who deserve the very best in life. I do try and hide my sadness from the girls, but it's not always possible, and sometimes the tears roll down my face and there's nothing I can do to stop them. Amy is my little angel to wipe away those tears, and I can never thank her enough. I asked all my girls to write down their feelings about their adored brother and here is what Amy had to say:

Lee was the most cheerful, loving brother ever, and he was always a shoulder for me to cry on. Whenever I needed someone to talk to he was always there for me, no matter what it was. If I ever had trouble in school he wanted to go in and sort it out and protect me. He always told me he loved me and that he would always look after me, which makes me sad as they took Lee away from me so now he can never look after me again.

I believe he is always looking down on me and my family and I always tell my mum that too. We both believe he is up in the stars keeping a watch over us and that helps us feel a bit better when we miss him and wish he was with us.

I still miss him all the time and when Lee died I was heartbroken and couldn't stop crying. I started having nightmares that his killers were going to break out of prison and come for us too. I used to be bubbly and happy but I lost my confidence in myself and became scared all the time. I still don't like being on my own and I'm frightened of lots of things, like crossing the roads and being near cars. I feel safe when I'm at home with Mum and Dad but I hate to see my mum crying because it upsets me.

I will never get over losing my big brother Lee, even though I have had a lot of help from my family and a trauma therapist, who I spoke to about the way I felt. I think I've got a bit better at learning to live with my sadness. I used to get so upset in school when people would talk about Lee and ask me questions about what happened to him, or tell me things

about his killing. My teachers are always so kind and protective at looking after me when I'm in school. Just like Lee
used to be.

I try to remember the good things about Lee – the things
that made me laugh because he was always joking about and
that made me giggle. He could also be a pain in the bum
because he would wind me up to the point he would make
me cry. He was the biggest mickey taker ever and if he got
me upset he would stop and give me a cuddle. If a boy called
to the house for me to go and play, he would wind me up and
tease me that it was my boyfriend, even if it wasn't. Then he
would get all strict on me and say I had better not get a boyfriend till I was much older. He also said I deserved a rich,
handsome and famous boyfriend. The last Christmas we spent
together, he bought me a pair of boots which fell apart a few
days later and we laughed so much at that. He would play
football, kerby, cards and Ludo when he was home and then
we would bounce up and down on the trampoline together,
which I loved. Sometimes he was a bigger kid than me!

He would take me to the local park and I still remember
him taking me to the markets when I was much smaller to
buy me a doll. I loved that doll so much I wish I still had her
because it would remind me of Lee.

He always told us that he loved us. Whenever he phoned
or was about to go away, he would always say: 'I love you,
little Amy.'

'I love you too, Lee,' I replied.

I wish with all my heart I could tell Lee how much I love
and miss him forever and always. He was the best, most
cheerful big brother in the world, and he did so much for
other people. He loved his family and his country. I couldn't
bear to go to his funeral because I wanted to remember Lee
happy and smiling and not in a wooden box.

It's been so hard to listen to my daughters, and their pain at the loss of their big brother, but they all loved him deeply and they miss him every day like I do. Courtney is Amy's elder sister and she was just eleven when Lee left us. Like Amy, she has found it incredibly hard to cope with his murder. Being that little bit older, she had a better understanding and grasp of what had happened, but it completely shook her world apart. She idolised Lee and couldn't cope when he was murdered. She really needed trauma counselling and that had a very positive impact on her. She had all sorts of overwhelming emotions after the murder, but one of the strongest was anger, an explosive and toxic fury that threatened to destroy her young life. How a youngster of eleven coped with such an avalanche of feelings I will never know, but Courtney is a very clever and sensible girl. She has always had a clear vision of what she wants from her life and I've no doubt she will achieve what she sets out to do but, unlike Amy, she internalised a lot of her emotions and it was obvious that she was struggling to process such a violent crime committed against the brother she adored.

Courtney loves her sport, as did Lee, and they had a fantastic bond over football, despite the fact that Lee was a die-hard Manchester United fan and Courtney is a Manchester City devotee. They would tease each other mercilessly over football results and were alike in lots of ways. She likes to rough and tumble and have a giggle and they would play-fight all the time. But she's also a very emotional person, again, like her big brother, so you can imagine how his murder knocked her sideways.

Courtney is growing up really quickly and has a brilliant head on her shoulders. She is quite a deep thinker, so I keep my eye on her to make sure she's coping. At one point she wrote in her diary that she wanted to die too, because the loss of her brother was so painful for her. I was terrified when I read that because I couldn't imagine the idea of losing two children. I spoke with her about it and it was all tied up with her anger. That's how the trauma therapy has helped her, because it has given her tools for dealing with everyday incidents and feelings. She is also highly protective of me and my emotions, and I feel the same way towards her. It was Courtney who first told me she thought she had lost me too after Lee died.

She said: 'It's like when Lee died, you died with him, Mum. It's like you're not here with us anymore.'

'I'm so sorry, my darling, but I feel like part of me was killed when they took our Lee,' I replied.

'But we are still here and we need you to be with us. Don't make us lose you as well as Lee.'

They were heartbreaking words from such a young girl, but Courtney was right. My daughters didn't deserve to lose their mum as well as their brother, so I tried to hide my emotions as much as possible. You have to wear invisible body armour just to get through the day sometimes but, when I'm alone, I can take that defence off and be left with my thoughts about Lee.

Courtney helps me a lot to see things clearly when I start to lose my way. On the last Mother's Day she sent me a message which made me sob my heart out.

She told me: 'Happy Mum's Day, Mum! I love you so much and I can't thank you enough for everything you have done for me, You've been my rock these past twenty-two months because you have always been there if I've needed anyone to talk to or cry or rant to. You are the bravest woman I know, even though I realise you have to keep a brave face on for us. You are the best mum I could ever ask for, and I wouldn't change you for the world. Thanks for looking after me. Lee will be so proud of you, Mum. I love you.'

They were such powerful words and reminded me of how much I owe my girls and how much they need me to be strong for them. Here Courtney talks about her love for Lee:

Lee was the best big brother I could ever have asked for. He was so funny and a huge wind-up, but the moment any of us needed him he was there. He would wind up all four of his sisters to the point where we would be in tears or Mum had to step in and tell him to behave, but it was always good-natured. He would tell me that I wasn't allowed to have a boyfriend until I was at least twenty-five years old and even then he joked that he would keep his baseball bat close by. I remember once Lee had two tickets to a tour of Old Trafford, and he took me with him even though I'm a City fan. We both loved our footie. When Lee came back from the Army to visit, we would always play football together outside the front of our house and he would take us all for days out to different places, shopping or meals out.

He was always so kind and he loved spending time with us all. Every time he went away he always said he loved us and that he wanted us to be safe. I loved Lee so much. He was my only brother but he was the best brother ever. When Lee was killed my heart broke. My big brother was dead and wasn't coming back. That took so long to sink in. I remember when we first saw it on the news but we didn't know it was Lee. I was praying that it wasn't him but then I found out in the middle of the night it was him. My feelings were all over the place and I didn't know what to do. I was only eleven at the time and it hurt so much. I got very angry about his death, and then I became angry at just about everything. I would hear my mum crying every night and knowing that I could do nothing about it or take her pain away made me even angrier. It was a really deep and painful anger and when it flared up I would start punching and destroying things until the point where I just broke down in tears.

I started locking myself away from other people and became withdrawn because I didn't want to hurt or upset anyone when

I was angry. The trauma therapy I was offered was a big help because I learned from my therapist about the emotions I was going through. She gave me ways to handle my anger. It didn't make my pain go away, because that's always still there. I know it's made my family a lot stronger because if we don't stick together it will be so much harder for all of us.

I won't ever get over losing Lee. If I could have spoken to him before he died, I would have told him how much of a great big brother he was. I hated being stared at in the street when people recognised our family, but I have also found out who my true friends are because they stuck by me the whole time and are still supporting me even now. They have helped me so much these past two years and I will never be able to thank them enough.

Lee was a brother I really looked up to because he had done so well by joining the Army and we were all so proud of him. Now I want to do well at school and get a good job so that Lee can be proud of me too. The worst part of all of this is trying to come to terms with the fact I will never see him again and that he is never coming home. I keep expecting him to walk through the door with that cheeky grin and then I remember that he never will. Losing Lee has made me grow up quickly, and has forced me to become a stronger person, but I still hurt so much on the inside. I hide a lot of my feelings away. I remember Lee as this amazing, kind and cheeky person. He was my big brother and my hero.

My two eldest daughters will have completely different memories of Lee because they were much closer in age and so grew up together. Sara, Chelsea and Lee were very close as children, and that special bond followed them into adulthood. Sara especially was like Lee's shadow, and they did everything together throughout their lives. She was completely and utterly distraught when Lee was murdered and it left a giant void in her life and always will. Lee was a huge family man, so he was thrilled when Sara began a family of her own and he became an uncle to her three children, as well as being delighted to have his own first son, Jack. They were so happy that their kids would all grow up together and look after each other. Sara has since had a fourth baby, who Lee never got to meet, but he would have been just as happy to welcome more children into the family as he was with all the others.

Sara's newborn with her husband Rob Sarjeant made quite an entrance into the world, with a drama that could have been scripted by Lee himself. Just two days after the first anniversary of Lee's murder, Sara went into premature labour and delivered her baby boy eight weeks early. He weighed just three pounds and fourteen ounces, and it was touch and go for a while for both mum and child. Thankfully they both pulled through.

Sara and Rob's perfect little baby was called Bobby Ian-Lee James in memory of the uncle he would never meet and my husband Ian. It was a perfect tribute and the first time our family had felt any joy since Lee had been murdered. Bobby Lee was perfect in every way and we all fell in love with him instantly. I couldn't have been prouder of him if he had been my own. He came out screaming his lungs off and my first thought was that he was just like our Lee – noisy, loud and full of life!

This tiny scrap of life signified a sliver of hope for us all because the last year had been hell. I had spent every day pouring out my grief for my lost son and now this bonny baby bounced into the world and allowed me to rejoice again. Even the date of his arrival – desperately early and just two days after Lee's anniversary – made me think that Lee had been directing the show from up above. Maybe he was trying to say that this was a new life for old, and this gorgeous child was a sign of celebration to help us through our worst days. I swear it was his

way of trying to make us all smile again. Poor Sara had a hor-
rendously difficult birth and I'm convinced Lee kept his sister
safe throughout. The only sadness at this fabulous new arrival
was that Lee was no longer with us to welcome him into the
world. He was a fabulous brother and uncle to all his nieces and
nephews and it is tragic that he will miss out on seeing them
grow up.

Sara was thirty-two weeks into her pregnancy when Bobby
Lee arrived, but the week before had been filled with drama.
Just a week before the first anniversary of Lee's murder, Sara
was rushed into hospital when she endured days of agonis-
ing pain. She was finally released home but, despite still being
in terrible pain, she insisted on being with us all for a private
memorial service on 22 May 2014. Just forty-eight hours later,
she returned to North Manchester General Hospital, where she
gave birth at 1.01 p.m.

It was really scary because we thought we might lose Sara or
the baby, but by some miracle they both survived. Lee would
have been so proud. We made a pact that we would celebrate
this wonderful gift, because even though we can never replace
Lee, we like to think he will live on in Bobby Lee.

I remember speaking to Sara after the birth and it was a very
emotional time for us.

She said: 'Mum, he's perfect in every way. My beautiful baby
son. I just wish Lee was here to see him.'

I tried to comfort her. 'I know, sweetheart, but I'm sure he is
with us in his own way.'

'He was such an amazing brother to me and I miss him so
much. I would do anything to have him here now to hold his
baby nephew.'

Sara was so choked up and very tearful and all I could do was
hold her close and hug her.

'Lee would want you to be happy and celebrate your new

baby,' I told her. 'He will want you to cherish him forever and not let sadness get in the way of such a wonderful day in your life.'

'I know, Mum, but it's hard not to be sad when he's not with us. When I thought I was going to die during the birth, I thought of Lee and it kept me fighting. I just wanted my baby to survive and I knew Lee was with me in spirit, guiding me through it all.'

'I don't doubt it for a minute. He would be so proud of you and Bobby Lee right now.'

'Mum, do you think Lee will live on through Bobby?'

'Oh, definitely. He's already shown he's a fighter and just as loud as Lee. And we will adore him just as we did Lee.'

It was a joyous but equally heart-wrenching time for me because I was relieved that Sara and Bobby had survived, but it also took me back to when I gave birth to Lee, and that was a stark reminder of how precious every child is. My boy had been stolen from me forever, but my daughter had pulled through with her beautiful new baby and that was something to celebrate.

For the first few months of Bobby Lee's life there were some difficult times to cope with. When he was eventually allowed home, he continued to suffer some health problems and so Sara and Rob were up and down to the hospital regularly until things eventually settled down. Today he is doing grand and is up to all sorts of mischief, just like his cheeky uncle who was the same at that age. Sara will certainly have her hands full when this little imp begins to grow up.

As Bobby continued to grow stronger and healthier, Sara and Rob decided to get married. On 6 August 2015 they made their vows together in front of close friends and family at a gorgeous ceremony in a hotel near Bury. It was a bitter-sweet occasion for the same reasons as when Bobby was born. Here was a fantastic family celebration, but once again we were missing Lee. As Sara explains:

It should have been the loveliest day of my life, marrying the man of my dreams, but the brother I adored so much was not there to see me walk down the aisle and it felt like a hole in my heart. I kept asking myself how I could get married without my brother being there but, deep down, I knew Lee would want me to carry on with my life and be happy.

We were so close, and he would have been thrilled to watch me marry someone who makes me complete. I was determined not to let my sadness ruin my big day, but I think the whole family was choked all day long. We wanted to do something really special to show that Lee was not forgotten, so we kept an empty chair for him at the top table of our reception. We placed a candle and our favourite photo of him at his seat to symbolise that his spirit was very much alive with us. We also displayed a plaque with some special words that read: *Forever in our thoughts, you have never gone away, we just wish you could be here, to share our special day.*

The day was absolutely perfect, apart from Lee not being there. Lots of tears were shed that afternoon – some for joy and some for sadness – but I carried Lee in my heart all day. We had the most wonderful party and celebration of our marriage that night, and I know Lee would have been right at the centre of all the fun and revelry if he could.

Sara's wedding was a roaring success and went without hitch but I wept buckets that day. I can remember watching my darling daughter looking so radiant in her wedding gown and that made me the proudest mum in the world. Then I would find myself drifting off to that place in my mind where I think of Lee and all that could have been. When Ian walked Sara down the aisle I broke down and wept. She looked stunning but both she and Ian were crying too. We were all highly charged and emotional. We were missing a member of our family and we could never bring him back.

Like her younger sisters, Sara has been profoundly affected by Lee's murder. She has her own young family, a new husband and a job to hold down, so she is always busy, but sometimes it just gets too much for her and she breaks down when she can no longer keep her pain inside. Here she talks about her beloved brother:

On May 22nd 2013 Drummer L J Rigby became public property when he was murdered on the streets of London in a crime that shocked the world. Before that day he was just like the rest of us – a normal bloke getting on with his life. He was my big brother and he had been there from the day I was born. We started our lives together crawling on the floors at our first home in Rochdale, and stayed close to each other for evermore after that. We had loads of rough and tumble toddler fights but we were good together. When we didn't fit in with other kids, we always had each other. We learnt to climb trees together, made new friends together. In fact, we did everything together! He was my brother and my best friend. We would have fights but we always made up and always had each other's backs. When we left school, we even got part-time jobs together, working at Burger King. When I got a job in a local bingo hall, Lee would come along to see me and to eye up all the girls, ha! He loved the ladies, did our Lee.

When Lee joined the Army I was seventeen, and when he left home to go to Catterick for his training I was distraught. I couldn't even say goodbye because my best buddy who had been there for my whole life was leaving me, and I felt so alone without him. I was thrilled that Lee was making something of his life, but it was the first time I had been without him. I was as proud as punch when I watched him pass out as a Fusilier, and he would return home as often as possible. That's when we started going out together into town with friends; they were such carefree, happy times. If a Whitney Houston song came on in a pub or club, Lee would be the first onto the middle of the dance floor, even though he couldn't dance for toffee! He didn't care though. He just loved to have fun and enjoy himself. These are some of my favourite memories of Lee, as well as the times he would give me piggy-backs home because my feet were hurting in high heels. He was a pure diamond who would do anything for those he loved. He was just so kind and loving.

The day Lee was killed I saw the news on the television and spent all night waiting to hear that family of the murdered soldier had been informed. I thought when I heard that I could be sure it wasn't Lee who was dead. But that was not to be. It was 2 a.m. on 23 May, almost twelve hours since Lee was killed, that my life fell apart. That was when police arrived at my mum's house to give us the worst news ever. The man murdered in Woolwich was my big brother Lee.

I spent days and days just lying in bed after that, refusing to eat, refusing to listen to anyone, and refusing to accept that Lee was gone. I thought that if I refused to believe it, somehow it would go away. My grief hit me like a sledgehammer, and in ways I never thought possible. I got drunk every day for months. I spent a stupid amount of money but, worst of all, I stopped being a mummy, a proper mummy that my babies needed more than ever. I had three young children and I could barely look after myself. Anger took over my life for a while and it destroyed Lee's funeral, my job, my relationship with my kids and lots of relationships with friends.

Every mistake I had ever made became magnified and my regrets ate me up slowly but surely. I raged at myself for all the things I should or shouldn't have said to Lee, for everything I wished I had done before he was taken away. I was falling apart and it wasn't until some eight months later that I looked in the mirror and realised I had two choices. To continue as I was and destroy myself or start to rebuild the life I still had. I accepted help and began therapy to deal with the overwhelming pain I carried inside. It helped me a lot, but it certainly didn't make it go away. I have now returned to work and am trying to be the best mummy I can for my children, but I will never be the person I used to be. In some ways, losing Lee has made me stronger and wiser, but in others it has slayed me. I can no longer trust anyone and I struggle to feel or share any kind of meaningful emotions.

Outside my family I find it hard to care about anyone or anything and I was never like that before. I often find myself petrified of the world I've brought my children into and I've had real problems in visiting Lee's grave. I feel that I shouldn't be there because, in my head, it signals that I have accepted what has happened. It doesn't get easier and I know it will never go away. The brother that was my rock all my life is never coming back. Inside, it has killed every part of who I used to be, and no amount of therapy will ever change that. I have to hold onto the hope that Lee was too shocked or unconscious to have felt any pain. My love for Lee will never go away and I can never forget the amazing, selfless and caring man he was. I now value every day I'm alive and know that I am blessed to be here with such a fantastic family. I still have so much to be thankful for, but Lee will stay with me in my heart for the rest of my days.

Lee's final sister is my wonderful daughter Chelsea, who we call the quiet one. Lee's murder affected her just as much as all of us but she has dealt with it very differently. She has always preferred to stay in the background and not say too much, but her grief runs as deep as everyone else's. Just reading her tribute to Lee taught me just how devoted she was to her brother.

I loved my brother Lee so much. He was such a funny and outgoing guy who used to make everyone laugh. He had so many friends because, once you met him, you couldn't help but like him. And he was never happier than when surrounded by his family. He used to call me the midget because I was so small and this always made me giggle. He also said that if I ever wanted to get a boyfriend when I grew up that he would have to approve them first. I found out that he said this to all us sisters because he was so protective over us. I have so many favourite memories of him but I always remember the time he tried to light a barbecue and it was a disaster. He smoked everyone out, and we were all laughing our heads off. He may have been the eldest of us all, but even when he was an adult he still ran around play areas or wherever we went as if he was still a little kid. It was lovely because it was like he never grew up in his mind, but he always looked after everyone else around him. He really was one of a kind. He walked into any room and it was like the sun had come out inside, but he was a bad loser and that always made us laugh. When we played cards at Mum's, we always used to say he fiddled the cards so he could win! We didn't mind though, because he was such fun to have around.

He treated all his sisters equally and looked after all of us. He never left without telling me he loved me, especially when he had to go away on tour with the Army, or when he rang home to let us know he was safe. He didn't just say he loved us, he made us all feel so loved, and that was something I miss so much. I think all the time of the last day I saw him. He took me to see his son Jack, so we could deliver our Easter eggs to him and he gave me a hug.

'Take care of yourself now. I love you and I'll see you in a couple of months.'

'I love you too, Lee. Stay safe.'

Those were the last words we spoke to each other, and I can still see him smiling at me as he left that day. I was working nights when Lee was murdered. Sara came to my work at 3 a.m. to tell me and take me home and I just froze. I was in total denial and I couldn't take it in at all. It has changed me forever because life can never be the same again. I have anger and sorrow and I cope by throwing myself into work and trying to keep busy. If I stop and think too much it's too painful.

I try to hold on to the precious memories of Lee, like the times he would take me shopping and buy me presents and play outside in our street. I just wish I could tell him one more time how much I love him.

14

Beautiful Aimee

One of the greatest tragedies of Lee's murder was that he was killed at a time in his life when he had never been happier. He had so much to look forward to, and was incredibly excited about the future that lay ahead of him. He had served seven years with his beloved regiment of the Fusiliers, and had an Army career to be proud of, but it was his personal life that was bringing him the most joy.

After meeting and falling hard for Aimee, who Lee said was 'The One', he asked her to marry him and they were so excited about tying the knot in the future. And so the status quo when he died was that he had a wife and a fiancée, but it wasn't as if he was in a relationship with them both.

It wouldn't be fair for me to talk about Lee's marriage to Becky because that's something that remains between them. I don't believe anyone knows what really goes on between a couple behind closed doors so, out of respect for them both, I won't go into details. I do know that when they first met as teenagers, they fell in love and were married and were both delighted when Becky had their baby son. They were both very young and

Lee was away a lot with the Army, so whatever changed for them my son was not happy in the marriage and he eventually left the marital home in the summer of 2012. He remained a fantastic dad to Jack, though, and visited all the time when he was not in barracks in London, to the point that this gorgeous little boy was like Lee's shadow. They idolised each other and you couldn't have met a prouder dad than Lee.

It's sad when any marriage breaks down, and I was devastated for him when he and Becky broke up, but I also realised that he was a grown man who had to make his own way in life. He had to do what made him happy and not make decisions to please everyone else. It was hard for Becky because I believe she truly loved Lee and always had done. She had doted on him when they were together and her grief at his death was genuine. It was obvious she still loved him dearly and, no doubt, always will.

It was in August that same year before he died that Lee met Aimee, and he told me it was like a thunderbolt from above.

'I've never met anyone like her before,' he told me. 'She is the one I want to spend the rest of my life with. I have never felt like this about anyone before. These feelings just grabbed me from nowhere and I want to be with her all the time.'

I was delighted to hear him so excited and passionate about his future with Aimee, and I told him so: 'I'm so glad she makes you happy, Lee. You deserve that more than anything.'

As a mum, that's all you ever want for your kids, to know they're safe, healthy and happy. I never wished for riches or stardom for my children – just that they were having great lives with people who loved and cared for them. He had certainly found that with Aimee and he was utterly smitten. I'd never known Lee like this before, because he always had an eye for the pretty ladies. He couldn't help himself because he was a natural-born flirt and with his easygoing, cheeky charm, the women loved him too! Aimee changed all that when she captured his heart lock, stock and barrel.

'I don't ever want to be with any other woman, Mum,' he insisted. 'She's everything to me. I never thought I would feel this way about anyone.'

It's so cruel that Lee was robbed of the life he had dreamed of with Aimee as it is for her. She will never have the chance to marry and grow old with the man she adored. When Lee's life was cut so horribly short, she was cheated of having beautiful children and a family with him. She has been forced to endure a life of never knowing what her dreams could have been made of, and it fills me with sadness for them both.

Aimee remains very special to our family because so many people overlook her grief and what she has lost. She was never given the respect or dignity she should have been offered as the woman who was Lee's partner when he died. She was relegated to the back row, as the spotlight fell on the rest of his family, including Becky and Jack. None of us wanted that attention but, because she was not his formal next of kin, her love was almost dismissed out of hand by the authorities and that, to my mind, was wrong. My family knew how important she was to Lee and how much he adored her. She never had the chance to gather memories of a life with him, but I will always be grateful to her for the pure love she gave to him before he died. I know how happy she made him and, for that, I will be forever in her debt. Here is her heartbreaking love story:

I was just twenty-one when I met Lee and I can honestly say that meeting someone I wanted to spend the rest of my life with was the furthest thing from my mind. I was still at University and I was also a member of the TA Military Police and Army Cadets.

In August 2012, I went away with the cadets for two weeks to the Brecon Beacons, to help as an instructor at an Army Cadets training event. The first time I set eyes on Lee he was

leaning against a minibus, fag hanging from his mouth, grinning like a Cheshire cat. He looks cute! I thought, trying to stop
myself from smiling.

'Alright?' he shouted across at me in his broad Manc accent.
'Yeah,' I shouted back. 'You?'

And that was it! From that moment on we became inseparable. For the first two days I didn't even know his real name. I
just knew him, like everyone else did, as 'Riggers'.

The thing about Lee is you couldn't fail to notice him. Yes,
he was drop-dead gorgeous and had the most fantastic smile
ever, but he was so loud that you could almost be in the next
town and still hear him! He was a presence that everyone felt
and I clicked with him instantly. I'm a lot quieter than Lee, and
so I was happy for him to be the noisy one. He was so crazy
and over the top you couldn't miss him, and he was so expres-
sive, talking with his hands all the time.

Our time at the cadet camp did not spill into romance and
we just rubbed along as mates, getting to know each other
and spending free time together. We wound each other up
continually and I would tease him by saying that he wasn't
a proper soldier and that he was just the unit's driver. He
never got cross and took the banter with such good nature,
but he would always plot to get me back somehow. I learned
quickly that everyone loved Riggers, and it wasn't hard to see
why. He was a whirlwind of energy, a real force of nature, but
he was also the kindest and funniest bloke I had met. Apart
from the wind-ups, I recall those days in the hills as being
filled with laughter and that was how our relationship would
continue.

When it was time to leave, after a fortnight, Lee wrote his
number down for me on a crumpled piece of paper and said:
'Can I take you out when we get back?'

'OK,' I said, trying to play hard to get, but it was game over really because he just stood there grinning at me and I knew I couldn't resist him. Not that I would have told him that!

When I got back home I had this warm feeling in my tummy. I realised that I didn't just like him, but I physically missed him being around. He had already set my world alight and had become a part of my life. For days I just missed hearing his booming voice and laughter, and life seemed so boring and mundane without him. It was like I had been at the best party ever and someone had come along and turned the music off. He made everything funny and fantastic.

Lee was very much a lad's lad, who loved spending time with his mates but, once we started dating, we couldn't get enough of each other. Our first date was in Staines, and we went to Frankie and Benny's Italian/American diner. We both loved it there and it would become of one of our regular haunts. Lee would always have his favourite pepperoni pizza with a bit of tomato and brown sauce on it.

We became inseparable from one another and every spare moment we had was spent together. I would visit him in Woolwich, where he was stationed at the barracks with his regiment, or he would come to my house where I lived with my mum in Staines. Lee was a huge hit with all my family and friends and he turned out to be the most romantic and affectionate man I have ever known. I was much more reserved, so he brought out the best in me by his loving and caring nature. I felt safe expressing how I felt to him, and I'd never had that before. I wasn't guarded or suspicious of him because he was so open and kind.

He called me his Princess from the start and, on my birthday, he bought me a cuddly rabbit from the Bear Factory, which was dressed in a floaty Cinderella dress. When you pressed her she said: 'I love you'.

That was Lee all over – thoughtful, sweet and considerate. I thought I was the luckiest girl on the planet to be with him because we just felt so natural together. It was like we had been born to meet each other. He told me he loved me all the time and I never got bored of hearing it. I always told him that I loved him back too.

Three months later, in November, I volunteered to go to Afghanistan with the Military Police and Lee was stunned when I broke the news to him. He dropped down and began sobbing and begged me not to go. I hadn't banked on him being that upset and it really took me aback. Looking back, I shouldn't have been all that surprised because Lee had already done a tour of Afghanistan and had been on the frontline, where he lost several friends and comrades in some of the worst firefights with the Taliban. I know it had affected him deeply and that he returned from war as a changed man, but he tried to keep those feelings hidden.

I tried to reassure him that I would be safe because I wouldn't be fighting on patrol like his regiment. I would be in the relatively safer environment of Camp Bastion, which was the giant airbase and military base camp built to house troops from across the world. Nonetheless, it did nothing to persuade him I wasn't going to be in danger.

'I don't want you to go, babe,' he cried. 'It's a terrible place and I won't be there to look after you. I don't want you to get hurt or killed. I've already lost friends out there and I couldn't bear to lose you.'

'Don't be daft,' I tried to reassure him. 'I'll be a lot safer than you were because you were out on the frontline. I'll be fine, I promise you.'

For weeks after that I was more worried for Lee than I was for myself, because he took it all so badly. He was hardly eating and he lost a lot of weight worrying about the trip, which was getting ever closer. I would ask him about Afghanistan and he would tell me lots of things.

'When you're over there, the skies are so clear that all you can see at night are stars. If you look up at the stars and speak to them then I will receive your message,' he told me.

It was beautiful and romantic because it came from the heart and he made me melt inside. We talked at length about me going to Afghanistan and, although he was scared for me, he also accepted that this was something I had always wanted to do as part of my Army career. He knew I was independent and so, in his own way, he supported me one hundred per cent. He also knew my mind was set and he helped me in every way possible to prepare for the trip ahead.

'You know you can ring me every day,' he must have said dozens of times. 'And you can email too!'

The days flew past and, before we knew it, it was time for me to pack up and go. I had to attend a training course for a fortnight before flying to Afghanistan, so, in early February, we organised a family meal at home a couple of nights before I left. There was me and Lee, my mum Karen and her partner Pete, and my little brother Chris. I was nervous and excited at the same time but we had a lovely evening all together.

Lee stayed the night with me and in the morning we went shopping together in Staines to get last-minute essentials and toiletries. We walked home to mine, hand in hand, through the park where we would always go running together. It was a really cold day and all of a sudden Lee spun me round and got down on one knee!

'You are the most gorgeous princess in the world and you make me so happy,' he declared. 'We fit together and I will never love anyone else like I love you.'

Lee was crying, and I could see him opening a box and getting a ring out of it.

'I want us to have a proper life together forever, to live together and travel and have a family of our own. I have never been this happy. Please marry me?'

'Yes, yes, yes,' I squealed, as we stood there hugging each other in the freezing park, both crying our eyes out.

He was so worried the ring wouldn't fit, but he slipped it on my wedding finger and it was perfect. The ring was stunning and I still wear it to this day. It was a white gold band with a big central diamond set in a cluster of smaller gems. We were deliriously happy and almost skipped home to announce our big news to the family. We burst through the front door giggling with each other because we had a big secret. Not that this was anything particularly new, because we were always up to mischief, but Lee couldn't contain himself.

'We're engaged!' he blurted out to the family, with a mile-wide smile. 'Me and my Princess are getting married!'

Everyone was cheering and hugging and it was a moment of pure joy. I can still remember feeling as if I was walking on air. We all went out that night to Frankie and Benny's to celebrate. It was my last night at home and everyone was happy and carefree.

The next day I travelled alone to Nottingham for training and I got stuck into my work. Lee and I chatted every day and then, the night before I flew out, he booked a local hotel so we could spend some time together. He brought me a special surprise present of a book made up of my favourite photos of me and him and family. It was beautiful, and he had obviously spent a lot of time and care in creating it.

It was a night of many emotions. We laughed together, cried and held each other, and spoke about our future life when I returned.

'Please be careful and come home safely for me, Princess,'

he pleaded. 'I can't live without you.' He then joked: 'And don't you dare "Dear John" me!'

'Of course I won't! I love you too much!' I told him.

I tried to make sure there were plenty of people to look out for him when I was gone because I knew he was going to find it difficult. I'd confided in his closest friends in the regiment at Woolwich and asked them to keep his spirits up, and Lee also promised to go to my mum's for dinner when he could.

I was scheduled to be on tour for three months, which is shorter than the normal six months that regiments usually serve in war zones. Lee had marked up his Manchester United football calendar for every day I was away, and he said he would tick off each day, one by one, until I was back in his arms. Neither of us slept well that night. Our heads were racing with so many thoughts and feelings, and we were both dreading the morning light when we would have to say goodbye.

When Lee dropped me back at the military camp it was time to say our farewells. He parked up and took a deep breath and then just started sobbing hysterically. It was truly awful and I didn't know how to comfort him.

'Please don't go, Princess, please,' he begged.

'I have to go, Lee. I will be fine, I promise you.'

'Come back to me safely, please. I love you so much.'

'I love you too. We're going to have a brilliant life together. I promise I'll come home safely.'

When I think about those heart-wrenching conversations we shared, I can hardly believe the cruel irony of what was to happen. Who would have guessed that I would be safer in a war zone than Lee would prove to be in our own country? Life is so unkind and I still struggle to understand how this could have happened.

We held on to each other for dear life in that car and it seemed like we had sat there for hours instead of a few minutes. We kissed each other and, as I walked away from him, I saw him slumped over the steering wheel crying his heart out. That really broke me and that was the last time I would ever see Lee alive.

The situation is often so much worse for the loved ones of soldiers who are away, because they feel so helpless. When you go on tour, you have work to do and it occupies your mind, but for partners at home they are just left wondering if you are safe. It was even worse for Lee, because he had been in Afghanistan and had lost comrades in fighting, and so it was no good me trying to tell him that the war-ravaged country I was heading to was a nice place. It was true that I did have the protection of Camp Bastion, but even so, Lee was beside himself with worry that he was going to lose me. We went from being inseparable to being forced apart for three long months. I was excited professionally to finally be heading to Afghanistan, but we would both be counting the days until I touched down in the UK again.

The journey is a long and hard one and we touched down in Cyprus for a refuel after a few hours. I took the chance to text Lee immediately, even though we had only been apart a short while. He was thrilled to hear from me and said he was already ticking off the boxes on his calendar.

When we finally landed in Bastion it was a world away from anything I had ever known before. I thought about Lee and his regiment and how he had been there before me but, unlike him, I didn't have to risk my life going out on patrol. I had tried not to build up any expectations of what it would be like there, so I had a completely open mind, but I was amazed at the random things that struck me. The biggest thing in the beginning was the heat, dust and sand. Everything was covered in dust and sand, even in the shower, and it got everywhere in your eyes and ears and hair. It was horrible.

Our flight had landed in the middle of the night, so it was the next day before I could ring Lee. We were both thrilled to chat and what made it great was that I didn't have to waste time explaining little things to him because he had already been there. This meant we could use our talk time to catch up with what we both had been doing. I rang Lee every day unless there was an 'op minimizer', which is when outgoing calls are restricted for a number of different reasons, including when there is a fatality, so that families can be properly informed without information leaking through from the media or other soldiers.

We chatted about silly things really. He would tell me if he had been to McDonald's and scoffed down a Big Mac and I would tell him about my dinner too. Sounds daft but we were both big foodies and we always joked that if we didn't do so much exercise together we would grow old and become big porkies together!

Aside from my phone calls to Lee, I also received so many parcels from him that it became a standing joke in camp. The boxes came thick and fast for me and were crammed with so much stuff. Lee would send me crisps, cakes, magazines and games, and even went to Boots and bought me some of my favourite Sanctuary body products. When the post came, everyone had one or two packages but the rest would be for me from Lee. People in camp would shout out: 'I see it's delivery time from Lee again!'

These were people who had never met him, but they still knew about him. Things settled down for us and I got on with my work and acclimatised to the conditions there, apart from the sand! When I reached the half-way point of my tour, Lee was so excited and I think he had even accepted I would be coming home safely to him. That was one and a half months into the tour and I was trying to make the most of the military experience.

Every day I would ring Lee at a similar time around 6 p.m. local time for me. I would have to attend a briefing at the end of each day and afterwards I would go and call him. We also spoke on email when we could. We got into a routine of our daily chats and we excitedly 'gabbed' away at how we wanted to go to Center Parcs for a holiday and tear around on the buggies and Go Karts. We planned a string of different shopping trips, places we were going to eat together, and he said he was even prepared to go on a girlie spa day so we could be together. We wanted to make up for so much lost time and we were desperate to be back together again. We plotted to book a villa in Spain and so many more plans.

The parcels that really touched my heart were the ones in which Lee sent me cuddly toys and wedding magazines. I already had my Princess cuddly rabbit but he sent me more fluffy toys and dozens of wedding magazines. I think he had bought every one in the shop, and he had clearly been through every page marking certain ones with Post It notes with remarks written on them. He would pick out dresses he liked and even flowers for my bouquet. It was amazing because then, when we spoke on the phone, I had already read his notes and we didn't have to waste time explaining things. Not that I liked all the dresses he selected, but it was the sweetest and most adorable thing to do. After one such delivery I told him:

'Hey you, you can't go anywhere near the wedding dresses! I get to choose that and you aren't allowed to see it until the big day!'

He loved the whole thing – the planning and fantasizing about how our perfect marriage was going to be. We had decided we would marry in 2016, after he was divorced, and we both wanted it to be the most amazing day ever to start the rest of our lives together.

It was just two weeks before I was due to finish my tour that all our worlds were turned upside down. Lee's calendar was almost ticked off and he was so happy and upbeat because I would be home soon.

'I won't be able to breathe easy again until I hold you in my arms again,' he told me just days before he died. 'My Princess is coming home and I will be the happiest man in the world. I'm never gonna let you go again. Ever!'

On 22 May 2013 I went to work as normal and was looking forward to speaking with Lee later on after I'd knocked off from my shift. With just a fortnight to go, I was feeling really homesick and was tired of the relentless heat and the sand. I also missed Lee so much and couldn't wait to be reunited with him. When we spoke in the mornings on email, we would always try and work out the time for me to ring him so that he was in a place where he could answer.

Around lunchtime in the UK he emailed to say he was on his way home early from the Tower of London. He ended by saying he loved me. He then sent me a text which read: *Princess, keep smiling for me. I know it's hard and you really want to come home, but just remember I am always there for you and I will always love you no matter what. We are on the home stretch ... you will always come first in my life. Xxxx*

Lee knew I was fed up and he was trying to cheer me up. It was the last text he would send me, and it was only twenty minutes before he was cut down and murdered. As soon as I could I went to call him but, unusually, it just rang off without answering. At first I wondered if he had been in a tube on his way back but, after a while, I started to panic that something was wrong. This kept happening, so in the end I rang my mum and told her I couldn't get hold of Lee. She then asked if I had seen the news out there and I said no. Realising she may have said the wrong thing, she made up some story about another issue because she didn't want to frighten me.

I returned to my quarters and pulled up the BBC Homepage on my tablet and there it was: 'Murder in Woolwich,' the headline screamed, with a pixelated image of a dead man on the ground with his arms above his head.

I could see the outline of his body, the way he lay on the floor, and his jeans and Timberland boots. I knew it was my Lee and all I wanted was to go home to be with him.

It was a huge shock and I remember being struck quite numb by what I had seen. I was quiet and speechless and it was now night time in Afghanistan. A friend tried to reassure me that I couldn't be sure it was Lee but, as the hours ticked by, she went to see one of the commanding officers to inform him of my fears. No one knew anything at all and so, for the entire night, I was left all alone, staring at my tablet and continually refreshing the BBC news feed for even a crumb of information. I felt sick and so very helpless and alone. It felt like someone had bored a hole in my chest and I just felt empty. There was no one I could call and, when I spoke to my mum the next morning, she told me she had spoken to 'Robbo', who was one of Lee's closest regiment friends but he couldn't tell us anything either. There was clearly an information lockdown because the dead soldier had not yet been named.

It was about 6 a.m. when the silence was finally broken. I saw my boss and the padre outside my room and I knew that was the final confirmation. I steeled myself for what I was about to be told.

The padre came to my quarters and sat gently with me. He was softly spoken and gentle but the news was anything but.

'I'm sorry to tell you that it was Lee who was murdered in Woolwich yesterday.'

That's when I broke down and became hysterical. I was screaming and crying and totally out of control. The padre tried to bring some comfort but it was no good. I was inconsolable and I think I screamed and shouted most of the day. There are quite a lot of blanks after that moment because my body just began to shut down from the outside world.

Emergency plans were made to get me home with the RAF to Brize Norton air base, but the flight is a bit of a blur. When I did get home I was plunged into an even bigger nightmare when Army bureaucrats effectively tried to write me out of Lee's life. Not only had I lost the love of my life, but now I was being told I would not be included in any plans to lay him to rest. Because Lee was technically still married, his estranged wife was still classed as his next of kin. Lee had forgotten to change his will, which was made out in 2008. She inherited his estate but, far worse, was that I was not able to have any say in how my beloved fiancé, the man I was going to spend the rest of my life with, should be laid to rest.

The Army basically took over everything, because the spotlight was firmly on this horrific murder which had stunned the world. They tried to tell me I couldn't go to Woolwich where Lee was killed, and that I couldn't go to his funeral. I wasn't even invited to say goodbye to Lee the day before his burial, as he lay in the Chapel of Rest in his home town of Middleton. I was made to feel like a burden because I got in the way of them presenting a cosy and tidy picture of a nuclear family of husband, wife and child. The reality was that I was living my life with Lee and we were going to be married, but the doors were shut firmly in my face.

Lee's family were outraged when they realised how I was being treated, and they took me to their hearts and tried to help me. Lee's amazing sister Sara had to sneak me into the Chapel of Rest, so I could spend some time with him, and I will always be so grateful to her. It was such an awful time because all I wanted to do was grieve for Lee, but I was facing problems at every corner.

It made me so angry when Army bosses spoke to me, as if I was a naughty child instead of a woman who had just lost her beloved partner. In the end I was cast aside to sit at the back of the church at Lee's funeral, behind Prime Minister David Cameron and Boris Johnson, because I wasn't considered as part of my fiancé's family. I know Lee would have been horrified.

After the funeral, the real devastation kicked in. Anger was a huge factor for me, because Lee had been robbed of his life and he had been taken away from me. I was struggling so badly to get a grip of everything that had happened, not least that I was the one who had been in the so-called dangerous war zone when Lee was murdered in London. It wasn't supposed to be this way. How could Lee be butchered on his way home from work?

I became so depressed and some days I couldn't get out of bed to face the world. But then I would hear Lee's voice gently whispering to me in my head:

'Come on, my Princess, please don't cry. Get out of bed and have a cup of tea. You have a life to live for both us. Please don't be sad because I love you and I always will.'

I tried so hard to pull myself together but every turn I took seemed to set me back. If I went to Frank and Benny's with friends I couldn't cope because I felt that Lee should be there. If I went running it reminded me of my times exercising with Lee, and if I walked across the park where he proposed to me it was just too painful to bear.

I would find myself shouting out loud: 'He had a life and you took it from him!'

Eventually I had to seek help for a grief that was so deep I didn't know how to cope. Doctors diagnosed a number of

conditions, from severe depression to PTSD, but I have tried
to resist medication as a way out of dealing with it. Running
has been a huge salvation for me, because it gives me a drive
to go forwards and achieve something. I have to focus on the
good and not the bad. Lee and I were going to run the Paris
Marathon together the year after he died, and so I promised
myself I would complete it for both us, which I did. I raised
£20,000 for the forces charity SSAFA and I thought of Lee
every step of the way.

If I let myself hurt then it really drags me down, so I try to
keep going for me and Lee. If I give up on life then what happened to Lee means that these warped people have killed two
people. I have to live for both of us and cram as much fun and
love and laughter in there just as if Lee was still here.

I know my beautiful man is still saying to me: 'You have to
have fun, Princess. Go out and enjoy life. For both of us.'

I still talk to Lee and tell him about my day and how I'm
feeling. I tell him I love him and ask how he is doing. I try not
to think about Lee's killers or dwell on the attack. For me, it's
all about putting the focus on one person and that is Lee. He
was a man you could rely on, and he was loved by all who
knew him, from his family and friends to the lads in his regiment. I know his closest pals in the Fusiliers really struggled
with Lee's murder.

I'm a completely different person now because I'll take on
challenges I never thought possible. I think it's because I'm
no longer scared of anything, because the worst thing that
could have happened already has. Lee was perfect for me and
I was perfect for him. He was my best friend, my lover and my
future. Every day I still ache for him constantly, both physically and mentally, and it has taken its toll on me.

I miss him beyond words, and when I get too sad I pull on
my running shoes and train as hard as I possibly can. The

pain of running reminds me that I'm still alive and I think of Lee, who hasn't got that privilege. And then his beautiful voice pops in my head and says: 'Stop being silly, Princess. Go put the kettle on and make a brew.'

I talk about Lee because I want everyone to know how brilliant he was. He was a real person to me and his family – not just a victim of a crime or a photo in a newspaper. I learn to live with the pain and sadness, but I will never get over it because in my eyes Lee was just perfect. We were so in tune with each other and I know I will never have that connection with anyone else.

15

'Besties' Forever

I have been asked so many times how I have got through the grief and trauma of losing Lee and the simple answer is that I have absolutely no idea. I didn't know it was humanly possible to experience such pain and still be alive, but I guess the body is a remarkable machine that helps us cope in even the most profound and horrific of circumstances. Some days it's all I can do just to breathe and put one foot in front of the other and, on those occasions, it's not living, it's simply existing. When the tidal wave of grief floods in I can barely function and it feels like I'm drowning in my sorrow, but then it slowly ebbs away again until the next time.

I have often said that if I didn't have my other children and grandchildren to look after then I would be down in the ground with Lee now, without question. It's only my deep love for my daughters that has constantly reminded me that I have to get through this for their sakes. I'm their mum and they have all suffered enough, so that is ever present in my mind every day I wake up and dread another twenty-four hours without my darling son. That's my reason for surviving, because Lee would want me to take care of his sisters and I love them all dearly.

That survival can be really rough sometimes. The dark days that you think will never end and the hours spent lying in bed or staring at the sky trying to speak to Lee. My husband Ian has been a rock for me, although he has his own grief to manage as well. Together we get through it, even though it is far from easy.

I have also been lucky to have a very special lady by my side throughout this whole terrible ordeal – my truly best friend Sandra. 'San', as she is known to everyone, has been my 'bestie' for eighteen years. She has been there for me through thick and thin. She is a larger than life character: strong, wilful, fearless and very, very funny. She is the most loyal and dependable woman I know, and we consider each other as family.

San has lived across the road from me in Middleton for almost two decades. She was already living there with her family when I moved in all those years ago with my kids, so it's hard to remember life without her. She has shared in all of my family's joys and heartaches, and has watched my children grow up; it's the same for me with her family. My children have only ever known her as 'Auntie San' and I am 'Auntie Lyn' to her kids. I love her so much and I need to acknowledge her in this book because I simply wouldn't have made it without her. She helped bring Lee up and, even when he was going through his terrible teens, she never gave up on him. Like me, she knew it was just a phase and that he would come good again one day. My eldest children are best friends with her children, and that was the same for Lee before he died. They have all suffered Lee's loss too, but San picked me up off the floor every time I fell down and helped me to carry on. I will always be indebted to her for her unswerving love, courage and friendship, and I have asked her to write a little about our lives and her memories of Lee.

Sandra Lord: I'll never forget the day Lyn and her family moved into our road. Ours is a typical northern working-class street with terraced houses, and not much gets past anyone around here! Most of the time folk are outside in the warmer weather, with the kids playing up and down the pavements. I can remember Lyn trundling up the street with her brood like it was yesterday! It was always exciting when someone new came in, but I had no idea that Lyn and her kids would become such an important and valued part of my life.

Lyn had only her three eldest kids at this stage – Lee, Sara and Chelsea – and it was Chelsea who piped up first when she arrived. Lyn was as quiet as a mouse and I remember hearing this cheeky little voice shouting over to me.

'I like them shoes you're wearing!'

'Thanks, love, and who are you, then?' I replied.

'I'm Chelsea. My mum's inside. Do you wanna drink?'

'Why not, my love!'

And that was it. I went into Lyn's house, she offered me a beer and we have never looked back since. Ours was a very typical working-class lifestyle. Lyn was a full-time mum and I had a part-time job in a local pub, and as time went on Lyn would mind my kids for me when I was at work, and I would return the favour when she needed some time to herself. There was no question that I was the 'gobby' one with the big mouth, while Lyn was very quiet. Almost shy but, as we got to know each other, she began to come out of her shell.

What I hadn't realised until later was that Lee and Sara were already mates with two of my daughters, Katie and Natalie, from school before they even moved here, so we were all incredibly close and we formed our own tight-knit community together. Lyn and I would chat daily and share a brew or a drink in the evening while continuing to care for and bring up our kids. Lyn was single at the time, so I would help her with the kids where I could. One of the first things I learned about Lyn is that she is such a kind person. She really would give you the clothes off her back, and she was content to just stay home and be a mum with her children. She was never interested in going out socialising and partying, she was too reserved for that, and so chose instead to live a simple life at home.

All of our kids were smashing children but I'm not gonna say they were perfect – far from it! They were just like normal youngsters, tearing around and making merry hell from time to time. Sometimes they would scrap with each other and it would end in tears, but they always made up, and any flash-points were quickly forgotten the next day. These kids couldn't be any closer to each other if they had all been brothers and sisters.

None of us had a lot of money and both families survived on a pretty tight budget, but we got by and, when there was money spare, Lyn would always spend it on her children where she could. Life wasn't perfect but we were all pretty happy and the kids were loved and well cared for. It was like me and Lyn and our kids against the world.

So, the kids were all pretty boisterous but Lee, being the eldest and a boy, was livelier than the rest. I think Lee was around nine years old when they came here and, as he started to get a bit older, he became a handful for Lyn on her own. I don't think there was any one particular reason – it was just part of his journey growing up. It was only later, when he struggled at school, that he became so frustrated. His dyslexia would go undetected throughout his school years, and Lyn is convinced it had a huge impact on his confidence and ability to express himself. He was a smart and vibrant boy, but he hated school because he didn't understand why he was having problems. So, as well as the normal frustrations of hormonal teens growing up, he was angry because of his inability to grasp stuff.

Luckily Lyn had Ian for Lee's teenage years, and he was a really calming influence on him. Lyn had met Ian when we all went bowling with the kids one day. I remember saying to Lyn: 'Eh, that fella over there keeps looking at you, Lyn. Either that or he's got a bog eye!'

'Sod off,' she laughed. 'He's not looking at me at all.'

'Yes he is and I'm gonna prove it!'

With that I went over to Sara and said to her, 'See that bloke over there, well go and tell him that your mam fancies him!'

Cocky and cheeky as ever, Sara did just that, and the rest as they say is history! Lyn and Ian have been together ever since and have made the perfect couple. He's also been amazing with Lyn's kids, and treated them all like his own, including Lee, who adored Ian and saw him as his real dad.

We've shared so much together as families. When I got married Ian walked me down the aisle and Lyn was my maid of honour. Lyn and Ian went on to have younger children of their own to join the Rigby family – first Courtney and then Amy – both of whom are my goddaughters. I remember Chelsea getting jealous at this because she said she felt left out! So I thought, right, if that's the way you feel. I went into their bathroom and filled the tub up with cold water.

'Chelsea,' I hollered downstairs. 'Come here quickly, I wanna show you something!'

I heard her legging it up the stairs excitedly and then I grabbed her and threw her in the bath. She was screaming her head off and everyone came running up. We were all just laffin' our heads off, including Chelsea, when she got over the shock.

'Now,' I told her. 'You have been baptised as my goddaughter too!'

None of us ever forgot that day. The years when Lee was struggling were tough for Lyn and Ian, and they certainly did everything to support him but nothing seemed to work. Lee was always a lovely lad. He was full of life and so loud and in your face, but he had a heart of gold and would always do the kindest things to help out. He would tidy his bedroom, offer to go shopping for you, and make you a brew whenever you wanted.

When he was good he was fantastic but when he was bad he was horrid. He would sometimes flare up with anger and frustration and lash out at people close to him. It was like a mini drama, sometimes over nothing. If he couldn't get his own way he would make a big scene, shouting and cursing. Sometimes it was over something simple, like Lyn not being able to afford to give him some money he wanted. He would storm out of the house and Lyn would be frantic with worry trying to find him, and often he would just sneak back in and hide in the garden for hours. He exhausted Lyn and I felt really sorry for her.

'I don't know to do for the best, San,' she would cry to me. 'Nothing seems to work and I don't know why Lee is like this.'

'Don't worry, love, he'll come round soon enough,' I tried to comfort her. 'It's his age, you'll see. He's a great lad but he is just going through a horrible spell.'

I truly believed in Lee, because I knew what a lovely boy he was, but I could see that Lyn was finding it really hard to deal with and I felt very sorry for her. She loved her children more than anything and to not be able to make them happy was destroying her. Lee had said for years that he wanted to join the Army, but when he went through his stroppy phase I did wonder if he would ever go through with it. I just kept thinking that you need a lot of discipline to be in the Army, and Lee certainly didn't have that in his early teens. Back then it was Lee's way, or no way!

It was more about attitude than criminality. Lee never stole or became involved in gangs or drugs or anything like that. None of our kids went down that path because they were just not allowed to be exposed to that lifestyle. He never brought the police to their door but he certainly stretched Lyn emotionally.

After a couple of years, Lee grew up enormously and his tantrums seemed to stop when he left school and started working. As soon as he was eighteen, he joined the Army and it was one of the proudest days of Ian and Lyn's lives. Boy, were they chuffed for him, because he had turned out to be the fine young man we always knew was in there.

Lee was a real chatterbox and a livewire. It was part of his personality, and why so many people took him to their hearts, but as he grew up he also became softer and even kinder than he had been before. He was able to express his feelings and he would constantly tell his mum and dad how much he loved them. He had an unconditional love for them and his bond was so strong. The Army took a teenage boy and turned him into the most fantastic young man. He was cheeky still, but he didn't talk down to you. He treated people nicely, even if he still took the mickey, but that was just who Lee was. The horrible attitude that had dogged him growing up was gone, and he had grown into the most handsome and adorable man. Lyn totally idolised Lee and I could see why. She never gave up on him when he was troublesome, and now he was repaying that love and patience in heaps.

Everything Lyn ever had she gave to her kids. She was, and still is, an exceptional mum who is loved by all her children. She put a roof over their heads, gave them a warm and loving home, clean beds and good food on the table. She couldn't afford big fancy toys or games back then, but she gave them whatever she could afford.

Lee took to Army life like a duck to water. He loved to come home on leave and see his family but, at the same time, he couldn't wait to get back to Army life too because he loved it so much. He was strong and committed to the Army but he always remained a big softie all his life. Everyone teased him about his love of Westlife ballads, but he didn't care. He wasn't embarrassed to show his emotions at all and that was the wonderful thing about him.

He loved to make people feel good and he was the life and soul of any party. When Lee was in the room you knew all about it and everyone would be laughing. He always had a smile on his face, and if he wasn't joking about, teasing his baby sisters, he would be doing stupid dances or daft things to cheer everyone up. He was the joker of the family, and I like to think of him as a completely loveable rogue. That's what I always used to call him because he didn't have a bad bone in his body.

Lyn followed his Army career with great pride, and she was over the moon when Lee finally passed out. She and Ian went to the barracks to watch his parade and she was the proudest mum on the planet! She was watching her and Lee's dreams come true.

When Lee had to do a tour of Afghanistan, Lyn was in bits. It was the worst time ever for her, and I remember she needed a lot of support back then. It must have been dreadful to lie awake at night for months on end worrying about whether your son is safe in a war zone.

'What if something happens to him out there, San?' Lyn sobbed.

I remember just giving her a hug and a kiss and telling her he would be fine.

'Don't worry too much, Lyn. This is Lee we're talking about. He will be back before you know and he will be safe again. '

Little did I know then that these words would come back to haunt me. No one could ever have predicted what terrible fate was in store for Lyn's only son. We were all worried about him fighting in Afghanistan but, in the end, the danger was far closer to home.

The day Lee was murdered was just appalling. I don't think any of us will ever erase the events of that day and how it panned out. There was a lot of confusion that evening, because although everyone knew a soldier had been killed in Woolwich, his identity was still unknown. Lyn was very worried but I remember saying to her that it definitely wasn't Lee because she would have been told by the police or the Army. I remember having a cup of tea and going to bed. The next thing I was woken by this mega screaming. There was literally screaming all down the street, and I thought it was a massive fight after the pubs had spilled out.

I looked out and I saw Lyn on the floor in her front garden. My heart turned over and I threw on a dressing gown and ran over to her. I picked her up off the floor, as she was still wailing and screaming, and I got her inside the house and put her on the couch. The noise was awful. Lyn was hysterical and it was quite terrifying. She was crying and shaking beyond control and there was nothing I could do to stop it.

'What's happened, Lyn?' I shouted at her.

"They've cut his f****** head off," she screamed back in my face.

I tried to hold her but Sara was screaming now and Lyn was deranged with shock and disbelief. She was swearing a lot and making strange noises. I was trying my best to sort everything out when Ian came in from working nights.

'They have cut my son's head off,' Lyn kept repeating.

Ian fell to the floor by Lyn's side and tried to wrap her up in his arms and comfort her. Courtney and Amy were awake and on the stairs and they were petrified. It was so scary, and it felt like waking up in the middle of a horror movie. It just didn't seem real.

The police officers were absolutely fantastic. They looked after that family so well that night and, despite the screaming and shouting and hysterics going on, they stayed calm and kind and took whatever was thrown at them. They knew Lyn was in deep shock and was not having a go at them. They are all still friends to this day.

Lee's murder was an earth-shattering moment for Lyn and her family. None of them will ever be the same again, even though I think Lyn is so brave trying to cope every day. Deep down I know she is a broken woman. She has her own mask, which she keeps on for her children and the rest of the world but, when darkness falls, she removes the mask and has private grief time that she doesn't want everyone to see. She was never a really noisy woman but now she's much more withdrawn and doesn't talk as much as she once did. Sometimes we can have a brew together and she will sit in silence, lost in her own thoughts in some place far away. Her house was once filled with noise and laughter and fun. There was always music playing, and it was a happy place, but now she even finds it hard to put the radio on.

She has even said that she hates going out now because sometimes people stare at her if they recognise her as Lee Rigby's mum. She finds that very hard and just wants to run home to the safety of her house. I've tried to explain they stare because they recognise her but they don't know what to say.

We still spend time in each other's houses, and will often have coffee mornings together, or one of us will do a big breakfast for everyone, but she will never be the same again.

Lyn's home has become like a shrine to Lee and it feels like she's scared to leave the house in case she forgets what he looks like, or that she will in some way disconnect with him if she isn't there with his pictures and memories. As her friend, all I have been able to do is love her and put my arms around her, so she knows I'm always there for her, but I've also learned it's important to allow Lyn her own space.

We still talk about Lee, and I think she likes to do that so he's always part of our conversation and daily life. But, more than two years on, every day is still a struggle for her.

I have also tried to explain to her children that they have all lost someone very special but they can't relate to what Lyn feels. They've lost a brother but Lyn has lost her first-born only son. I don't know how that must feel, because I have never been through it, but Lee will never leave her heart. She will grow stronger as time goes by, but her heart will never mend and I wish I could do more to help her because she is the best friend any woman could wish for.

16

Could My Son Have Been Saved?

It's a question I have tortured myself with many times over and I still don't have the answer. Could anything have been done to prevent Lee's appalling murder? Could the security services have done more to intercept his killers before they targeted him on that fateful day? And how were two known terror suspects able to operate so freely, without being checked, to be able to brazenly slaughter Lee in the street?

There was quite a lot known about both Michael Adebolajo and Michael Adebowale by the time they were arrested for murdering Lee. They were clearly on the radar of MI5 and MI6 security operators after a history of radical behaviour in and out of the UK. Much of their background and journey to violence came out during the trial, and there were startling revelations of how two ordinary Christian boys from London were lured in by hate preachers and turned into killing machines in the cause of Islamic terror.

The more dominant one of the pair, Adebolajo, came from a Christian family in Romford, on the border of London and Essex, and it seemed he had a wide mix of friends from many different racial backgrounds, including a pal called Kirk Redpath, an

Irish Guard who was killed by an insurgent's bomb in Iraq. His mum and dad were hard-working Nigerian immigrants who took their son to church every Sunday, and he was taught by his mother how to pray by candlelight.

As he grew older, it was reported that he was known to have a problem with authority – telling the jury at his trial 'unless it was with his parents or God'. It was when he was in his late teens that his love for Islam was sparked, and he converted during his first year of studying politics at Greenwich University. He began to attend protests against the Iraq War and loudly vented his anger during those meetings.

He told the jury: 'It was Iraq that affected me the most. I saw Operation Shock and Awe and it disgusted me.'

Michael Adebowale, six years younger than Adebolajo, had a turbulent upbringing and was in trouble long before he embraced Islam. By the age of fourteen he was already involved in gangs in south-east London. In 2008 he was dealing drugs and caretaking a flat that was used as a crack den. A violent argument in the flat with a drug user ended in a fatality, when the man plunged a kitchen knife into the neck of one of Adebowale's associates. A third man launched at the attacker to stop him but was cut to pieces and killed in front of Adebowale, who was then stabbed twice before the killer fled.

The killer was jailed for life, while Adebowale was convicted of drug dealing and jailed for eight months in a young offenders' institution. After his release, he disappeared for about a year but, when he returned to his family in Woolwich, he had become a Muslim, wearing traditional Islamic dress and a white skull cap. He had given up alcohol and began distributing radical leaflets near his mother's home in Greenwich.

It is believed that around this time the two Michaels met around Woolwich, as they both attended radical Islamic rallies and meetings in the same area. They were two converts in the same neighbourhood and shared the extremist views of radical Islamic preachers. Adebolajo had, by now, been kicked off his degree course and aligned himself closely with preachers of hate, who influenced scores of disaffected young men in south London. He was seen and photographed loudly demonstrating at a number of protests across the capital. He would eventually be jailed for fifty-one days for assaulting a police officer.

After Lee was murdered, it emerged in the news that MI5 had known of both the killers for at least three years before they targeted my son, but it was never fully explained why they were not more closely monitored, until a report was finally published in November 2014 into the security services and their handling of the terror suspects.

It was on 25 November 2014 that the House of Commons Intelligence and Security Committee published its findings into Lee's murder. It had been set up to examine the background, and to establish whether the security services could have possibly stopped the murder of my son. This was an extremely difficult time for my family because it brought everything back into the news again, and we were thrust into a media spotlight we never wanted to be in. The report was huge, and a lot of it went over my head, but there were several key areas that would become the focus of the findings. It also highlighted more details about Lee's killers and their journey in the run-up to Lee's murder.

It emerged how, in 2010, Adebolajo had tried to travel to Somalia but was captured in Kenya and brought back to the UK. It was reported that an SAS unit 'snatched' him as he prepared to enter the war-torn country for terror training and to fight for Al-Shabaab – a group linked to Al Qaeda.

Having failed to make it across the border, he ended up in a Kenyan court before being deported to Britain, and it was at this time that MI5 tried to recruit Adebolajo as an informant, asking him to relay intelligence back to them about other extremists in return for cash. The bid failed, but Adebolajo was flown back to the UK and allowed to roam the streets unchecked for two and a half years before he murdered Lee.

He told the jury at his trial: 'I attended demonstrations in the hope it might make a difference. I was somewhat naïve and I realised I was prepared to do much more.'

The biggest scandal of the entire episode was that MPs appeared to lay the blame at social media giant Facebook – insisting that the web giant may have been able to foil the murder of Lee. The parliamentary report said that Facebook failed to flag up how one of Lee's killers crowed on the social media site of his lust to murder a British soldier 'in the most graphic and emotive manner'. It referred to messages on the site passed from Michael Adebowale to a foreign extremist in the Middle East.

Adebowale made his twisted vow five months before he and his sidekick slaughtered Lee, but the report says the exchanges were never brought to the attention of the anti-terror authorities. According to MPs, the American web giant uses powerful filters to detect terror chatter and had already automatically closed down a string of other accounts held by Islamic convert Adebowale.

My family has never engaged in the politics of Lee's murder because our grief was too profound. I would rather never watch the news or hear of any further tragedies, but there were some things we couldn't avoid, and this was one of them.

Prime Minister David Cameron responded to the report saying: 'Terrorists are using the internet to communicate with each other. We must not accept that these communications are beyond the reach of the authorities or the internet companies themselves. Their networks are being used to plot murder and mayhem. It is their social responsibility to act on this and we expect them to live up to that responsibility.'

The report – which ran to a staggering 192 pages – concluded that MI5, MI6 and GCHQ were in the dark about the murder plot on Lee. That meant, MPs insisted, the spy agencies could not have prevented the savagery on my son. However, they were criticised for not keeping closer tabs on the two killers, especially after Adebolajo was arrested in Kenya and attempts were made to recruit him. The spy agencies only learned of Adebowale's boast on Facebook to a foreign jihadist after an unidentified party notified GCHQ after Lee's murder. The extremist advised Adebowale on different methods of murder, including using a knife. Facebook maintained throughout that it knew nothing about the terror plot online.

It was a deeply distressing time for my family because we were left with the knowledge that vital online information could have alerted our security services to the plot to kill Lee. It was also very confusing because so much was said, and I think, to a large extent, we were left with more questions after the report than we'd had before. Sara and Ian spoke publicly at the time.

Sara said: 'It's too late now for us because nothing can bring Lee back but we must do everything we can to try and prevent this happening to anyone else – and that includes new terror laws to make internet firms more accountable.

'We all feel let down because things could have been different for Lee if we had known about the terror plot on the internet. I think we all wanted to have someone to blame but that's not really what we have come away with. It has been like opening a can of worms but knowing it may have been prevented makes it all the more painful in our grief.

'It's like being back at square one – it feels as if we are reliving our grief all over again. It takes away from the fact that Lee was a person – he was my brother, a son and a father. Everything has changed for us. This will never leave us because it is impossible to shut it out. The report has not made us able to move on any easier because we still don't have all the answers and I doubt we ever will. We have all become more wary and scared in everyday life – I know I feel like I'm looking over my shoulder the whole time.

'Yes, we are glad that a thorough investigation has been carried out, but Lee's family is still left in the same place at the end of it. Lee is gone and is never coming back.'

Ian also spoke of our family's pain, saying: 'Every time we try to move on with our lives, something flares back up again. If this can happen to Lee, this can happen to anyone. All we can do is take each day at a time but the misery never goes away.

'We all miss Lee so much – he was a real prankster and a great laugh. Often we laugh together as a family about all the antics he got up to but we struggle to talk about his murder and what happened on that terrible day he died.

'If we talk about it, it's almost like we have accepted it and I'm not sure that day will ever come for us.'

Talking in any way about Lee's killers is a nightmare for me and my loved ones. We try to avoid it at all costs because it just makes our grief even worse. I know Lee's story is not complete without exploring how his murder came about but, on a day-to-day basis, I don't think about them or give them any space in my head. All my thoughts and emotions are always with Lee and that will always be the way. At the end of the day, he is the most important person in all of this because he was the one who lost his life and the chance of a happy and fulfilling future. I don't forgive Lee's killers, and never will, but my heart is too broken to carry around hatred. I just wish every day that he was back here with us.

It is not for my family to get entrenched in the politics of what went on but some things are unavoidable. I know that this report had to be done, and I hope if it achieves anything it will be that lessons will be learnt. I know there is a huge problem worldwide with people becoming extremists, but I'm not going to lay criticism at our security and spy forces because, at the end of the day, they are the good guys. They are on our side and they're trying to protect us around the clock. If there is one point my family would make, it is to ensure that our security services, our emergency services and armed forces get all the support they need. We have always supported them all and continue to do so. If they need more resources, more money and officers to do their jobs to the best of their abilities, then that should be made available because if it prevents just one more murder like Lee's, then it will be worth it.

I speak later in the book about our visit to see Prime Minister David Cameron and how he has looked me in the eye and promised that he does not believe the security services could have prevented Lee's murder with the knowledge and intelligence they had at the time. I accept his words as honest and, I think if anything, the whole report made us realise just how difficult a job it is to know exactly what would-be jihadists are doing at all times. But that is why our intelligence services must be given all the support and money they need to increase their strength, so we can hopefully stop another family being handed the life sentence we are going through.

17

The World's Gone Mad

Since Lee was murdered my life has been divided into two clear categories: Before Lee Died and After Lee Died. Beforehand, I was just an ordinary mum and wife who lived for her family and no one had ever heard of my or my son's name. Since he was killed, it's like I've been yanked from Earth and planted in a hostile universe where nothing is recognisable.

I have never pretended to be an expert at anything and I never will. I am not a politician or a professional news pundit – on the contrary, I have always tried to shield myself and my children from the terrible things that happen in the world. Even when Lee was in Afghanistan, I tried to avoid the television and news bulletins because it scared the living daylights out of me just hearing about the deaths and casualties of our soldiers. It doesn't mean I don't care about world affairs, but the constant stream of bad news on a daily basis can be overwhelming at times.

Lee's murder changed all that to an extent, because I suddenly became a focus for the media when terror atrocities kicked off in the UK and around the world – and the kind of violence being carried out by extremists certainly appeared to be getting worse. Lee was the first person who was the victim of an attempted beheading, but this became more and more common with the emergence of a new terror group, the so-called Islamic State in Iraq and the Levant (ISIL).

A little over a year after Lee's murder, the world was stunned again when news broke that a brave American journalist, James Foley, was beheaded by ISIL jihadis. On 19 August 2014 his vile execution was videoed and placed on the internet for the world to see. It was totally shocking and immediately brought back chilling echoes of my own son's murder. James had been captured by the group on 22 November 2012, as he was covering the civil war in Syria, and he remained a hostage until his death, despite international calls for his release from both politicians and his loved ones.

I was stunned when I heard about his murder and I burst into tears, thinking about my own son, this poor man and his family. I knew only too well what they were about to go through. I didn't go into the politics of the event, because I couldn't comprehend how such a dreadful thing could happen, but I knew that I was filled with dread for the future of the world. I just wanted to reach out and comfort James's mum and dad and his loved ones. No mother should ever have to face the agony of a child meeting with such a violent end. It doesn't matter how hard I had tried to rid my mind of the savagery inflicted on Lee, it didn't work. I still live with those nightmares, which constantly work overtime in the back of your brain. All I knew at that moment was that James's loved ones were facing the double agony of not only losing him, but that they would be tortured with the knowledge that he suffered so greatly. That was one of the hardest parts of my grief with Lee.

My heart was heavy with the news, and I couldn't help but wonder how this poor family was going to cope – I knew the pain they were facing is something not everyone can survive because sometimes it is so overwhelming you think you are going to die yourself.

The video of this dreadful act recorded the young man's final moments, as he was forced to read from an anti-US script, which had been written by his captors. The recording was so gruesome and disturbing that it was not shown on British television but it was, sadly, widely available on the internet. At the time I backed Mr Foley's parents, who urged people not to watch the appalling propaganda video. I don't understand how anyone would want to see something so gruesome but many people did, and I knew this would compound the misery for his family.

I had been through something similar myself when amateur footage of Lee's murder was seen around the world, and it's almost impossible to explain how much it hurts that people willingly watched the execution of my flesh and blood. It wasn't a fictional horror film made in Hollywood. This was a real person, experiencing real pain and suffering. Refusing to watch such films is one of the few ways that families and good people can make a stand against the evil people of the world, who want nothing more than to push a nasty and violent agenda. Even now I am stunned to know there are evil individuals who can easily carry out wicked acts of barbarity on fellow human beings. It is heart-breaking. How can such hatred burn within those who inflict so much pain on innocent people?

Many people have said that Lee didn't suffer on the day he was killed, and that he would have been unconscious from the moment the car knocked him down, but the truth is no one knows that for sure. I will never know what he felt, what he was aware of, and if he felt any pain. At one stage, I visited a trusted clairvoyant in my desperate bid for answers, and she told me that Lee had sent me a message to say that he didn't suffer. I hold on to that because it is what I want to believe, but my nagging doubts will always be there.

James Foley must have endured hell before he died, and it makes me weep to think of the fear he would have gone through. He knew he was about to be executed and he was mocked and taunted beforehand. At least his suffering is over now, but his family have now inherited the suffering, just as I have. The pain never leaves you – it seeps deep into your bones and your blood because you never forget what happened to your precious child. Worst of all is the recurring feeling that I failed my son because I wasn't there to protect him in his hour of need.

It broke my heart to look at television images of James's parents because I could see how hard they fought to retain such magnificent dignity for their son at the same time as trying to disguise their raw and desperate pain. All I know is that you have to keep love in your heart for your lost child and never let hatred hijack its way into your soul. It's that same hatred that is the cause of all the madness and mayhem, and it has no place in the lives of decent human beings like mine and the Foley family. I wish them all the peace in the world, even though I am still searching for mine.

James's murder was tragically one of several more to come, and the next couple would be much closer to home. David Haines was an English aid worker who was captured by ISIL early in 2013 and held hostage until he too was beheaded on 13 September 2014, a few weeks after James Foley. A former Royal Air Force aircraft engineer, the Yorkshire-born peace campaigner turned to humanitarian work in 1999 and helped many in conflict zones including the former Yugoslavia, Africa and the Middle East. It was while he was working in a Syrian refugee camp that he was kidnapped near to the border with Turkey.

The pattern was the same, with wicked videos of the execution being paraded on the internet. And next it was Alan Henning, an English cab driver who became committed to humanitarian aid work. He was captured in December 2013, in Syria, as he attempted to deliver aid. He was executed on 3 October 2014. In both cases the British Foreign Office withheld news of the men's capture while officers attempted to negotiate their release, but sadly the efforts failed. It was reported that Alan knew the dangers and had been warned not to cross into Syria, but he was determined to make sure his essential supplies got through to those who needed them most. He was working as a driver for an organisation called Rochdale Aid 4 Syria, which delivered emergency aid to the desperate and displaced. His murder stunned the world yet again and even American President Barack Obama made a statement.

He said: 'Mr Henning worked to help improve the lives of the Syrian people and his death is a great loss for them, for his family, and the people of the United Kingdom.

'Standing together with our UK friends and allies, we will work to bring the perpetrators of Alan's murder – as well as the murders of Jim Foley, Steven Sotloff and David Haines – to justice.'

Yet again, his murder followed the same sickening format as the previous video showing the death of David Haines. A man with a British accent, who was dubbed 'Jihadi John', spoke on the video before carrying out the murder. This time, he declared that Mr Henning's blood was 'on the hands of the British parliament.'

It was truly horrifying moment. These two British men had done nothing but try to help orphans, women, and sick and hungry children, and they were murdered in such a brutal manner. They were kind and compassionate men who had simply gone to help others, and the fact that Alan had put his life on the line to help these people, knowing the risks, shows just how courageous and selfless he was.

Alan and his wife Barbara and their children lived in Eccles in Greater Manchester, which is only fourteen miles from my own family in Middleton. By chance, we shared the same Police Family Liaison Officer and, over time, we were introduced to each other, bringing what small comfort we could to one another. Ian and I were honoured when Barbara invited us to attend a memorial service for Alan in Eccles in October 2014, and it was a highly emotional occasion. When I embraced Barbara, I could see how much grief she was in and I knew how she felt. A loss like this, in such violent circumstances, floors you, and you are never the same person again. Part of you is lost forever with the loved one who has been taken so cruelly from you.

By now, an international manhunt was on to find 'Jihadi John', who had carried out these awful executions with the help of his team of kidnappers. The identity of the English-speaking man was still unknown but it was only a matter of time before he was unmasked.

That happened in February 2015, when it was revealed that the British man behind the beheadings was Mohammed Emwazi. A further shock to us was that he knew Lee's killers and that they had attended the same extremist meetings and worshipped at the same mosque in London's Greenwich.

My heart went out to all his victims, especially as it was officially confirmed he was from the UK. Just like Adebolajo and Adobowale, he had grown up as a normal boy in this country with English values before being radicalised into a killer with no mercy or humanity.

We felt sick to the stomach learning yet more misery, but I had no answers as to why these men were becoming so hate-filled and hell bent on the destruction of all things good. Like Lee's killers, Emwazi had been on the radar of the security services but had slipped away from them and out of the country.

It felt like the whole world was out of control and in the grip of a global terror that no one seemed to be able to stop. My biggest fear is, what comes next? How many more innocent victims will there be of this kind of violence? And how are we going to make it stop? It certainly doesn't feel as if things have got better since Lee's murder and if anything, the violence around the world seems to have got worse. It is not a problem for just one country, and I pray that one day peace may be restored.

The beginning of 2015 brought renewed violence across the world, starting on 7 January when two Islamic terrorist brothers forced their way into the offices of French satirical weekly newspaper, *Charlie Hebdo*, in Paris. Using assault rifles and other weapons, they killed eleven people and injured eleven others. After leaving, they killed a French National Police officer. Four days later, on 11 January, about two million people, including more than forty world leaders, met in Paris for a rally of national unity. 3.7 million people joined demonstrations across France, and the phrase *'Je Suis Charlie'* became an iconic slogan for unity. It was a clear message that people everywhere wanted change and an end to the senseless violence and murders worldwide.

The summer of 2015 brought no respite when, on 26 June, an armed gunman attacked a hotel in the Tunisian tourist resort of Port El Kantaoui – ten kilometres from the northern city of Sousse. A staggering thirty-eight people were killed, thirty of whom were British holidaymakers.

At around noon on the day of the massacre, terrorist Seifeddine Rezgui, disguised as a tourist, socialised and mingled with innocent sunbathers before taking out a Kalashnikov assault rifle he had concealed in a beach umbrella and fired on terrified victims. He then ran amok in a nearby hotel, shooting at people he came across. He was killed by security forces as he fled the hotel. The result of his onslaught was sheer carnage and mayhem and stunned people across the world.

The year ended as it had started – in terrible violence. On 13 November 2015 news broke that Mohammed Emwazi, the so-called Jihadi John, had been killed during an airstrike on Syria by western forces. But that was not to be the most shocking news of the day.

That evening, Islamist terrorists once more brought horror to the streets of Paris when they attacked the city, murdering 130 people. Cafés, restaurants and a rock concert hall were targeted as innocent people enjoyed a night out. Among the victims were eighty-nine people killed at the Bataclan Theatre, where gunmen held music fans hostage during a shoot-out with police. Many more were seriously injured, as gunmen and suicide bombers rampaged across the city. The whole world was stunned by the scale of terror and violence. The world held its breath, and some cities went into lockdown as more attacks were feared.

ISIL were, once again, behind the attacks. French President Francois Hollande declared them an act of war. The atrocity struck fear into so many, including myself and my family. We had lived through the consequences of acts of terror, but Paris felt like the sky was falling in. That night so many families lost innocent loved ones, just as I had lost Lee, and it left me feeling bereft and grief-stricken for the victims. I just wanted the world to stop and for the violence to go away. It felt completely overwhelming and I was so scared for the future. The slaughter was so senseless and brutal. The threat to our country remains high and I dread that yet more families will face heartbreak and misery. I wish I knew how to make it stop, but I don't.

People often ask me my opinion about the global terror that is affecting us all and I can honestly say that I am not qualified to pass an opinion because I'm just an ordinary mum who lost her beloved son. The only thing that I'm an expert in is grief and heartache. This has been inflicted on me without choice, and there isn't much I don't know about the misery that results after these kinds of senseless attacks.

I still believe there are more good people in the world than bad, and I know the majority of decent people want to see a more peaceful and loving world than the one we are all facing at the moment. I hate what's happening, but I don't have an answer to the problems. That's a job for politicians the world over to try and come together to tackle, as the forces of evil affect so many people.

To that end, I would like to praise our security services for the outstanding work they do to try and make us safe in the face of sometimes overwhelming odds. They work in the dark so often and don't always know when the next terror will strike. For all the occasions when terror has struck and the bloody damage has been done, there are so many other instances when attacks on innocent people have been averted.

One particularly poignant result for my family occurred at the same time as the Tunisian bloodbath. The day after holidaymakers were slain, it emerged that security services had successfully averted a terror plot to blow up soldiers in the UK during an Armed Forces Day parade on 26 June. IS fanatics were planning to explode a bomb during a march in which Lee's regiment, the Royal Fusiliers, were taking part. The procession, which also included Gurkhas and military veterans, was in Merton, south London, and was picked as a target by the terrorists because it was closest to the barracks of the Fusiliers in Woolwich. The plot was destroyed when terror chiefs unwittingly recruited an undercover reporter online and the *Sun* newspaper alerted counter-terror chiefs at Scotland Yard.

It sent a shiver down my spine when I learned of how close it had been. I was just so thankful that it had been stopped by vigilant reporters and our fantastic police force. I know from personal experience that this would have brought nothing but a lifetime of misery for the loved ones of those who could have been killed – just as it has for all victims' families in atrocities around the world.

It was almost unbearable for me to think that the lads from Lee's beloved regiment were being targeted yet again. I have no idea why the world has erupted in this madness but I do know it changes nothing apart from hurting many innocent people who lose loved ones. An attack like this could have killed and maimed so many ordinary people in the crowds, as well as those on the march, just like the innocent people who were killed and hurt during the Boston marathon in 2013.

Sometimes I feel suffocated by grief to the extent that I fear I will stop breathing. I sometimes ask, why was I chosen to be persecuted in this way? Why was my son the one who was killed? And then I remember that it's not just me. With murder and chaos all around the world, as in Tunisia and Paris, I remember all the poor souls who, like Lee, have become victims of such senseless violence.

As a family, we have never been involved in, or believed in, any form of extremism. The very notion that there are people around the world who want to kill and maim for a cause is alien to me, and I despair when I see so much needless suffering and bloodshed. My message will always be one of peace, because anything else is pointless and futile. It's a cruel mind that plots to kill people to make a political point, and we are the living consequence that it solves nothing. Words often fail me when I see acts of barbarity, and the grief of such loss eats away at you each day. I don't know the answer to the madness in our world right now, but I do know violence is not the solution. All it does is perpetuate the suffering.

18

Memorials For Lee

I have already touched on how moved I have been by the general public in their support for my family. Lee's murder stunned so many people and they shared our deep abhorrence and sorrow by showing in many different ways how much they cared. Among those incredible strangers is a woman called Lorna Taylor, who is also a soldier's mum. Her son Luke served in the same Fusiliers' regiment as Lee, and the two lads knew each other. They didn't work alongside each other, so they weren't close pals, but would often stop to chat and catch up when they bumped into each other. Even still, Luke was devastated when he learned of Lee's murder for, after all, he had lost one of his 'brothers in arms'.

Lorna shared her son's distress and realised from the beginning that it could just have easily been her son who was picked out on the day of the killing.

'There but for the grace of God, that could have been Luke that day,' she often told me. 'We had lost one of our own and people were shaken to the core. Many didn't know what to say or do in response to something so horrific, but I knew straight away that I had to do something. I wasn't sure what, but doing nothing wasn't an option. I believed our country had to do something to honour this brave soldier and send out a message that this was a truly heinous crime.'

Luke later left the Army but supported him mum as she set about launching a huge online petition on Facebook to install a memorial in Woolwich to commemorate Lee. Lorna lives nearby, in Thamesmead, and the geography of Lee's murder and the soldier's barracks in the same town made her even more determined to make a mark. Greenwich Council is the ruling body for Woolwich, and chief officers there had already made it extremely clear that they would not seek to provide a memorial unless it was instructed by the Army. Enraged by their apathy and insensitivity, Lorna was galvanised into action.

'It was pretty clear from day one that Greenwich Council had no interest in taking a lead to honour Lee,' she said. 'For them, it was a highly political situation and they tried their hardest to steer clear of it. I thought it was pretty despicable they hadn't volunteered to remember Lee in the town which has a proud military history. If the Council wasn't interested, then we would have to find another way.'

Lorna launched the campaign on social media and was immediately overwhelmed with public support, from people around the world, who agreed that a memorial should be erected in Woolwich. It was a fantastic early response, but she had no idea of how long a fight it would prove to be.

I first met Lorna after she had started her petition through friends at Charlton Athletic Football Club. The amazing supporters at the club have been a tower of strength, love and support to us. The club's home ground is only about a mile from where Lee was murdered, and is the closest local club to Woolwich. He may have been a passionate Manchester United fan, but Lee also had a soft spot for his local side, which plays in the Football League

Championship. As far as the club and its supporters were concerned, Lee was part of their community, also one of their own,
and took to heart his brutal slaying.

It was the wonderful Lee Rose from the club who started the
campaign to have my Lee's first memorial at their ground. My
family will always be so grateful to Lee and his friends, who
have done so much for us and become such wonderful friends to
us all. We can never thank him enough for leading the way so
early on and showing us how much people cared about my son.

Desperate to show their loyalty, Charlton supporters, led by
Lee Rose, began raising funds to pay for their own memorial at
their ground. When he first got in touch with me, I was delighted
by such a heartfelt gesture. In February 2014, the very first permanent memorial to Lee was unveiled by the generous football
fans who spearheaded the tribute. The plaque was laid into stone
outside the west stand of the club's Valley stadium. The fans took
to raising the money after Greenwich Council had refused to
provide a fitting tribute to Lee.

The black plaque, bearing the club's Charlton Athletic logo,
reads 'RIP LEE RIGBY – FANS UNITE.'

We will always be so thankful to Lee Rose and Gavin
McClean, a Charlton fan for thirty-six years, for such a beautiful memorial. Gavin had appealed to other supporters on social
media and was thrilled when scores of people backed him and
donated cash. Even fans from rival clubs such as Millwall gave
money to the cause.

'We just thought it had to be done. It was such a dreadful
thing to happen and Lee was killed just down the road from
here. We thought it was the decent thing to do to provide a
permanent memorial in the area to remember him by. No one
should forget what this poor lad went through,' he said.

On 26 March the following month, we were invited down to the
Valley to see the memorial ourselves, and it was a deeply moving

occasion. I felt so honoured that these wonderful strangers had taken us all under their wing and shown how much they care. Ian was with me and we laid some single-stem red flowers on it as a mark of respect. I cried so much when I laid the flowers because it was the first time Lee had been honoured with his own permanent memorial in public, and it struck a deep chord within me.

I often felt like I was being bounced from to pillar to post. One minute we were in the deeply uncomfortable confines of the Old Bailey, and the next we were at a football stadium honouring my dead son. It was a world away from the life I had once known of anonymity.

To this day I remain so thankful to Charlton Athletic and its fans. As sad as any memorial is, they gave me and Lee's loved ones a real boost of confidence with such a beautiful gesture. They spoke to us from the heart and I will never forget that. After laying our flowers, we were invited to the Millennium Suite at the stadium, where we met celebrity comic and lifelong Charlton fan, Jim Davidson. He was fantastic to us and gave me a hug and a kiss and shook Ian's hand.

'I have so much respect for our troops and what happened to your son was pure evil,' Jim said us. 'If I can do anything to help you, in any way, please get in touch and I will be there.'

I found Jim to be a really lovely, down-to-earth bloke. I know he gets himself into bother with some of his riskier material, but he was very kind to Ian and me that day and made a real fuss over us. He gave me his glass of wine and, when he couldn't find another glass, he poured his glass into a tea cup, which made us all giggle. He put us at ease and we even managed to have a laugh with him. We found him hilarious, and the afternoon proved to be a welcome respite from all the misery we had been through. Jim also promised he would help with a charity that we had spoken about launching in Lee's name. Ian and I came away feeling proud and very humbled by the kindness of strangers.

After meeting Lorna for the first time, we became good friends and I applauded and welcomed her petition on Facebook. She had my full endorsement to shout from the rooftops to try and get a memorial sanctioned in Woolwich, but the local council had really dug their heels in and remained adamant they were not going ahead with one. They kept shying off because they said they were concerned that a permanent memorial would be inflammatory to Muslim extremists, and may even attract further jihadi attacks in the town.

Since when has this country ever bowed down to terrorists on our home soil? I thought this a cowardly and very un-British way to respond, and I was deeply disappointed not to see Greenwich Council stepping up to the mark to do what so many people clearly wanted. I was humbled by the sincerity of so many ordinary people who wanted to honour Lee, but the council, at that stage, was having none of it.

By now, Lorna had attracted 12,850 people to support the Lee Rigby Memorial, and that figure was growing daily. Lorna and her team were like a dog with a bone and refused to back down, continually writing to the Army, MPs and Mayor of London Boris Johnson. The council insisted their preferred tribute to Lee was to add his name to the National Arboretum in Staffordshire – in other words, no responsibility for Greenwich chiefs. Eventually Lorna received a letter from the council and Woolwich MP Nick Raynsford, warning that a memorial could cast a shadow over the area and might attract undesirable interest from extremists. Lorna was not going to be dissuaded.

'Almost a year had gone by and, as the first anniversary of Lee's murder approached, nothing had been done in Woolwich to recognise such a terrible act,' she said. 'I knew from the thousands of people joining us that the majority of decent people wanted a memorial and were determined to get one.'

I joined Lorna and began writing to the council in support of her campaign and helped out wherever I could. On 25 May, just over a year since Lee was killed, the *Sun on Sunday* newspaper waded in and gave the online petition a huge boost by launching its own campaign. Its voice joined growing unrest, as the previous week the council had further rejected a permanent site of remembrance in Woolwich.

The paper called on its Army readers to join the fight for a tribute near to the barracks, and the campaign was seen not just in the UK, but across the world. Westminster politicians led the way to back the campaign.

Communities Secretary Eric Pickles said: 'A memorial has attracted broad support from the public. We disagree with those who suggest a public memorial would encourage extremism. Extremism in all its forms should be challenged and we should not cave in. We should uphold British traditions.'

I also publicly voiced my support for the campaign, saying: 'We feel Lee deserves to be honoured not just by his loved ones but by the wider public in our country, who were all so shocked to see what happened to Lee on our TV screens. It remains of huge importance to me to make sure there are lasting legacies to Lee and that I do everything possible to ensure his sacrifice as a proud soldier of this country is honoured.'

Within a week, 17,000 people had backed the campaign and staff at the *Sun on Sunday* delivered a giant mail sack bulging with petitions and letters from its readers. Stunned staff at the town hall refused to receive the bag, claiming they were not authorised to take it, so the bag was left by the front door to send a message to the council. A further 15,000 readers went on Facebook to register their support, with thousands of others writing letters and contacting the paper via its website.

Boris Johnson responded again: 'Lee died doing a job he relished for a country he loved. He was a hero and his killers are cowards. We can't change his family's sense of loss and injustice, but we can honour Lee's sacrifice.'

It was an extremely frustrating situation and I shared the sense of injustice that Boris had spoken of. Why didn't my son deserve this tribute? I was also receiving so many mixed messages from the council. One minute they were promising me a memorial and the next they turned their back on the idea again. In the summer of 2014, with the campaigns continuing, two lovely women from the council came to my home from London to see me.

Denise Hyland, the chief executive at the time, and the borough's 'leader elect', Mary Nee, spent two hours chatting with me about the different possibilities in the town, and what I would prefer to see happen. It was a productive but very emotional meeting.

'I just don't want my son to be forgotten,' I beseeched them. 'He lived and died in Woolwich and, as his mum, it's my job to make sure he is honoured for all time after what happened to him.'

By the time the ladies left, the atmosphere was very kind and gentle and they reassured me that a tribute *would* now be organised for Woolwich. It felt like a great success and they told me they would come back to me as soon as possible once they had a chance to draw up plans for suitable memorials. I knew this would take some time, but I was confident that, finally, a tribute would be installed. We agreed that we would work together to agree appropriate details. I was delighted with the outcome and thanked them sincerely.

The one thing I was certain of was that I didn't want the memorial to be placed at the roadside where Lee died, or anywhere that you could see the murder scene. That would be far too distressing and not somewhere I would feel happy to visit. I suggested somewhere near to the barracks instead. The officers agreed to a plaque bearing Lee's name in a position just outside the barracks.

The news clearly lifted my spirits, to know I would soon have the chance to honour Lee in a permanent manner that could also be shared with the people of Woolwich. I waited patiently for confirmation of our discussions and some detailed plans, but, as the weeks ticked by, the proposals I had discussed with Denise and Mary began to come back to me very differently to what I believed was going to happen.

After all the promises that were made to me, the council had backed down and reneged on their deal. Instead of a memorial for Lee, the council said they were now prepared to install a memorial in the town for all fallen soldiers. My heart sank when I got the bad news. Don't get me wrong. I'm all in support of a memorial honouring all armed forces, but this was not the same as a specific memorial for Lee. I was heartbroken to have the decision reversed and I couldn't understand why. With such a proud military history, the reluctance from this particular council was at the very least baffling and very upsetting. I also knew Lee would be proud to be honoured in Woolwich. I was insistent that he should not be forgotten in the town where he lost his life.

My son was not an extremist. He was a peaceful, fun-loving lad who wanted to help people and care for them, not harm them. He didn't care about the colour of your skin or your religion. He judged people on whether they were nice and, if anyone needed support, he would be the first to offer. I wanted the chance to cherish this wonderful son of mine and public recognition for him in Woolwich would have helped. It was important more than ever for me to highlight and praise the good people of the world, instead of the bad. This was yet another set-back from Woolwich, but the fight was to carry on. It would be some months before I would speak with the council again.

In March 2015 I was invited to Downing Street to meet with

David Cameron. It was a big occasion and it was an opportunity to ask him questions about Lee's murder, and whether it could have been prevented. I travelled to London with Sara and we met with Aimee and her mum to go into the meeting. I didn't know what to expect but Mr Cameron was extremely kind and pleasant, and I warmed to him quite quickly. He seemed to care very much about Lee's murder, and told me that he didn't think the security services could have done anything to prevent the killing on the information that MI5 had at the time.

It was quite a short meeting but Mr Cameron told us that if there was anything else we wanted to ask him, then we could write to him and he would respond. It wasn't far off the General Election in May, but even so I wrote him a letter begging him to try and influence a decision to have the memorial built in Woolwich. I never heard back from him. So far, Woolwich had let us down completely but we were very honoured to be invited to an alternative memorial for Lee in our home town in Middleton.

I had been in discussions with Rochdale Borough Council for some time, as I had asked them to consider a tribute for Lee in Middleton. The response of their officers and councillors couldn't have been more different from Greenwich. They pulled out all the stops for an amazing memorial that was finally unveiled during a beautiful ceremony on Sunday 29 March 2015. The memorial itself took my breath away.

The council had commissioned a large bronze drum and a giant plaque bearing Lee's name. It was installed at Middleton Memorial Gardens and was stunning. The council had also arranged a spectacular private unveiling during a dedication service at the gardens, before later being opened to the public.

It was the most miserable day in Middleton that Sunday, as usual, and the heavens had opened. We were drenched by the time we even got to the service, but nothing would have kept us away. It was a very proud moment. Colonel Mike Glover, regimental secretary of the Lancashire Fusiliers, spoke some beautiful words during the service.

He said: 'The afternoon of May 22nd 2013, Fusilier Lee Rigby paid the ultimate sacrifice when the horror of the battlefield was brought to the streets of Woolwich. That day will forever be embedded in our nation's history, and for many here today it will remain forever in our hearts. Lee's death sent shockwaves around the world, especially in Middleton, where Lee had grown up.

'As a nation, as a member of his family, as a friend or a fellow Fusilier, it is important we do not forget the sacrifice of Lee and those who served the Crown. All too often as time passes we close our eyes, forget the faces, forget the names, forget the stories. But this magnificent memorial will ensure we never forget.'

I sobbed throughout his speech, as I sat in the pouring rain with local dignitaries who had worked so hard to make this a special day.

He continued: 'On September 1st 2014, Lee Rigby was honoured by the nation at a ceremony in Staffordshire, where his name was added to the Armed Forces Memorial at the National Memorial Arboretum, but today it is his hometown; his family, his friends, his fellow Fusiliers, at the site of this memorial can reflect upon the tragic loss of a son, a father, a friend and, above all, a Fusilier. We will remember.'

It was such a moving ceremony and I couldn't have been more proud. Councillor June West, chair of Middleton Township, also spoke some lovely words on behalf of the town.

'The Middleton community and the township were very clear in their support for a permanent memorial here in his hometown – a lasting legacy where Lee and other soldiers can be remembered not only by their families and friends but by so many others who owe them such a debt. I would like to thank our local residents and those who have worked hard to make this happen.

'I would also like to thank Lee's family for their support and I know they too are pleased that calls for this local memorial were answered.'

A short reception was held afterwards in the warmth of a community centre and it gave me a chance to show my gratitude for the wonderful tribute that had been created for Lee. My son had put his life on the line for his country, and now his home-town had said thank you. It is a stunning place, and I see it as a celebration of Lee's life because that is what he would have wanted. It's also a place for quiet reflection and peace.

It inevitably saddened me when I thought about the snub we had received from Greenwich. If it could be done so willingly in Middleton, then I knew it could be done in Woolwich town too. New leaders had taken over at Greenwich since my last discussions with them, and I had received no calls, letters or emails from them in over six months. It felt like they just wanted the whole issue to go away. It felt wrong to have such a fantastic tribute in Middleton, but absolutely nothing where he lived and died. Lee was one of the good guys and he still deserved better than this.

As for the Middleton Memorial, I cried like a baby throughout the dedication service but I felt enormous pride in my heart because this was the community where Lee grew up. It was an honour that our community felt so committed to showing Lee such love. It was nothing less than he deserved.

By now, the second anniversary of Lee's murder was approaching. I made the decision to return to Woolwich for the first time since he was killed. It was a huge undertaking for me because it only reminded me of my son's suffering. It held no sliver of hope or remembrance, but something was compelling me to go there. It proved to be as gut-wrenching as I had imagined.

I took with me a floral wreath of red and white roses bearing Lee's name, and walked with great trepidation to the road where so much carnage had unfolded two years earlier. I had never stood at the exact spot where Lee died, but this day I was determined to try to bury some of the gruesome ghosts that haunted me. Courtney and Lorna were with me too, and I valued their support. But when it came to walking to the place Lee died, I insisted on going alone.

As I carried this stunning arrangement of flowers, I felt bereft that there was no place I could lay them to honour my son. The only point of remembrance was some beautiful giant placards bearing Lee's pictures that had been tied to the railings on the roadside where he was butchered.

It was the last place on earth I wanted to be, and I felt sick to my stomach, but somehow I felt as if I was betraying Lee by not returning to this scene. I tried to find some poise as I stood looking at the flat grey road where, two years earlier, my son lay dead in a sea of his own blood. The horrors and the nightmares of everything I knew leapt into my mind, and I wanted to run away as fast as I could. It felt like only yesterday that he had been taken from me.

Perhaps I was trying to prove a point to Greenwich Council. Why should I be forced to lay flowers for my son at the roadside where he died? I had only ever wanted a place in Woolwich where I could take my children and grandchildren to remember Lee in the most loving and respectful way. Lee's baby sister Amy was ten at the time and there was no safe place I could take her in Woolwich for her to feel good about the brother she adored.

As the sadness and anger rose within me, I fell to the floor in a heap and sobbed into my hands.

'God, why did you have to take my son?' I questioned.

I thought I was going to throw up, as I tried to get back on my feet, but all I could see were the images of my son's body and the road awash with his blood. It was too much for me to bear and I don't ever want to return there again. I laid the wreath on the pavement beneath the banners and rushed back to Courtney and Lorna as quickly as possible. They hugged me in their arms and held me close until I could stop crying.

That trip brought me nothing but misery and sorrow but it also left me angry that the people who run the council for Woolwich couldn't see the suffering of our family. If they put themselves in my shoes for one day, they may get just a snapshot of what my grief is really like. If they cared enough, they could make some of that suffering go away by honouring Lee and providing a place we can pay our respects.

The trip to Woolwich was tough enough, but the week was about to get even worse. With just a few days before the anniversary, Ian suffered a massive heart attack at home. He had gone up to bed before me but, after a few minutes, he came back down.

'I feel really ill,' he told me. 'I'm in pain and struggling here.'

I laid him on the couch and saw that he had gone a ghastly colour and was clammy and sweating. I immediately rang 999 for an ambulance.

'Don't worry, Ian,' I tried to reassure him. 'The ambulance is coming and we will get you sorted. Don't you dare leave me, do you hear me?'

He was past being able to talk to me and I prayed for the ambulance to arrive quickly. As ever, the paramedics were outstanding and got to work on Ian as soon as they arrived. I went in the back of the ambulance with him and I held his hand and prayed that he would survive.

'Please don't take Ian away from me too,' I pleaded with God.

'I've lost Lee and I won't be able to cope without my husband too. I'm begging you to let him live.'

When a loved one is in peril like this, it's hard to know what to do. I just put my faith in the medics around us and hoped for the best. It was a long night, as doctors got to work on Ian without delay. They then rushed him to theatre for emergency surgery to implant a stent into one of his arteries, which was blocked. It was certainly touch and go, but Ian pulled through and the operation was a great success. Had he not got up feeling unwell that night, I fear he may have had the heart attack in his sleep and died. Losing my husband after my son would have been the end of me.

After a few days, Ian was allowed home to start a long and slow recovery, but it was obvious that the stress of the past two years had taken its toll on us all. Ian was paying a heavy price for the grief he felt for his son. I count myself very lucky that he survived a major illness, and now we have to try and keep him calm and away from tense situations.

My family was long overdue some good news and it finally came on 14 September 2015 with a phone call and an email from Greenwich Council. After more than two years of playing cat and mouse with us, they finally caved in and agreed to honour Lee with a personal memorial in Woolwich. I was over the moon and felt like I wanted to run around the room. It was a huge victory for Lee and it really was something to celebrate. So many people had fought for this, including over 100,000 *Sun on Sunday* readers who petitioned for the tribute.

Lorna had fought tooth and nail with her online petition and I had refused to give up emailing and writing to the council. It was a joint effort, with so many playing their role. I had almost thrown in the towel with the campaign because I thought it had failed permanently. Now we were back in business. I put out a public statement to share the news and my gratitude.

This means so much to me and my family because we want to make sure Lee is never forgotten. It also means I have a special and safe place to take my children and grandchildren to show our love and respect for Lee. The support we have received has been truly overwhelming and there are just so many people I need to thank for never giving up on this. Lee is loved and missed as much today as the day he was murdered, and I owe it to him to make sure no one forgets what he sacrificed. He was a proud and strong soldier who loved his country and his regiment. He was taken from us too early in the most horrific way and people across the UK have always wanted to honour him.

It shocked not just our nation but people across the world, and it is so important not to be cowed by jihadi terrorists and to stand up and honour those who paid the ultimate price.

Lee's memorial should now become a beacon of hope for the future because it says we will not be beaten by cowardly murderers who kill in the name of so-called religion. Lee was the complete opposite to the evil people who robbed his life. He was loving, kind and so much fun and we all utterly adored him. But he also stood for honour, strength and courage and that is why he must be honoured where he worked and was ultimately killed.

Lee was as brave as a lion and fought for his country on the frontline. He was fair and principled and didn't have a bigoted bone in his body. He always stood up for the underdog and helped others who couldn't help themselves.

This is how we should remember Lee. I don't just want people to think of that dreadful day when he was butchered to death. This was a man who had his whole life stripped from him. He had a young son and a family he was devoted to, and it's crucial that we remember what Lee lost and how his family will suffer forever after.

I want people to know that Lee's life was worthwhile and significant. I want people to know he was a great guy who was loved by so many and how he tried to make a difference in the world. I want people to visit his memorial plaque and be proud of Lee and all of our armed forces, including all the fallen, the injured, the veterans of all ages, and those who serve us still. These are the good guys who stand on our walls and keep us safe at night. We all owe them so much.

It's taken one hell of a fight to get this memorial but I couldn't be more proud as a mum and I am so grateful that Woolwich Council chiefs have finally changed their minds to allow the name plaques to go ahead.

This was a good day! There hadn't been many but this stood out from all the rest. Lee's name plaque will form part of a new war memorial for stricken soldiers, which has been created at the bombed-out shell of St George's Garrison Church. Separate plaques will also bear the names of other soldiers linked to Woolwich who have died in military conflict since 1945. The council has also agreed to consider an additional plaque featuring Lee's name on a park bench once the first memorials are complete.

St George's Chapel was built in the 1860s for the Royal Artillery Barracks, where Lee was based. The chapel was hit by a V1 flying bomb in 1944 but has been spruced up, thanks to a Lottery Fund grant. It contains monuments to battles and servicemen killed in action and the council hopes the chapel and its gardens will soon be opened more regularly to the public. Greenwich Council leader Denise Hyland was behind the decision to approve the £3,500 plaque for Lee in the chapel which is opposite Lee's barracks.

She said: 'After talks with Lee's family, I have taken stock of their views, as well of those of community leaders. As a result, I have decided we will ensure Lee is named on a memorial plaque, as will other victims killed in recent conflict. This will allow his family to commemorate his life and his connection with Woolwich from where he served his country.'

Staunch supporter Boris Johnson, who helped broker the deal with the council, added his delight: 'I'm so pleased Lyn's campaign for a memorial has been successful. The plaque in Woolwich will be a fitting tribute to Lee's sacrifice.'

Even David Cameron welcomed the decision, commenting: 'The brutal murder of Lee Rigby was devastating for his family and friends, and shocking for the country as a whole. It is fitting that he is remembered for the life he lived with a permanent memorial in Woolwich.'

There are endless people I have to thank for this momentous event. The *Sun on Sunday* played a pivotal role by campaigning nationally and applying so much public pressure with over 100,000 readers backing their petition. That's a staggering amount of people who took the time to have their voices heard. Lorna was also sensational with her online campaign, started not long after Lee died. She felt compelled to do something and she has made a huge impact in our lives and my family loves her dearly. By refusing to take no for an answer, she also instilled in me a courage to keep fighting the council.

There have also been a few outstanding individuals who have given me back some faith in the human spirit, including Chris Last, who has been a special help in collecting huge amounts of signatures for us, and was there till the end. Finally, Hamish Immanuel Barton has done us proud by designing and creating the giant banners that have hung proudly from the railings near to the road where Lee died. For the last two years he has made sure that my son was not forgotten by creating beautiful posters as a reminder of Lee's life. It was particularly poignant that on the day we learned Lee's memorial would go ahead Hamish had created a beautiful new banner that he'd hung at the petition site just hours before the phone call arrived.

Next to a giant black and white photo of Lee as a little boy, the caption reads: 'I am Lee Rigby. I lived in Woolwich. I served in Woolwich. I contributed to Woolwich. My life was taken from me in Woolwich. I am forever a part of this town's history and my story will be told over and again. I am Lee Rigby. I will never grow old. Nor will I be forgotten.'

It was by pure chance this wonderful banner was hung up, but the words are very special to me.

It was on Armistice Day last year, 11 November 2015, that I finally had the chance to honour Lee in the right way when we were invited to a private dedication and unveiling of the new memorial in Woolwich. It was one of the most moving days of my life, and it was both heart-breaking and fulfilling at the same time.

To be able to stand in front of a stunning plaque bearing Lee's name was everything I had fought for, and I felt like the proudest mum in the world. I cried for most of the day because it was so moving and important to me to have fought and won this particular battle for my son. But sitting right next to my overwhelming pride was the rawest of my grief. The significance of this memorial was immense, but it was also a tragic reminder that all I had left of my son were my memories and the dedications to him. This will be a very special place for us in years to come. We will always visit the memorial and pay homage to Lee and the wonderful life he lived to the full for twenty-five years. Lee deserves this memorial and it will help me to shine a little light into the darkness of those who miss and love him so much

19

Lee's Legacy

There are three things I vowed to do to keep my son's memory alive and create a lasting legacy for him.

The first was to write this book, so I had the chance to share the story of Lee's life and death with the world. It is so important to me that people learn more about the man Lee was, and not just know him because he was murdered in such a terrible way. Lee was just a normal, loving young man in the Army who had the terrible misfortune to be in the wrong place at the wrong time. But he was everything to our family because he was a part of us. We will never be complete again.

I hope that by writing about Lee I have shown what he was really like – the human being behind the soldier's uniform. From the moment he was born, he embraced life with gusto, and his joy and humour really defined him. I try hard to keep those precious memories of him laughing and happy in my mind, instead of the gruesome images of his death. I could talk about Lee forever because I adored him and he was a wonderful son who will always live in my heart. It has been hard to revisit some of the worst things, but it has also given me the wonderful opportunity to celebrate so much of Lee's life. It also reminds me to hold onto my memories tightly and never let them go.

The second achievement was to have a permanent memorial for Lee erected in Woolwich, and that has now happened. I was honoured to share in the unveiling of this poignant tribute on Armistice Day, 11 November 2015.

My final mission for Lee is to create a charity in his name that can help people in need. In the coming weeks, my family will be launching the Lee Rigby Foundation, a charity that I hope will make Lee proud. The aim of the trust is to look after bereaved military families, as well as injured veterans and their loved ones. I know how important this is because, when we lost Lee, we had no idea who to turn to when we needed help. It was a very lonely place to be.

The primary aim of the Lee Rigby Foundation will be to provide respite for those who really need looking after. We want to purchase a series of lodges or holiday homes around the country so that when people feel they can't cope anymore we can offer them a place where they can have peace and tranquillity to recoup some strength and carry on. I know how vital that rest can be when you fear you're about to go under from the weight of grief. In addition, the charity will grow to become a 'one-stop shop', providing help across the board for military families and veterans, as and how they need it. Every case can be taken on its merit because, when you feel all alone, in grief or in injury, even the smallest things can appear too difficult to cope with.

I'd like to use my son's name for good and, if more people were like Lee, there would be far less suffering in the world. No one should have to go through what my family has suffered. I still miss Lee and suffer his loss as acutely as the day he died, but I'm hoping that, by building a legacy for him, it will help me to heal in some small way.

I still visit his grave in Middleton every week, sitting with him in rain or shine, laying fresh flowers and tending his grave plot.

I also like to visit the memorial in Middleton because that has a special feeling of warmth and comfort for me. I try to remember to be grateful for the good things in my life, including the gradual recovery of Ian from his heart attack. But it's not always the huge events that floor me. Some days I get pulled up by the simplest of things that leave me sobbing my heart out. Recently I was looking after my young grandchildren and, as I looked in the hallway, I saw two little pairs of children's shoes belonging to Holly and Ryan, lined up against the wall. It threw me back to when their mum, Sara, and Lee were little toddlers, growing up together and, out of nowhere, I found myself crying at such tender memories of my own kids. It's like when I see Lee's son Jack. It always takes my breath away because he is identical to the way Lee looked at the same young age and I yearn to turn the clock back and protect my boy again, but I know I can never do that. Instead I have to try and make the future positive for Lee's memory.

Lee always wanted to help people and make them happy, and that is why the Foundation will be a fitting tribute to him. I am privileged to have a brilliant team of trusted friends and colleagues around me to ensure our vision becomes reality, and we are hoping to enlist the help of key sports figures across the country to reflect Lee's passion for all things sporty, in particular football. We already have two tremendous military patrons who are supporting our cause: Former Royal Marine Matt Croucher GC (George Cross medal holder) and former SAS hero Colin Maclachlan, who starred in the hit TV series, *SAS: Who Dares Wins*. I am so grateful for their patronage because they are hugely inspirational and heroic.

Speaking of his role with the charity, Colin said: 'The causes supported by the Lee Rigby Foundation are very close to my heart and I will do everything in my power to get the message out there so that people embrace the fabulous work it will do. I am proud and honoured to be a patron for this organisation and I hope everyone gets behind us and makes it a blinding success.

Everyone was deeply shocked and saddened by what happened to Lee and I am humbled to be a part of the team carrying the foundation's aims forward.

'Helping bereaved families and suffering veterans is so important, and the team at *Who Dares Wins* are trying to encourage people to be open and talk about PTSD. It is indiscriminate and affects so many.

'Organisations like the Lee Rigby Foundation are so important because they are there to help people who often feel they have nowhere else to turn. I have no doubt that Lyn and the team will reach out and be there for many people in their darkest hour and I am very happy to be a part of that.'

Colin and Matt have already given the Foundation a real boost. I don't doubt it will be a lot of hard work and graft, with hurdles and obstacles to overcome. But it has given me a focus to carry on in Lee's name. I know my grief will never go away, but I have good days and bad days and I'm learning to cope with my sorrow a little better. It doesn't make it less painful, but working on projects for Lee has made me stronger. It has given me a real sense of purpose to achieve great things for him. It keeps me connected to him. I know I have to live my life for the two of us now, and so I will never let Lee be forgotten.

There are so many others, too many to mention in total, who have helped to keep Lee's legacy burning brightly and I would like to send my heartfelt thanks to them, in particular, Julia Stevenson, from the Ride of Respect biker group; Gavin Vitler from the Rigby's Guardians biker group in Middleton; and Donnie Reid from the Rigby's Guardians in Scotland. Barnsey Bro is among the bikers who help with charity events and, everyday without fail, he wishes me a good morning on Facebook. These fabulous bikers and their teams turn out for so many occasions to respect and honour Lee. You are all amazing.

Gary 'Bambi' Hobson, a former Fusilier, and ex-Royal Marine

Steve Young bowled us over with an epic charity walk, which started from Lee's grave in Middleton and ended at his barracks in Woolwich. And finally we are so proud that Ford International in Derby honoured Lee by putting his name and photo on the front and sides of one of their lorries. It is the only operational truck bearing Lee's picture and it can be seen up and down the country on its travels. Thank you to manager Gary Harrison and driver Dave Springthorpe. Your tribute is wonderful.

All of these things help me because I want Lee's larger-than-life personality and joy to shine through in everything done in his name. I was lucky to have had him in my life for those twenty-five wonderful years. Lee's love for life was never more obvious than in a set of photographs I was given recently, which showed Lee the day before he died. They are some of the most stunning pictures I have ever seen of my son.

They captured a handsome young man, in the prime of his life, just twenty-four hours before he was murdered. Lee is shown happily posing and laughing at a wedding fair, where he was working as part of his Fusilier duties at the Tower of London. Never has he looked so vital and full of life.

Lee always loved being the centre of attention and this proved to be no exception. The wedding company at the event called for volunteers to take to the stage to pose as bride grooms! All his Army mates ran off, apart from Lee, who couldn't wait to hop onto the stage and strut around like a model. He was showing off for all he was worth, as his pals laughed their heads off. He loved every minute of it.

They are such vibrant and special images that they caught me off guard when I first saw them and I burst into tears. Now I treasure the pictures every time I look at his laughing face. They are a tragic reminder that, just a day later, he was taken from us, but I try to remember him as the smiling-faced boy who was happy in his life.

Part of Lee's job with the regiment at their HQ at the Tower of London was to provide hospitality with his Army colleagues. His friends have since told me they all had a blast from start to finish. Apparently Lee took to the catwalk like a natural, as if he'd been doing it all his life.

He laughed and smiled as his mates teased him from the sidelines, but that was Lee all over – always happy to make people enjoy life. You only have to see look at the photos to see the kind of lad he was – larger than life with a heart of gold.

When the lads all went for beers after work, having enjoyed a brilliant day, no one had any idea it would be the last time they saw him. Seeing my son so happy in those photos gives me some small comfort to know Lee was genuinely happy when he died. He was carefree and alive and I wish with all my heart I could see him like that just one more time. I said from the beginning of writing this book that Lee's smile lit up any room, and these pictures really show what I mean by that. I will treasure them forever, even though they evoke great sadness as well as happiness. What's important is that the world sees the kind of lovely lad Lee was – the true Lee. Handsome, funny, lively, loving and always smiling, and it is how I will always remember him. I have saved my last words for Lee.

My darling boy, thank you for being the best son any mum could have wished for. You brought so much joy to me that it's impossible to describe how much I miss you. I know you are still with me, by my side and in my heart. There are days I can feel your presence guiding me through this life and I feel blessed to know your spirit lives on. I know you always told me to keep a smile on my face, but I can't promise to make my sadness go away. I do promise to try and live life to the full for you, and to achieve my pledge to carve out a wonderful legacy for you. I hope you are proud of the work we are doing in your name. I am certainly truly proud of you. Heaven is lucky to have you, and I know you will be surrounded by friends and making them laugh. They took the best of the best when you left this earth, son, and now it's my job to make sure no one forgets the sacrifice you made. You gave so much to others and now we must give to you. Stay warm and safe and keep smiling, my beautiful boy. I will miss and love you always, but, until we meet again, night-night, God Bless, ever your loving mum xxxxx.